barefoot zen

barefoot zen

the Shaolin roots
of Kung Fu and Karate

Nathan J. Johnson

SAMUEL WEISER, INC.
York Beach, Maine

First published in 2000 by
Samuel Weiser, Inc.
P. O. Box 612
York Beach, ME 03910-0612
www.weiserbooks.com

Library of Congress Cataloging-in-Publication Data

Johnson, Nathan.
Barefoot Zen: the Shaolin roots of kung fu and karate / Nathan J. Johnson.
p. cm.
Includes index.
ISBN 1-57863-142-4 (pbk. : alk. paper)
1. Hand-to-hand fighting, Oriental—Philosophy. 2. Zen Buddhism and martial arts.
I.Title.

GV1112 J64 2000
796.8—dc21
00-034941
EB

Typeset in 10/13 Berkeley

Cover and text design by Kathryn Sky-Peck.
Photographs by Kevin Luce.

PRINTED IN THE UNITED STATES OF AMERICA

07 06 05 04 03 02 01 00
8 7 6 5 4 3 2 1

The paper used in this publication meets the minimum requirements of the American National Standard
for Information Sciences—Permanence of Paper for Printed Library Materials Z39.48-1992 (R1997).

Dedicated to

Thomas Smith
Barbara and James Johnson
Mitsusuke Harada
R. J. Gardiner
Meng Ken Too
Rose Li
Wong Shun Leung
Samuel Kwok
Yip Chun
Steve Rowe
Greg Klein (Ajahn Anando)
Ajahn Vajiro
Randolph Weinberg (Ajahn Kittisaro)
Ajahn Munindo
The Venerable Titapania
R. A. Schwaller de Lubicz
The Reverend R. Straugn
THE THREE UNKNOWN MEN
and for Father Anthony Gatt

Many thanks to

Mike Stobart, Martin Johnston, Dryw Wyvern, Jeff Mitchell, Dave Franks, Matthew Tasker, Dale Williams, Huy Djeung, Mark Bishop, Patrick McCarthy, Simon Lailey, Graham Noble, Chris Rowen, Simon Budden, Declan Johnson, Andrew Comley, Kan Wah Chut, Simon Lau, Shanir Patel, Steve Nowacki, Hayden Ebert.

Finally, I would like to thank Kevin Luce, for his excellent photography, and the editors and staff of Samuel Weiser for making this book possible.

Contents

He who injures living beings is not noble.
By non-violence towards all living beings one becomes noble.

—DHAMMAPADA CANTO XIX, 270

Preface

During a period of twenty-five years, I have met many Kung Fu and Karate practitioners who felt, intuitively, that there must be, within these arts, "something else"; some way to progress beyond physical and technical ability alone. I shared with them, and many others, a belief that there is more to these mysterious and elegant arts than the downing of an attacker in a self-defense situation. This belief encouraged and sustained me in my own search for meaning in the martial arts. Far from being the published account of subjective experiences, however, this book presents groundbreaking material.

Kung Fu and Karate, arts both known for their dynamic and flamboyant displays, originated with non-confrontational Chinese Buddhist monastic practices, practices such as "pushing hands"—the passing of force between two people who keep their arms in contact yielding-to and neutralizing force. Its methods involve a whole range of techniques, including pushing and pulling, and civilized and nonbrutal methods of escaping from arm or wrist restraints.

The purpose of the pushes, pulls, and restraints, and their counters, is to physically illustrate Buddhist notions of harmony and nonviolence. As practitioners developed skill in testing each other's physical and psychological balance, a "way" of harmony grew. This "physical Buddhism" was a logical development of the Zen "wordless gesture." As we will see later, Zen wordless gesture is a profound and practical way of teaching certain skills or abilities that avoids the limitations of words and the pitfalls of intellectualism. The application of these (physical) skills was governed by an Eastern code of chivalry, replete with courtesies and ritual behavior unrelated to the harsh realities and uncertainties of actual conflict. The evidence is within.

In this book, you will discover that the traditional movements of both Kung Fu and Karate record these practices. The whole is inexorably linked with Chan/Zen Buddhism

The empty-hand art.

and the pursuit of wisdom, peace, and enlightenment, values and possibilities that far exceed the limitations of sport or pseudo-self-defense.

My commitment to the art did not begin with an interest in Zen or spirituality. I simply wanted to be able to apply the movements found in traditional forms that actually looked more like ritual dances to me!

Initially, like many others, I sought application in combat. This presented several problems. Real fighting is brutal and does not require the use of a vast array of refined and enigmatic movements—fifty-plus Karate kata from which to choose before we even consider Kung Fu! Furthermore, I became aware that I could only attempt to use the full range of skills offered in these forms if I had a training partner who knew what I was doing and could meet my requirements (stand in the right positions, attack a certain way, etc.). The degree of cooperation (choreography) required to work things out was always considerable and seemed a far cry from real fighting. The final and most irritating problem was in learning how to apply all the traditional movements spontaneously and continuously. They seemed to be applied only as choreographed pieces. I think that, like many other practitioners, I just hoped I would be able to connect it all together—to come up with the right response at the right time, should it be necessary.

The only time the actions were linked in any continuous way was during free sparring. During free sparring, however, the scope of technique was always limited (despite varying styles) and the techniques employed bore little relationship to the movements in the traditional forms. It was like observing at least two different systems being practiced within the same style. This has led to a serious neglect of the meaning and value of traditional forms. Currently they are used primarily for showy displays or merely to pass grading examinations. Although traditionalists still maintain that these forms play a pivotal role in the various styles, some teachers are changing them beyond recognition, while others are abandoning them completely, throwing the baby out with the bath water, so to speak.

I persisted with the traditional methods and continued in dedicated practice, deciding along the way to commit myself to understanding the forms. Later, it occurred to me that, if I were to succeed, I would have to learn to think like the people who created them; so, I set out to discover what kind of people they were.

Initially, I thought I was seeking warriors of old. It came as quite a shock to me, therefore, to discover that the art originated with Buddhist monks and nuns! Consequently, I spent seven years learning about Buddhism from the monks and nuns of a contemporary monastery.

It wasn't my intention to fit Kung Fu into a Buddhist or religious mold. Like others, I wanted to be able to interpret the forms in my own way. Moreover, the Buddhist teachings seemed to be restrictive and divorced from the realities of modern urban life, not to mention those of self-defense. Through my studies and practice, however, it became apparent to me that the legendary courage of the Shaolin (Chan/Zen) order was not developed by fighting with enemies, but by *not* fighting! Their bravery lay in embracing the path to peace and all the challenges and difficulties that this entails. Indeed, it seems the Shaolin teaching was designed to free us from fear, the only true enemy.

Throughout this book, I hope to indicate the possible benefits for those prepared to follow in the footsteps of the great Shaolin masters. It is my hope that this book will contribute to a renaissance of their "way," for, in reality, this is their story.

At the outset, I must state that this is not an academic work, but a book written from the heart. The research for it was carried out as objectively as possible. I believe the book makes a strong case for an incomplete or broken transmission of the traditions behind the key and antique Karate and Kung Fu forms. If there is any fault therein, it is mine, and may be the result of attempting to present a subject that was (for traditional reasons) never written down. Having made that plain, let us begin.

Introduction

Most books about Kung Fu or Karate deal with their techniques and history. Few examine the underlying purpose of these arts, or approach them as tools for spiritual (as opposed to physical) development. There are countless styles of Kung Fu and Karate, yet I think I can say, without fear of contradiction, that most Oriental styles trace their origins, however distant, back to the Shaolin Temple (Cantonese, Siu Lam or Siu Lum), considered by most to be the birthplace of Chan (Zen) Buddhism and the empty-hand art. Jou Tsung Hwa, a prominent writer and teacher of T'ai Chi Ch'uan (Chinese, grand ultimate fist) informs us that, "All the styles, names and clans of Chinese martial arts are generated from Shaolin Chuan, the prototypical Chinese martial art."[1]

The eminent Okinawan Karate teacher, Horoku Ishikawa (born July 1922), trained hard in Karate under the famous Shinpan Shiroma. Ishikawa spent five years living in Taiwan, where he had ample opportunity to study Fujianese (Fukienese) White Crane boxing. He is reported to have stated, "All Okinawan Karate is derived from Fujian Shaolin boxing." (Fujian is a southern Chinese province said to have inherited the Shaolin tradition.) The Buddhist origins of the art cannot easily be refuted (see chapter 6), and the art is inexorably bound up with traditional healing. This connection even extended to pre-war Japan, where the teaching of certain arts required a bone-setters license (as was held by Hironori Otsuka, the founder of Wado-ryu, one of the first Japanese Karate styles). This license was not required for first-aid skills, but was simply a matter of associating certain arts with, and classifying them as, healing.

The art was developed at Shaolin. From there, it subsequently spread. Any serious study of the art, therefore, must look to the temple to understand the philosophy, beliefs, and ideals that shaped it, since Buddhism was the cultural and moral foundation upon which it was constructed.

While the need to practice and perfect the physical aspects of the various arts must be recognized, it is also apparent (through both the nature and history of the Oriental empty-hand art) that physical proficiency is only one aspect of their study. Although this may be obvious to most readers, there are several specific questions I would like to address in this book—questions like What is the fundamental philosophy that permeates most Oriental styles? and What relevance does this philosophy have, not only for the arts, but for our lives?

Barefoot Zen is presented in three parts. Key concepts are given intentional emphasis and sometimes repeated. Broadly speaking, the book sets out to accomplish two things: to provide information and instruction, currently unavailable, on how and why members of the Shaolin order devised the prototypical empty-hand art; and to de-bunk

---

[1] Jou Tsung Hwa, *The Tao of Tai-Chi Chuan* (Boston: Tuttle, 1981), p. 5.

the impractical and misleading theories attached to the study and practice of traditional Karate kata, replacing them with clear and unambiguous applications.

Part One addresses some popular misconceptions. It challenges many interrelated misconceptions concerning Karate's origins, purpose, and classification, and comments on the effect of cultural presentation and the dangers of teacher attachment.

Part Two contains a brief summary of the spiritual disciplines that contributed to the creation of the Chinese "martial" arts. It seeks to clarify the thought processes that contributed to the construction of the empty-hand art. It includes a full explanation of Sanchin, the primary form or kata for both Kung Fu and Karate, as well as vital research material on the complete and restored solo form Naifuanchin, better known to modern practitioners as Naihanchi or Tekki. This kata was the foundation of the original Shuri-te Karate (Shuri-city Karate), later known as Shorin-ryu Karate (Shaolin-family Karate), from which much popular Karate is derived. Later, we will see that this type of Karate was actually founded on kata illustrating techniques intended for grappling!

Part Three acts as a summary, reinforcing the views expressed in the first two Parts. It also contains a short work of fiction dealing with the historical period that saw the destruction of the Shaolin Temple and the formation of many of the world's Kung Fu styles.

Throughout this book, I have tried to use familiar terms (Kung Fu, Karate, Zen) wherever possible for ease of recognition. I have tried to avoid the use of jargon. Inevitably the inclusion of some was necessary. Kung Fu, for example, is a slang (Cantonese Chinese) expression that can be translated as "hard work." It has, however, become a common term used to designate empty-hand arts of Chinese origin.

In Japan, there are many fine indigenous martial arts, but Karate, mainly a cultural import, has been a way of life for many Japanese people since its introduction by the Okinawans in 1922. Karate is in fact a modern term that is useful here. It means, literally, "empty hands" (Japanese, Okinawan). I will use both these names, replacing them where necessary with the term "empty-hand art." This term I use to describe the Zen Shaolin prototype and distinguish it from modern Kung Fu and Karate styles and weapon systems. I will also use "Zen" in preference to the less well-known term "Chan," although both mean the same thing.[2]

When I refer to the solo sequences of choreographed movements practiced in Kung Fu, I will generally use the word "form," instead of the less well-known "quan," "kuen," or "hsing." Karate forms will be referred to as "kata." The terms "key" and "antique," in reference to forms or kata, will be used independently, but occasionally in combina-

---

[2] Zen is the Japanese translation of the Chinese word *Chan*, which in turn is the Chinese translation of the Indian word *Dyhana*, *Jnana* or *Janna*, which refers to meditation. So the Zen school is the meditation school, which traditionally began with its founder and first patriarch Bodhi-Dharma (*Daruma* in Japanese) who allegedly left India and crossed into China in approximately 528 A.D., eventually to take up residence in the Shaolin Temple (Japanese, Shorin-Ji).

The reader may question the use of the Japanese term Zen when it appears alongside the Chinese name Shaolin. The purist may prefer the use of Chan with Shaolin, and Zen with Karate. However, I mix them for convenience and to indicate the connections between Kung Fu, Karate and Chan/Zen.

tion. A key kata will always be an antique kata, but an antique kata will not always be a key kata. I also use the term "partner" in preference to "opponent." If you can understand why, you will have already entered into the spirit of the essential Zen philosophy underlying the empty-hand art—a philosophy that aims at the liberation of all sentient beings from suffering.

PART ONE

Zen Shorin Do

The Roots of
Kung Fu and Karate

Kung Fu and Karate: Modern Progeny of an Ancient Art

1

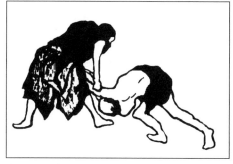

O*nly by following the path of non-violence can defeat be avoided.*

Kung Fu and Karate are widely popular in the West. Combined, their practitioners would make up a nation-state of several million people! Moreover, despite the decline of traditional martial arts in China and their replacement with Wu-Shu (a type of theatrical "martial" gymnastics), there are millions of Chinese people actively engaged in related arts today.

Unfortunately, because these arts have been classified and promoted as methods for staying in shape, as sports, self-defense, or performance arts, teachers have placed strong emphasis on physical and technical development, at the expense of the philosophical or spiritual teachings that these arts were actually intended to convey.

The general public has its own ideas concerning the value of Kung Fu and Karate. Unfortunately, many of these ideas are drawn largely from fiction and misrepresent the true nature of these arts. If we are to understand the original purpose and potential benefits of the empty-hand arts, we must distance them from sports, self-defense, and films, particularly those modern, violent screen images that have already exerted such a negative influence, putting off many people (the majority) who might otherwise have been interested. Regrettably, violence is the "stock in trade" for many films, and part of an entire generation has come to accept such scenes as normal, almost in the way that the crowds in ancient Roman arenas viewed fighting matches.

In modern times, "high kicks" have become representative of both Kung Fu and Karate. The stereotypical image of a martial artist, emitting a piercing shriek, face contorted, executing a high kick and presumably venting some bloodlust, is common. Such images also adorn badges, logos, and letterheads, and are very commonplace on posters—and the more spectacular, acrobatic, or gymnastic the kick, the better. Yet these techniques are not representative of the bulk of source material found in the key and antique (traditional) forms or kata. Furthermore, overemphasis of these modern kicking techniques is detracting from the study and application of the proper skills recorded and passed on through traditional forms and kata.

For those who are, or have been, involved in popular Kung Fu or Karate (or related arts), part of the initial attraction may well have been these high kicks. I was fascinated by them as a youth and remember eagerly setting out to try to master them. Earnestly believing in their alleged devastating potential, I was soon pounding a kickbag with fairly agile kicking combinations. Hitting a moving target proved to be very different, but, with the zest of youth and some expert tuition from a Korean stylist, I persisted, firm in the belief that I was mastering something ancient and profound, not to mention deadly. Later, I learned otherwise. I learned that:

1. While they are very evident in modern Wu-Shu and styles influenced by it, high kicks do not appear in the traditional (antique) southern Shaolin forms or the antique Karate kata (see Appendix, page 241) in which the leg is used only fourteen times in the hundreds of movements comprising nine antique kata.

2. Karate practitioners, returning to Japan after being absent from 1935 to 1945, had never even learned the side kick, a popular kicking technique in which the leg is abducted by being thrust or snapped out to the side. The side kick is now considered as basic to Karate. Taiji Kase, a prominent contemporary senior Japanese Karate instructor, informs us that the side kick was developed in the absence of Karate-ka (Karate practitioners) overseas. When they returned, they would not accept it as a legitimate Karate technique!

3. High kicks have a poor track record of success in interdisciplinary full-contact Karate bouts, and those who claim to teach "real self-defense" generally disregard high kicks or give them little credence.

The martial arts and, by implication, the empty-hand art have become associated with scenes of violence. Indeed, this is the only exposure some people will get to them. In the way, however, that Clint Eastwood films do not depict the real life of a cowboy or a police officer, martial arts films are clearly not about real life. There may still remain a need for self-defense, but the term "self-defense" is as much a generalization as the expression "the average shoe size," something that obviously would not fit the majority of people.

Despite the many people worldwide who practice martial arts, there are many more who do not. In the age of modern technology, communications, law enforcement, and weapon usage, a barehanded duel is (statistically) an unlikely event for most adults. The average citizen, in fact, seldom thinks about self-defense until threatened (for example, by an aggressive drunk). Although some imagine that all good citizens could be protected against mugging by learning a few "tricks," those tricks could not possibly cover the full range of potential scenarios. If you try to examine all the possibilities, you can end up becoming obsessed with confrontation scenarios. Confrontation and violence, however, do not obsess the seeker of the "way," who requires more legitimate reasons for practicing.

In chapter 2, we will examine the notion of "kill or be killed" and discover just who is the most likely to be concerned with self-defense, and why. Indeed this is the crux of the matter. Please do not confuse the needs of professional warriors (both ancient and modern), law enforcement officers, practitioners of Shaolin, and the rights of the general public to go about unmolested. Each face different problems, and each require different tools.

There is, in the West, an incessant drive in martial arts toward "making it work." This is another factor leading to the distortion of the empty-hand way. Many courses are being run in which participants seek reassurance by rehearsing perceived common scenarios. Similar scenario-based training has also, traditionally, been the focus of self-defense courses for women. There is now a popular emphasis on tactics and methods connected with confrontation—for example, at a nightclub door. These methods bear no genuine relationship to the material found in the Shaolin-based forms and have nothing at all to do with the Zen foundation of the art.

I think it's a pity to see the empty-hand arts monopolized by the urban combat "specialists" and promoted as something violent, confrontational and negative. This book asks deeper questions: What if the original (Shaolin-based) Kung Fu is more than fighting? What if it is not even for fighting (as we perceive it) at all?

A Little Bit of Zen

If the Shaolin empty-hand art was created by Zen monks, how can we reconcile the so-called martial arts with the peaceful aims of Zen Buddhism? How can physical activity (martial arts) lead to Zen enlightenment? And, what is Zen enlightenment, anyway? Later, we will see that the attainment of Zen enlightenment, or even Zen self-improvement, through physical means unfolds in a way that differs from other physical activities.

Self-discipline is required for improvement or success in any sport or activity. Zen enlightenment is different. It cannot be achieved in an atmosphere of competition, aggression (even controlled aggression), image obsession, or self-defense anxiety. Traditionally, Zen training is not about the control of others; it is about the control of self. The road to enlightenment is an inward-turning pathway leading us back to our original nature.

Zen and Meditation

Zen is not a philosophy or a religion in any strict sense. Simply put, Zen is initially concerned with doing the right thing at the right time and in the right way, with a clear head and a good heart. Indeed, one of the early benefits of meditation practice is that it occasions *mindfulness*, which is perhaps best considered as involvement rather than thinking. Zen is the superlative, mindful way of doing things, because it is an efficient state of "being." In fact, it is *the* most efficient state of being, approached and experienced through meditation before gradually permeating out and embracing all aspects of life.

Contrary to popular stereotypes, meditation was not invented by hippies. It is not anti-establishment nor is the use of joss sticks obligatory. Meditation can be carried out perfectly well without any paraphernalia, for that matter. It does not make you docile and passive, nor does it encourage you to "drop out." For many of us, Zen represents quite a challenge in our modern, "hyper," must-get-something-done culture. It must be experienced to be understood.

> *"I see what you mean". . . said the man who was blind*
> *As he groped about in a narrowing mind.*

An Example of Meditation

The example given in figure 1 is for those with no prior knowledge of meditation. It takes place in a quiet solitary place and may last for ten minutes to an hour, or longer. Sit either cross-legged or on a straight-backed chair, keeping your back straight. Swell out your abdomen and put a little strength there, then relax. Close your mouth and let your tongue touch the hard palate of your mouth. Leave your eyes slightly open, with your gaze cast down. Make sure that your chin is not sticking out. Relax your face and then your entire body. Continue to keep your back straight; do not sit tailor fashion (round-backed). Breathe through your nose and become still. In this stillness, begin to "let go"; first by emptying out and clearing away distractions such as impatience, doubt, fear, even curiosity, and then by detaching from all thoughts, emotions, ideas, and beliefs. Discard them all, even your identity. After reaching an initial state of calm, gently focus your attention on either the feeling of the breath at the tip of your nose, or the rise and swell of your abdomen, particularly at the point one inch below your navel. You can also practice counting from one to ten, simply returning to the number one every time your mind wanders.

It is amazing how many tricks the thinking mind will play during meditation. For instance, after having settled well, your mind may break in on the quiet moment and congratulate you with an "Oh, I'm doing okay

Figure 1. Seated meditation.

with this meditation thing! OOPS, better start counting again, or should I try feeling the breath at the tip of the nose, or should I concentrate on the swell of the abdomen, I wonder what it's like to be a Buddhist, to be strong to be happy, wise, I wonder . . ?" Presto! You have become a victim of classic thought-drift and you are thinking, not meditating.

Beginners may well find all this quite tricky, as doubt and suspicion also challenge the mind. If you are sitting cross-legged, pain (mostly in the knees) can reduce the resolve of even the most determined. Questions concerning the usefulness of sitting still, apparently doing nothing, are also particularly common at this stage. These and other obstacles can only be smoothed out with practice—by continuing to detach from thoughts and emotions, merely observing them and letting them pass, neither accepting nor rejecting them. As for the pain in your knees—well, it's advisable to move them, give them a rub, and settle back down to meditation!

What Happens Next?

If all conditions are shed, let go of to become "no-things," and if these limitations actually fade, your true nature or true self will be revealed. As the Zen expression goes, you will begin to see your true face before your parents were born.

This true self can be regarded as a pristine consciousness, an indwelling intelligence. Unlike mere intellectual intelligence, the indwelling intelligence is a force within that watches and knows. It is made manifest when the focal point of consciousness has been withdrawn from the external world of objects and becomes focused on the internal world of being.

If you get this far, you will have entered the internal world of being (the subjective realm) that is a vast and continuous mirror of the external objective world. Mistakenly perceived as a great "nothing" by those who have never traveled its broad expanses or plumbed its great depths, the subjective realm can profitably be compared to the relatively vast space inside an atom (nothing tangibly or truly concrete, alas, for the materialists). Within this space, the exciting potential of all creation exists. Here, we can find echoes of Taoism and parallels with the great vast "emptiness" of the Tao, or "Way" (see chapter 4).

In this sense, all potential exists *within* the individual, hampered only by ingrained habits, mind clutter, and ill-devised belief systems. In a simplistic sense, Zen meditation provides a means of zeroing the registers, cleaning out the "room of mind," and returning to a pure and unsullied state of consciousness. Freed from the objects of consciousness, we are conscious only of being conscious and free to experience (*insperience*) our true nature.

Western thought, concerned as it is with adding things—wealth, power, status, speed—sometimes turns a deaf ear and a blind eye to the possibility of embracing simplicity, graciously letting go, and no longer grasping. It often confuses Zen letting go with giving up or giving in. This is a mistake.

Metaphorically speaking, spiritual misers hoard everything—compassion, goodness, altruism, open-mindedness, and particularly their own spirituality—refusing even to empty the rubbish, so to speak. Dressed in rags, they live a miserable, impoverished, and purposeless life. Happily, the Zen ghosts of past, present, and future have helped many to let go of suffering, neurosis, fear, doubt, judgmental attitudes, and other impediments, and move progressively toward a more fulfilling way of life.

Indeed, during meditation, by letting go, you can "gain the way," find the center, and sit fearlessly within. This still center is a place of great balance and power. It is peaceful, yet dynamic; tranquil, yet eventful; instant, yet eternal. It was these high levels of meditation ability, rather than martial prowess, that gave the Shaolin monks and nuns their reputation for fearlessness.

In sitting, sit (still) like a mountain; above all, don't wobble!

Freedom from Fear

The Zen mind has a true (practical) value for the martial artist.

> It is wrong to think that misfortunes come from the east or from the west; they originate within one's own mind. Therefore it's foolish to guard against misfortune from the external world and leave the inner mind uncontrolled.[1]

As plants spring forth from seeds, so thoughts spring forth from minds. It is the ability to let go of these thoughts and cease to identify with them that truly liberates. In the book *Buddhist Scriptures*, we read:

> For whatever a man thinks about continually, to that his mind becomes inclined by the force of habit. . . . For unwholesome thoughts will grow when nursed in the heart and breed misfortune for yourself and others alike.[2]

At one time, I taught Kung Fu professionally and was considerably preoccupied with my combat efficiency in any potential confrontation. I had a hectic (hazardous) social life in which I kept regular company with fear, doubt, and egotism, my own and other people's. Although my quest to be a completely efficient martial artist only increased my unwholesome preoccupation with (potential) conflict, the turmoil this caused was a product of my *mind*.

In the second of the Buddha's four noble truths we learn:

> Physical discomfort and suffering are not the same thing. We suffer in the mind, and the mind produces the conditions of life which are unstable and unsatisfactory.[3]

Indeed, the suffering I experienced at this time was psychological. From a Zen perspective, however, such emotional damage can become dangerous if it becomes habitual. I suffered from too many days in the company of fear and paranoia.

---

[1] Bukkyo Dendo Kyokai, *The Teaching of Buddha* (Tokyo: Buddhist Promoting Foundation, 1979), p. 420.
[2] Edward Conze, *Buddhist Scriptures* (London: Penguin, 1959), p. 109.
[3] Edward Conze, *Buddhist Scriptures*, p. 109.

You may wonder what this has to do with Zen in the martial arts. Well, the usual platitude employed at this point is: Zen helps a warrior (or a fighter) to calm and focus his mind, making him more efficient. The cultivation of Zen however, should not be undertaken to make you a cold and mechanical person, devoid of passion and humanity. Zen was born from the Mahayana (Sanskrit, Great Vehicle) school of Buddhism and founded on compassion. This is incompatible with any notions of "warrior Zen."

The idea of warrior Zen, common among martial artists, eulogizes the activities of samurai warriors, particularly in 16th- and 17th-century feudal Japan, a period during which Tokugawa Ieyasu (1541–1616) unified Japan. This is a romantic period for novelists and samurai enthusiasts alike. The Zen of that time did not, however, reflect this romanticism. As early as the 15th-century, the celebrated Ikkyu Sojun (1394–1481) burned his certificate of enlightenment and wrote this poem:

A lifetime under the broken eaves of crumbling huts
Free from the vanities of glory and fame,
While in the temples greed and lust are made at home,
Long-neglected, the walls and roof of Yang-chi's house.[4]

According to Arthur Braverman in *Warrior of Zen*, during most of the 16th century, Zen practice in Japan became so formalized, and ritualized, that true Zen experience was rarely seen.[5] In fact, as early as the 12th and 13th centuries in the Nara and Kyoto regions of Japan, there existed private armies of so-called warrior monks, a contradiction in terms if ever there was one.

I remember, as a young man, being captivated by the romance, mystery, and reputed power of the historical Samurai warriors. I remember the morbid fascination that gripped me when I read of the most formidable Zen-trained warriors who, with perfect composure and Zen mindfulness, could impassively decapitate someone in an instant!

Remaining mindful while you cut off the head of another with a sword may indeed constitute an act of mindfulness, but it is still killing. It is still highly karmic (see chapter 4) and it remains opposed to the Buddhist Dharma (teaching). In short, the so-called Kamakura Zen of this and later periods was a social, cultural, and political adaptation of Zen values and should not be viewed as a pristine model. On a more positive note, that time period also saw the virtual end of hundreds of years of bloody civil war.

In contrast to the warrior Zen of Japan, the Zen Shaolin way of China was not designed to defeat anything other than the aspirants' own fears and delusions. Created out of Zen wordless gesture, as an adjunct to other meditation methods, the empty-hand art taught how to seek and find the middle way, by physically letting go and not contending with any force, physical or mental. As stated earlier, it is important that you do not see this as a means of giving up or giving in. Later, we will see that giving in is as poor an option as fighting.

[4] Arthur Braverman, *Warrior of Zen* (Tokyo: Kodansha, 1994), p.6.
[5] Arthur Braverman, *Warrior of Zen*, p. 6.

Figure 2. "Incense shop" Monk-fist Kung Fu from Fuzou, China.

In my own experience, the more I pursued Zen training, the less preoccupied with confrontation I became. Recognizing that the bogeyman in my own mind was doing more damage to me than any external enemy could, I simply stopped living that way.

If, by renouncing a lesser happiness one attains to a happiness that is greater, then let the wise pursue that happiness which is greater.[6]

In the practice of solo moving meditation, you find sheer pleasure in the skillful management of your posture and movement.(See figure 2.) Mastery of emotions such as anger, depression, and frustration, is, in itself, very liberating. Also, the positive stimulation of breathing and blood circulation, and the pleasant feeling of the *qi* (*chi*, *ki*, vital force) circulating unimpeded throughout your body, are experiences well worth the time and effort spent in practice. These things, however, are merely a beginning.

Physical exercise and intellectual considerations aside, practice is energizing and stimulating. It leads to an incredible feeling of well-being. Harmonizing with another person during pushing-hands gives perhaps the greatest insight into the true psychological and spiritual value of the empty-hand way as a means to resolve duality, (con-

[6] *Dhammapada: Wisdom of the Buddha*, Harischandra Kaviratna, trans. (Pasadena: Theosophical University Press, 1980), p. 115. Further references to this work will cite title, chapter and verse.

tradition). I suggest that, from a Buddhist perspective, this has a grander and more pressing importance than any immediate needs for self-defense, imagined scenarios of confrontation, or regrets about previous encounters.

I am not alone in supporting the inherently spiritual characteristics of the original empty-hand art. Patrick McCarthy, hailed by many as one of the world's foremost Western Karate historians, says the following:

> The most successful *spiritual* factions within man's ancient communities effectively cultivated remarkable doctrines that provide illuminating paths upon which followers *through methodical self-diagnosis* discovered the source of human suffering. In an effort to protect their spiritual beliefs and maintain a robust health, spiritual recluses cultivated herbalism, physical exercise and self-defense to protect their beliefs. The legendary place that cradled this unique synthesis is reputed to be China's Shaolin Monastery. Yet when introduced outside its monastic sanctuary, the moral and spiritual elements of Quan Fa (Gong Fu or Kung Fu) became detached and reduced to a ritual of lip service. This resulted primarily because its defensive techniques were often sought after by secular disciples many of whom placed little or no importance upon its *moral or spiritual purpose.*

He goes on to say:

> It would be ludicrous to even consider that self-defense methods did not exist in ancient China prior to the advent of the Shaolin order, however, the advent and subsequent development of a codified self-defense system with *spiritual characteristics* and a moral philosophy with which to govern the behavior of those who mastered its secrets, remains purely a cultural phenomenon *cradled in the confines of austere Chinese monastic sanctuaries.*[7]

In China today, even though the art of Zen is divorced from its roots, the positive life-enhancing potential is stressed, and there is far less emphasis on self-defense and "making it work" than in the West. Millions of Chinese people "play" T'ai Chi Ch'uan every morning, without a single enemy in sight! (T'ai Chi Ch'uan is primarily a slow-motion, flowing, choreographed solo sequence of quasi-martial-arts movements.)

With a proper understanding of Zen we can come to see that what causes the enemy without to appear is fundamentally the same as that which causes the enemy within to appear. Zen teaches us (among other things) to deal with the universal, not just the personal. Aggression, mood swings, error, and crisis are experienced by all of us to a lesser or greater degree, and are not restricted to a few miscreants. I hope to point out, in the pages that follow, that there is much more to the empty-hand art than learning to deal with those at the extreme end of error.

---

[7] Patrick McCarthy, from notes sent to me from his 1995 European seminar. Italics mine. Later, I will postulate that the exercises and so-called self-defense techniques *contained* the Shaolin beliefs.

We all have lessons to learn. A nation not in control of itself can hardly wage effective war against another. Likewise, an individual must master self before ever considering the mastery of others, even if such a notion is valid. We must first settle what is within, before looking without! Then, when we do come to look outside, we will do so with clarity and understanding. What's more, we will have overcome the largest impediment to success . . . ourselves.

Fighting Monks?

There are many films and stories about the Buddhist Shaolin order. They were masters of the martial arts, fearsome warriors whose aid was solicited by emperors and warlords alike. Contrast, however, the nature and requirements of warfare with the aims and objectives of Buddhism. Buddhist monks and nuns (of any denomination) who prefer not to harm even insects. Obviously, it doesn't make much sense to avoid treading on ants, only to practice slashing people with a broadsword or attacking them in close combat. None of these offensive techniques appear in the foundational or key forms or kata.

Actually, there is nothing inherently martial about the methods that are traced directly back to the Shaolin tradition (methods such as pushing hands, shown in figure 4 on page 13). The very existence of such methods, their arrangement and presentation, and the etiquette and moral admonitions involved all hint at a vision greater than

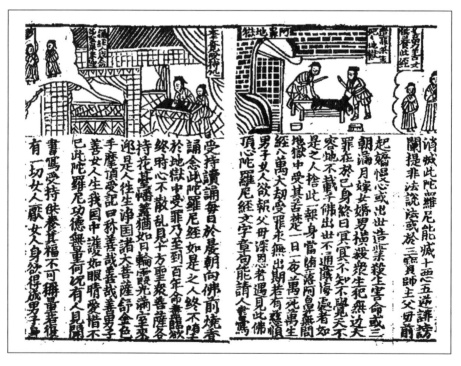

Figure 3. Non-canonical Buddhist text dealing with one of Buddhism's greatest crimes, that of killing living beings (Ming dynasty, 1368–1644: Fo ding xin da tuo tuo luo ni jing).

Figure 4. Pushing-hands.

warfare or mere self-defense. Military and combat-oriented versions of the Shaolin way are developments *away* from what was originally a type of kinetic meditation designed to objectify the meditative state.

In sharing meditation directly with another person, the Shaolin Buddhists were able to resolve duality (by reducing the feeling of "self" and "other"). The practice was devised to contribute directly to the achievement of enlightenment. (The rationale for this will be given in Part II.)

The Empty-Hand Arts Are for All

During the course of my own training, I have encountered certain nonprofessional opinions, biases, and sheer prejudices among teachers and students alike. These, as well as being unfounded, make very little sense. I address this issue early in the book, because the authentic empty-hand art, as conceived and practiced in the Shaolin Temple, is inseparable from Zen. Despite initially appearing to be culturally bound, authentic Zen transcends all racial and cultural barriers. As Master Hui-neng taught:

> There may be southerners and northerners, but in the Buddha nature, there are no distinctions.[8]

---

[8] Judith Blackstone and Zoran Josipovic, *Zen for Beginners* (London: Unwin, 1986), p. 40.

Figure 5. Juniors practicing Rokushu.

Cultural "difficulties" can sometimes be used as an excuse for lack of understanding or teaching ability (by teachers and students alike), or as a tool to establish or maintain superiority. For instance, according to some, it is essential to have a Chinese Kung Fu teacher in order to learn proper technique. How absurd! Even as I write, a wrangle is going on in the UK martial-arts press concerning two senior Kung Fu teachers. One of them is Chinese, the other is not. The Chinese teacher seeks to become the senior representative (of a master) and claims publicly that only he (by virtue of being Chinese) can impart the cultural subtleties of the art they both practice. He claims that the other teacher, while competent, cannot. Yet both teachers learned from the same master and have attained the same rank. When they both appealed to the master, the *non*-Chinese teacher was selected as the official representative.

That must have been quite a wise master. Both teachers were the same grade, and these grades were awarded by the master, who recognized both practitioners. Not accepting this, the Chinese teacher considered himself superior simply because he was Chinese! This indirectly questioned the master's ability to regulate, teach, or pass on his art, and amounted to an insult to his wisdom, the source from which both students drank. Further, it brought into question the motives of the Chinese teacher.

When the Shaolin empty-hand art was restructured and first called a "martial art," it attracted many patriots and nationalists. This tended to color the way in which others characterized an already inward-looking people. These xenophobic attitudes, however, were never a component of the Shaolin way. They stem, in part, from a nationalism that developed at the fall of the Ming dynasty in 1644/45, and from the strong anti-foreign feelings engendered in the build-up to the Boxer Rebellion of 1900. Today, these so-called "traditions" of exclusivity have all but disappeared. In fact, Chinese Buddhism had its roots in Indian Buddhism, and Japanese Zen had its roots in Chinese Buddhism. Moreover, the Okinawans and others learned empty-hand and martial arts from the Chinese, further demonstrating that these traditions are not only cross-cultural, but truly ecumenical.

Figure 6. Adults and juniors practicing together.

Many years ago, an extremely competent British second-degree black-belt Karate teacher visiting Japan was asked (by the chief instructor) to conduct a class. In that class was a young Japanese 4th *kyu* (four grades below black belt) who, a few years later, was sent to Britain to assist the Japanese chief instructor. The British instructor was sent to the airport to collect the new master, only to find his former student, who now outranked him and expected the appropriate treatment regardless of his or his former instructor's true, intrinsic merit! The empty-hand arts belong to all who practice and understand them, regardless of gender, race, age, creed, or color. Rank for rank's sake is pointless.

Wisdom, not Warfare 2

The wise give up winning and losing and enter the "way."

In this chapter, I will challenge many inter-related misconceptions about Karate's origins, purpose, and classification. It includes observations on the effect of culture-specific presentation and the dangers of teacher attachment. It critically examines the misinterpretation and misrepresentation of key Karate kata, and lays the groundwork for new criteria by which to evaluate key and antique forms.

Karate from China

Several misconceptions and difficulties arise with regard to Kung Fu, Karate, and related arts as a result of the considerable cultural emphasis placed on the way in which they are perceived and taught. For example, Karate has been promoted as a cultural product of Japan, yet its technical repertoire is essentially an Okinawan development of Chinese Kung Fu!

Okinawa is the largest in a chain of islands collectively called the Ryukyu Islands. These islands stretch between Taiwan and Japan, approximately 300 miles south of the Japanese mainland, 300 miles north of Taiwan, and 400 miles east of China.

Enthusiastic Okinawan recruits adapted the sophisticated techniques of the Shaolin empty-hand art to develop an early Okinawan version of Karate known simply as *Te* (hand). Te was categorized into three main schools—*Naha, Shuri,* and *Tomari*—

named after the three main cities of Okinawa. Tomari Karate has all but vanished as a distinct method or group, but its kata have probably survived in the other two branches. Later these three schools became known collectively as *To-te*. This was written as two characters, one meaning Tang (or Chinese) and the other meaning hand, thus identifying the Chinese origins of the art(s).

The late Masatoshi Nakayama, former chief instructor to the Japan Karate Association, had this to say about the origin of Karate:

> Kata are the formal exercises of Karate. They have been passed on from the Chinese origins of Karate centuries ago . . .

Later, in the same statement (actually advice on the performance of kata), we can see part of the Japanese influence on Karate through Nakayama's attempt to define the kata according to existing ideas on Budo (Japanese, warrior way).

> Imaginary enemies surround the Karateka as he executes the four fundamental movements of the Kata; uke (blocking) tsuki (punching) uchi (striking) and keri (kicking).[1]

Further on in this book, we will examine the effect that this interpretation has had on the way Karate kata are viewed and practiced today and the mistakes it has engendered. For now we can simply note Nakayama's acknowledgment of the Chinese root of his art.

It is well recorded that the Okinawan founders of prominent (and now international) Karate styles either studied in China or had Chinese teachers. For example, in the Naha tradition, Chou Tze-Ho taught Kanbun Uechi, the Okinawan founder of Uechi-ryu Karate. The Okinawan Kanryo Higashionna, the teacher of Chojun Miyagi (founder of Goju-ryu Karate) learned from several possible sources, including: Wai Xin-Xian, Lin Liang Hsing, Ryu-Ru-Ko (Japanese rendition) and possibly Xie Zhongxiang. Chojun Miyagi also traveled to mainland China to study.

Karate kata in the Shuri tradition (from the Shorin-ryu, Shaolin family, styles) were passed on by To-te Sakugawa (1733–1815) and Sokon Matsumura (1796–1893). These, including Naifuanchin (Nahanchi, Tekki), Passai (Basai), Chinto (Gankaku), Sesan (Seisan), Kosokun (Kushanku), Wanshu (Empi), and others are the foundation kata for popular modern Japanese Karate styles such as Shotokan (Shoto's Hall), founded by Gichin Funakoshi (1868–1957), and Wado-ryu (Harmony-Way Family, or Way of Peace), founded by Hironori Otsuka (1892–1982).

Some kata allegedly bear the names of Chinese emissaries, envoys, traders, and sailors. Key kata were imported directly from China, others are domestic Okinawan products, probably combinations of Chinese techniques, or approximations of them, combined with moving patterns (*embu*) possibly derived from or imitating the steps used in Okinawan folk dancing.

Although the kata listed above and in chapter 8 are generally acknowledged by Karate historians to have originated in China through the Shaolin (Zen) tradition, Karate as a whole is generally presented in a formal, semi-military fashion and tied to

---

[1] Quoted material from an article published by Master Nakayama in *Fighting Arts International* (F.A.I. 5, no. 6, 1985) as "Karate Kata Shotokan," p. 35. His book was originally published by Kodansha.

Japanese social customs and language. It is important to understand, however, that the traditional movements that comprise the kata were not practiced in that way in pre-militarized Okinawa, and certainly not in China. It would be unwise, therefore, to consider Japanese military customs as integral or essential elements of Karate practice. Although it may have been turned into a military art, Karate was never intended as such. Indeed, in seeking meanings for the traditional kata, it will become clear that they cannot be viewed from a military perspective with any real success.

It should be borne in mind that early promoters of modern Karate either taught Karate or received their Karate training in Okinawa or Japan in the fervor of the Japanese military build up of the 1930s and early 1940s. Influenced by the attitudes of the time, some teachers, along with their senior students (and other representatives), have perpetuated this mistaken characterization. This was supported by a determination to draw on Japan's ancestral warrior past. These militaristic attitudes, however, are more properly associated with pre-Kamakura Samurai attitudes that re-emerged in distorted notions of *Bushido* (Japanese, warrior-spirit way) that had lain dormant since the abolition of the Samurai class in 1868.

Sadly, history illustrates that the combat tradition developed by provincial, unarmed Okinawans bore little resemblance to the wholesale slaughter of World War II. In the capture of Okinawa, the Okinawans/Japanese suffered more than 90,000 deaths. Images of Okinawan peasants, successfully defending themselves against mounted weapon-wielding warriors (archetypically members of the well-trained mainland Satsuma clan) are fictitious and exist only in the realm of legend.

Nationalism and Karate

In the mid-1930s, up to and during the Pacific war, Japan displayed a military and political arrogance toward China, and cast a covetous eye on her territories. Attitudes among Karate practitioners were profoundly influenced by these nationalistic attitudes. By 1936, Gichin Funakoshi (among others) had renamed his approach to Okinawa-te (Okinawan hand), removing the *kanji* (Japanese character) for China from the expression and replacing it with *Kara*. Kara-te thus came to mean empty-hand, instead of China-hand. Although he acknowledged the Chinese roots of the nationalized Japanese Karate, Funakoshi wrote:

> However, because of the frequent confusion with *Chinese* boxing [Kung Fu] and the fact that the *Okinawan martial art* may now be considered a *Japanese* martial art, it is inappropriate, and in a sense *degrading* to continue to use the character China, as in China-hand/To-te . . .[2]

The political motivations in Funakoshi's writing, connected as they were with a strategy to downplay the Chinese origins of Okinawan Karate, made it more acceptable to the imperialistic mainland Japanese authorities of the day.

---

[2] Gichin Funakoshi, *Karate Do Kyohan* (London: Ward Lock, 1976), p. 4. Italics and bracketed material mine.

Not for Battlefield Use

The mistaken belief that Karate is for battlefield use was echoed, if not originated, by the Karate-ka Ankho Itosu (1832–1916), an influential teacher of Funakoshi. It was Itosu who wrote the following lines circa 1908:

> When you train in Karate you should train as though you were on the battle-field fighting the enemy . . .[3]

The late Donn F. Draeger, a noted martial arts practitioner, historian, and author, however, advises us in volume 2 of his *Classical Budo The Martial Arts and Ways of Japan*, that:

> The classical warriors had little use for any system of combat that did not use weapons. This was primarily because the opportunity for unarmed combat was rare, being favored by neither custom nor circumstances. And the necessities of the time in which he functioned required him to be well armed and trained in the use of deadly weapons. A warrior therefore was never without weapons, even when asleep, and was certainly never without his beloved sword. . . . For the warrior even to entertain the idea of success in combat, in the sense of killing an opponent, he could attack his foe only when armed. The fact that armor was worn influenced the manner in which a warrior would deal with his foe. Mere sparring tactics of a "boxing" nature, which must rely for effect upon the natural parts of the body—hand, fist, foot—in delivering *atemi* (blows directed at anatomically weak points) by striking, punching, or kicking, were hopelessly ineffective and would be likely to result in more injury to the attacker than to the intended victim.[4]

Patrick McCarthy agrees:

> An important point when considering [Karate] kata should be to know *that the techniques were never contrived to be used in an arena, against a professional warrior, or on the battlefield.*[5]

The erudite McCarthy clearly considers Karate to have been a civil art, originating (as we saw in chapter 1) from a monastic discipline. This sits well with the undoubted use of *Chi-Na* seizing and grappling techniques in China, where they were probably employed as secular civil arrest techniques from at least the late Ming dynasty on. Similarly, the bulk of weaponless arts created, or rather synthesized, in Japan from the mid-16th century onward were largely for use by and against commoners.

Historically, classical warrior training in feudal Japan did include close-quarters grappling-style engagements, but these were geared toward combat with an enemy wearing armor. Samurai "grappling", or *Yoroi-kumi-uchi*, Draeger informs us, did not

---

[3] Quoted material is from an article published by Graham Noble with Ian Mclaren and Professor N. Karasawa in *Fighting Arts International* (F.A.I. 50, vol. 9, no. 2, 1988), as "The History of Japanese Karate: Masters of the Shorin-ryu," p. 27.

[4] Donn F. Draeger, *Classical Budo: The Martial Arts and Ways of Japan*, vol. 2 (New York: Weatherhill, 1973), p. 107.

[5] Patrick McCarthy, from notes sent to me from his 1995 European seminar. Italics and bracketed material mine.

imply unarmed combat. Indeed, Draeger claims that *"No classical system of classical bu-jutsu [warrior technique] requires a warrior to be unarmed."*[6] These close-quarter methods were, in fact, secondary systems connected with the use of weapons, particularly related to the ability to deliver a strike with, for example, a short armor-piercing weapon. In civil law enforcement, on the other hand, it is evident that, in any civilized culture, an ethical law enforcement officer will seek to restrain or subdue a miscreant without resorting to brutality. However, this does not transfer to the battlefield, where such aesthetics are not part of waging successful warfare.

It is alleged that some Samurai knew Ju-jutsu, the Japanese art of locking, throwing, and striking, derived in part from Chinese techniques. According to Stephen Turnbull, however, there is only one well-documented incident concerning the battlefield use of anything even remotely resembling Ju-jutsu-type grappling. The incident occurred during the Battle of Shizugatake in 1583, and seems to have been initiated by the reckless act of a *wakamusha*, a young vanguard warrior named Kiyomasa, who confronted an experienced opposition general. Reportedly, both combatants abandoned their spears.

> It was a combat that has often been depicted in art, showing the young Kiyomasa and the other Samurai (whose name is unknown) locked in a rather graceless struggle, very far removed from the ideals of Aikido. . . . The two samurai fell off the edge of a cliff and Kiyomasa cut off the older man's head![7]

This account appears to be of note because it was so unusual. Notice, as well, that Kiyomasa has access to a weapon and uses it!

Actually, contemporary accounts of this and other periods record that among Samurai, the sword or sometimes the *bokken* (wooden training sword) were generally used to settle individual disputes. Unarmed street scuffling would have been an undignified and unwelcome embarrassment to a Samurai, particularly with a commoner. It must also be remembered that Samurai held the right of *kirisute-gomen*, which allowed them to cut down (with impunity) any member of the lower classes who insulted them.

It is, therefore, a major misconception to associate Karate with romanticized images of the Japanese Samurai warrior. In fact, neither Kung Fu nor Karate has anything to do with the medieval code of Bushido or the Samurai warriors of ancient Japan, except in cases where modern Japanese teachers have traced their personal lineage back to an ancestor who held that social or military rank. The Samurai class was abolished in the Meiji Reformation of 1868, the year Gichin Funakoshi, the man credited with introducing Karate to the Japanese mainland, was born! Further, Funakoshi did not export Karate there until 1922. Masatomo Takagi, a senior student of Funakoshi, had this to say about him:

> Funakoshi was not a Budo-Ka (practitioner of the warrior way) when he went to Japan, but he (soon) became one.[8]

---

[6] Donn F. Draeger, *Classical Bujutsu: The Martial Arts and Ways of Japan*, vol. 1 (New York: Weatherhill, 1973), p. 90.

[7] Stephen Turnbull, "Samurai Genesis: The Origins of the Japanese Martial Arts" (*F.A.I.* 46, vol. 8, no. 4, 1987), p. 20. *Aikido* (Japanese, harmony way) derived largely from Ju-jutsu.

[8] Graham Noble, "The Master Funakoshi and the Development of Japanese Karate" (*F.A.I.* 34, vol. 6, no. 4, 1985), p. 35.

In the hundred years or so prior to Funakoshi's birth, Karate was little more than an obscure, provincial Okinawan pursuit. It did not form part of the training of a Samurai warrior and any claimed connections with the Samurai are spurious.

Politics, Culture, and Confusion of Purpose

Many Karate associations outside Japan have been encouraged to keep affiliations and connections with Japanese Karate teachers and associations, while Japanese teachers have few (if any) connections with their original Okinawan teachers. In fact, Okinawan Karate is being eclipsed by modern (standardized) mainland Japanese approaches taught within the public education system. Nonetheless, in looking at the clean lines, sharp techniques, and general aesthetics of modern Japanese Karate, it is easy to see why it has become so popular. Also, its competition-based approach, through both kata and *kumite* (Japanese, meeting hands, sparring), tends to be well regulated and consistent, even across styles. High standards of organization and administration generally apply. The use of a clearly structured and progressive ranking system using colored belts has proven popular and is even emulated within some modern Kung Fu styles.

Since establishing their own traditions, the Okinawans themselves have had few connections with Chinese Kung Fu teachers until recently. Nevertheless, Okinawan Karate still tends to be closer in approach to its immediate parent (southern Chinese Kung Fu), and is relatively unconcerned with tournaments, competitions, or rank. Okinawan Karate also generally lacks the "corporate" image and standardization found in Japanese Karate. Moreover, although the same kata are practiced within the various Okinawan styles, the various *dojo* (Japanese, training hall) exhibit individual characteristics.

Despite this "individuality," the most radical changes to Karate kata have taken place since their export from Okinawa, with many changes occurring as a direct result of the impact of various host cultures. The Samurai veneer added to Okinawan kata on mainland Japan has already been mentioned, while in the West, as we saw in chapter 1, there has been an obsession with application and self-defense, particularly on the streets—something we will examine later in this chapter.

Groups with disparate interests normally take common material (kata) as a base and use it in completely different ways. Returning to the general theme of the book, however, it is necessary to question whether any of these approaches reflect the attitudes, philosophy, or technical applications intended by the originators of the forms. For now, we can note that the cultural presentation of a given art may provide part of the initial interest and motivation to practice, but that blind or misguided enthusiasm for a cultural model or a romantic period in history can divert attention away from more vital elements.

From a Zen perspective, this is like a teacher pointing at something he wishes a student to see, while the student, giving full attention to the pointing finger, fails to observe that which is being pointed out. Such a student may then go on to found a school based on the "teaching of the finger," in which he gives instruction in the authentic length, shape, color, number of creases, etc. of the "pointing finger of truth," and how to aquire a finger like the master!

There is much partisanship within the various arts. There are, for example, people who adopt or stick with an art just because it's Japanese or Chinese. In some respects, this is understandable. The cultural trappings are not the point, however. From a Zen perspective, placing too much emphasis on them can lead to a detrimental preoccupation with role-playing, escapism, or delusion.

I remember, with some amusement, two English Kung Fu students who turned up for training, having, by their own admission, dyed their hair black in order to look more Chinese! I also remember one of my Karate instructors in the early 1970s who, for several months, unintentionally convinced me that he was foreign because he always spoke pidgin English in class. In fact, he was a local man who spoke normal English. I later discovered that he had a habit of imitating the tone and diction of his Japanese Karate teacher when giving Karate instruction!

Of course, we are all influenced to some extent by factors that motivate us to behave in certain ways or to follow and indulge in our interests. I recall how I developed a passion for "things Japanese" after being fascinated by a full suit of antique Japanese armor in the hallway of my parents' house. I spent several years captivated by feudal Japanese (Samurai) culture. A growing interest in Karate intensified that passion. Later, I even started to collect (expensive) antique Japanese swords. There was nothing wrong with that, in itself. Despite my avowed passions, however, a cultural fickleness emerged when I switched my interests to Kung Fu. Then, I was encouraged to and did become pro-Chinese, and virtually abandoned my loyalty to "things Japanese." Did I collect Chinese weapons? Yes! (At least they weren't as expensive.) On a shoestring budget, I built a small Chinese-style training hall in the garden of my house.

In my metamorphosis from *gaijin* (foreign) "suburban Samurai" into "Kung Fu killer" (and culture junkie), I all but forgot my own identity and that I was born and raised in England. I fervently sought an unhealthy cocktail of exotic cultural trappings and paranoid urban-combat attitudes, pursuing both to distraction.

The perceived cultural divide between Kung Fu and Karate also drew me into cultural-superiority games and attitudes. My Kung Fu teachers largely derided Karate, labeling it as adulterated Kung Fu, while my friends from Karate considered Kung Fu weak and sloppy, and laughed at me for wearing footwear during training and for dressing in a manner they said resembled that of a Chinese refugee. Collectively, we experienced the phenomenon of the early 1970s Kung Fu films. These films were extremely violent, and promoted absurd and banal cultural stereotypes that unfortunately misguided us even further. If this all sounds a bit foolish, well, I was young and impressionable and, unfortunately, some of the questionable attitudes of the day were reflected in my training environment. I mention these influences because some of them still adversely affect attitudes and progress today, particularly as the students of those days have become the teachers of today.

Freedom of expression plays a part in self-determination, and image tends to be a part of identity. Nonetheless, real progress requires a lot more than merely "dressing up." The uniforms we wear or don't wear, the footwear we do or don't use during practice, clearly are of far less importance than what we are actually doing, why we are doing it, and whether we are using the right tools for the job. Buddhism encourages us rather to be ourselves and not to seek to become someone else.

The roots of the empty-hand art lie in Mahayana Buddhism, the express intention of which is to liberate all beings. It explicitly teaches the need to cut through illusions and appearances. Clarity of thought and action are fundamental traits of Zen Buddhism. Therefore, in connection with training, I think it unwise to "live" a novel or exotic culture, or to try to live out a fantasy, unconsiously or otherwise, if doing so detracts from the wisdom the art was designed to convey in the first place. The supporting culture of the empty-hand art should be viewed in this light, not as something itself to be "worshipped" or, for that matter, rejected.

Most Oriental styles that use forms are essentially developments of the unique Shaolin theme or approach (unlike, for instance, Western boxing). Their similarity cannot be explained merely as oriental cultural quaintness. With each "culture shift," something of the Shaolin way is lost, as the forms are modified to fit new interpretations. Chinese Kung Fu becomes Okinawan Karate, which in turn becomes Japanese Karate, Tae Kwon Do (Korean Karate), and so on. Such a modern and speedy proliferation of styles has little to do with natural cultural diversity, but attests instead to (modern) popularity, commercial potential, and rather a lot of unacknowledged borrowing.

Finding the Common Denominator

Eventually, I became able to transcend cultural stereotypes and founded a small multidisciplinary martial arts research group. Initially, we worked at Southampton University (England), and later at Oxford and Portsmouth Universities (also in England). Together, our group began to examine Karate anew, undertaking a critical examination of original source kata (illustrated in this book), alongside traditional southern Chinese Kung Fu forms.

The forms demonstrated in *Barefoot Zen* are important key Karate kata (as well as Kung Fu and empty-hand forms) from major Karate styles with worldwide followings. More specifically, these three kata are, in fact, historically the foundation (*kihon*) kata for the two approaches or groups into which traditional Okinawan Karate is divided (however questionably): Sanchin kata for the Naha groups (including Tensho/Rokushu for the Goju-ryu) and Naifuanchin kata (Naihanchi) for the Shuri group.

In a 1934 essay by Chojun Miyagi titled "Karate-do Gaisetsu," we are informed that the kihon (central or fundamental) kata of Okinawan Karate are: Sanchin, Tensho, and Naifuanchin. Morio Higaonna, a senior Okinawan Goju-ryu teacher, confirms this in his book, *History of Karate*.[9] Needless to say, I agree!

More importantly, these forms, as prime examples and illustrations of the themes outlined throughout the book, help to demonstrate the merit and specificity of genuine forms. Because of their clear and unambiguous nature, and because they are relatively unaffected by cultural overlay (some Okinawan kata do appear to be influenced by Okinawan folk dance), Sanchin, Rokushu, and Naifuanchin kata are studied

---

[9] Morio Higaonna, *History of Karate—Okinawan Goju Ryu* (U.S.A.: Dragon Books, 1995), p. 81.

almost exclusively in the Zen Shorin-do (Ko-do To-te, or Old-way China-hand) school I follow. Moreover, studying a limited number of forms is actually a very traditional (and enjoyable) approach to the empty-hand art. Indeed, later we will see that "less can be more."

Our research group was chiefly interested in the technical and functional aspects of the kata, rather than the names of styles, the politics and personalities involved, or long and often dubious lineages. Our adopted motto, coined by my friend, Dr. Huy Djeung, was "function dictates form." I believe he borrowed it from a clothing label.

We made steady progress. Our perseverance brought to light practical and functional evidence demonstrating that Kung Fu and Karate were from the same source. The physical similarities alone were enough to testify that the Shaolin empty-hand art was unmistakably the common parent of both. Ours was not a new field of research, but it did present us with fresh possibilities.

Having already accepted essential links between Zen and the Shaolin empty-hand art, I began to recognize that pervading Buddhist influences within the arts suggested that the original prototype had a primary purpose or objective completely beyond the surface credo of self-defense. I also recognized that the arts had been improperly presented as a method of entertainment and plundered wholesale to provide combat material. In fact, the arcane and enigmatic traditional movements of China's prototypical empty-hand art have been worked and re-worked so much that the original purpose for practice has been all but obscured.

Martial arts friends of mine recoiled in horror at the mere thought of anyone challenging popular beliefs in this way. They urged me to be cautious in suggesting that the empty-hand art might be for anything other than self-defense. I had no intention, however, of rushing headlong into a crank theory, nor did I. As a professional Kung Fu instructor, I had too much to lose. I earned my living teaching self-defense. I was faced, however, with something that was too important to reject or neglect. I uncovered (essentially physical) prima facie evidence that put the much-glossed-over, but vital, connection between Kung Fu, Karate, and Chinese Chan Buddhism (Zen) into proper perspective, revealing the Zen purpose of the prototypical art and making it both practical and accessible. My findings are summarized in chapter 6. They indicate *why* Chan (Zen) monks and nuns may have devised the prototypical empty-hand art in conformity with Zen wordless gesture.

On a technical level, non-spectacular Sanchin-like forms are clearly the centerpiece of the various Shaolin-based arts as they have been handed down (see chapters 8 and 10). A further connection between traditional styles and the common prototype (and its ethics) is found in the remnants of pushing-hands drills that many Kung Fu, and some Okinawan Karate, styles retain to this day, often disguised as arm-rubbing or pounding drills, sticking hands, or searching or tempting hands.

I am not, here, confusing Kung Fu with Karate, nor am I mixing them together to create an unpleasant hybrid. In reality, key Karate kata and possibly some antique kata *are* essentially Kung Fu forms. Modern Karate has simply sprung from Okinawan Japanese and other ways of perceiving, performing, interpreting, or restructuring them. The key Karate kata illustrated in this book are fine examples of Chinese forms time capsuled—transplanted—and well preserved on the small Island of Okinawa. Indeed, although they were mildly customized, they are less altered than many contemporary versions of traditional Chinese forms. Finally, the proper applications through pushing hands have a distinctly Chinese flavor, but that should hardly be surprising.

Dignity and Morality—a Clue to Purpose

Regarding Karate, the overemphasized differences between modern styles that use the same kata, along with the present tendency to justify minor stylistic differences as traditional, obscures the connections with the purpose of the original source, through the old Okinawan kata, and back to the Shaolin empty-hand art.

Understanding that purpose provides a benchmark by which we may determine what we are meant to be doing. Without this benchmark, we can easily be confused by the plethora of styles and uncertain about the proper use of the Shaolin art and, for example, dramatic stage fighting, fighting in an arena, against a professional warrior, on a battlefield, or even on the streets. Further, without understanding the Shaolin ethics, it becomes difficult (within the arts) to convincingly explain the emphasis on the cultivation of moral attitudes or, more fittingly, moral behavior not required or even desirable in actual fighting, and not, in fact, found in non-Shaolin combat systems. The creators of key and antique forms clearly promoted the attitudes and conduct of what the great sage Lao Tze referred to as "the superior man." The superior man demonstrates attributes such as, dignity, humility, courtesy, and uprightness. Remarkable methods of dealing efficiently with force, without resorting to undignified rough and tumble or brutality, were merely a vehicle to promote these qualities, and not an object in themselves. The mere presentation of key and antique forms exalts etiquette. For example, there is no need to bow before a fight! In kata performance, however, considerable attention is paid to bearing. The promotion of civility encountered in a traditional dojo is summarized in the following maxim:

Karate begins and ends with courtesy.

Further, forms include ritual hand and body positions originating in esoteric Zen. Reserved straight-backed and dignified formal movements demanding considerable practice comprise the major elements of traditional forms, along with many slow movements. Slow movements are often inappropriately described as intermediary movements, *kamae* (postures or guards), pauses for breath, intimidation tactics or strength-building exercises.

Partisan stylists who begin to investigate the ritual deportment and general elegance of a given art in order to understand its relevance to what is usually viewed ultimately as a deadly method of fighting, often find themselves becoming increasingly puzzled, so much so that they may, as I did, begin to investigate the supporting culture of a style in an effort to find answers and make further progress. An increased understanding of Japanese feudal warrior society or the activities of Chinese Triads in 1960s Hong Kong streetfights will not, however, improve our understanding of the formal methods devised by peaceful Zen monks and nuns in China, nor demonstrate how to utilize those methods properly.

The Shaolin empty-hand art originally constituted a rigorous program of self-discipline leading to self-discovery, self-improvement, and personal illumination through dignified ritual combat. As I repeatedly stress in this book, the art had little connection with the vanquishing of others in mortal combat or the training of weaponless warriors, despite popular romantic belief.

Misunderstanding Breeds Error

It is never easy to set aside partisanship. It is quite normal for individuals, teachers, or associations to stick to, and ultimately seek to spread, the particular style or version they espouse. Indeed, there is a need for such loyalty. I use the word "version" very deliberately, however, and apply it not so much to the styles, but to the soul of Kung Fu and Karate, the forms. Nowadays it is generally accepted that there are, and should be, versions or interpretations of given forms. I wish to challenge this way of thinking. I also want to question the degree to which the so-called traditional styles are, in fact, traditional.

Because theoretical explanations of forms and their applications are problematic, photographic evidence demonstrating the explicit functions of the three kata discussed in *Barefoot Zen* accompany this text. It should provide sufficient evidence for the open-minded reader and indicate that certain key forms are precise records of specific techniques that speak for themselves, although, admittedly, some antique or key kata are abstract. For example, in the Sanchin tradition, some versions remain formulaic paradigms. Others may be little more than martial dances, and, across the full range of some fifty Karate kata and hundreds of Kung Fu forms, no one knows for sure how to interpret them.

Because there is no general consensus in applications to forms or kata, ironically, what should unite the traditional styles often divides them. Despite the fact that many Karate styles share the same kata, not everyone agrees on exactly how to practice them. According to the late and well-respected Okinawan Karate teacher Shoshin Nagamine (9th-degree black belt),

> Some have theorized, for example, that the movements of the Kata derived from mimicking the protective movements of animals. Others have speculated that the Kata grew out of ancient dance forms. Consequently, the manner in which the Kata should be executed is also open to various interpretations. *Unfortunately the lack of a comprehensive theory of the movements and how they are executed* results in less interest in simple practice of the basic movements of the Kata . . .[10]

It is commonly assumed that versions of antique or key kata have grown naturally out of the interpretations highlighted, for instance, by Nagamine. Differing emphasis on speed, the heights of stances, rhythm, timing, the body types of individuals, personal

---

[10] Shoshin Nagamine, *The Essence of Okinawan Karate-Do* (Boston: Tuttle, 1976), p. 56. Italics mine.

choice, experience, the exaggeration of nuances in one style that are completely absent in another, the alteration, removal, addition, or improvement of techniques that are liked or disliked, and so on, are all used as reasons to explain the development of differing versions or interpretations. In a 1995 Karate publication from Japan, the author informed his readers that he had revised a particular and time-honored antique kata based on what he claimed were certain "weaknesses" in the original. As a result, he placed a long-range, high-level front kick in the middle of a kata sequence designed for close-quarters grappling!

In the rest of this chapter, and in other chapters, I will show that some forms (particularly Karate kata) have been altered and developed, or more properly restructured in modern styles, principally as a result of our unfamiliarity with the functions of the originals. I will argue that this, in turn, has given rise to styles that practice variations of the same kata, despite the fact that the old masters (until recently) wanted to preserve the classical techniques and insisted that antique forms must not be changed.

All antique forms were obviously compiled by someone. Despite often knowing who passed them on, however, in most cases we do not know the identities of the actual creators. This is a splendid example of letting personality and identity take a back seat, well in keeping with Buddhist attitudes toward egotism. Antique and key forms were never devised to be consumer products or platforms for individuality. There was no "my way" or "your way" within an authentic system. There was only *the* way. Indeed, forms were "sciences."

Later, we will examine the nature of their methodical construction. In traditional thinking, to vary or alter a form because it is not understood is an error, rendering great disservice to the discipline. If, as I suggest, certain key forms are carefully structured according to specific formulae (based on a distinctive philosophy) unquestionably linked to the rules governing human anatomy, physiology, and spirituality, and if these forms have explicit functions, then it becomes clear that they should remain as unchanged as possible. I am not advocating a "back-to-China" policy, but a "back-to-function" policy. Likewise some of us don't want to see works by the likes of Michelangelo, Leonardo, or Rembrandt overpainted by pop artists advertising fizzy drinks and chewing gum.

We are only human, however. We make mistakes. We forget things, or never learn them in the first place. The way to be sure about the proper sequence and arrangement of a form and how to practice it is to know its function, which means knowing the applications—a point I cannot stress often enough! A technical example, showing simple body mechanics, can illustrate this.

Figure 7 shows a classical stance from the kata Naifuanchin. Some practitioners of modern

Figure 7. Naifuanchin stance.

styles will have been told that this stance is from old-style Karate; it is certainly very distinctive. The in-turned feet grip the floor, the knees push out, and the hips are dropped back. Functionally, the whole stance makes a strong frame. Mechanically, this stance is designed to provide maximum traction and, as far as possible, to prevent you from being pulled forward and out of it. It is an ideal stance to use in grasping and restraining techniques. If used correctly, it helps prevent abdominal strain (or herniation) when you are "under load" during the application of grappling and locking techniques.

If you allow your feet to wander and turn out, the stance will become less effective, allowing you to be pulled forward; under load, you risk a groin strain or worse, as the strain on the inguinal canal can be considerable (see figure 8). Turning your feet out makes the stance useful only in pushing (for example, a car).

It can be surmised, therefore, that the stance illustrated in figure 7 was designed with a specific function in mind (prevention of being pulled over) and should be practiced in a very specific way, rather than just being a bent-kneed stance, open to variation. This is, in fact, the *correct* Naifuanchin stance, handed down from antiquity and only lately modified. In fact, the stance gives a huge clue to the function of the kata. Later, we will discover why (in Naifuanchin practice) it is necessary to turn the feet in to guard against being pulled forward or over.

Habitual factionalism between related styles, besides concealing the common links to original kata, also contributes to defensive explanations or attitudes that insist that there were never any "original" kata, that complete and

Figure 8. The importance of turning the feet in.

accurate kata have never existed, and that the art(s) have, therefore, always been in a state of flux. Just because an individual doubts the existence of such a form, however, does not mean that it does not exist!

Today, all sorts of implausible reasons are given to support the practice of forms that, according to some, have no definite applications. Consequently, forms are being relegated to a position of importance secondary to kick-punch basics when, in fact, the forms *are* the basics.

Many Karate styles use the same kata (or variations of them), yet each has different applications—or in some cases, none! Some merely use different names to describe the same things. The following photographs are not intended to show that specific styles are wrong, but simply that there is a need for clarity in the matter of *function*. Within styles, there is usually an insistence on a proper (uniform) way to perform the kata. This does not extend across styles for obvious reasons. In looking at figure 9, please bear in mind the Naifuanchin stance shown in figure 7 (page 28) and the explanation given on page 29.

The prevailing compromise regarding kata is that the applications are a matter of choice, being non-specific and therefore open to interpretation. This has become the normal attitude, and, until recently, few seem to question it. I do not support this modern opinion. The forms, I believe, were designed for a definite purpose. In fact, the creators of the antique forms were meticulous in assigning each a very specific purpose— a purpose that should remain constant, regardless of the style or the culture in which it's found.

Figure 9. Left: *Position from Shotokan Karate's Tekki kata.*
Right: *Position from Wado-ryu's Naihanchi kata.*

Karate-ka have, over the years, become accustomed to interpreting kata and inventing new applications for them, so their Karate (they believe) is always evolving, growing, changing. An outsider, someone not initiated into "Karate thinking," might be tempted to suggest that this behavior simply illustrates the uncertainty surrounding proper applications. This, indeed, is my view. Long experience and much research has led me to the belief that key forms do not evolve. Sometimes, new breakthroughs come from outside of established traditions. Sometimes it is only by dismantling many layers of cultural accretions and stepping outside of an accepted context that original source material can be viewed objectively. In fact, this is the approach that led to the important discovery outlined in chapter 12 (see page 175).

Modern and Traditional Styles

The quest for authenticity, connected with the need for confidence in what is being studied, often leads people to speak or write about styles of Kung Fu and Okinawan or Japanese Karate as being traditional. Does this include American, European, or other styles? Clearly, a process of evolution continues to take place. Yet, as we will later discover, an authentic system consists of far more than a random *ad hoc* collection of martial arts material, and should be defined by more than the national banner under which it is promoted. Minor cultural modifications in presentation and personal idiosyncrasies will be inevitable within styles. Indeed, they add richness to the experience. As we have seen, however, there are dangers inherent here. Much damage can be done by a lack of communication.

What makes a style traditional or authentic? Many so-called traditional Karate styles and their methods are not really very traditional at all. Most were, in fact, formulated during the period between the two World Wars. Gichin Funakoshi, the Okinawan father of modern Karate, argues that, by then, a process of change had already taken place. He illustrates fifteen kata in his book *Rentan Goshin To-te-jitsu*, yet ignores other fundamental elements of modern Karate.[11] Funakoshi leaves aside basics, sparring, and formal applications, and includes an odd collection of judo-like throws unrelated to the kata. One might find it strange to omit something as fundamental as the applications, yet it seems that a lack of applications is almost a tradition of its own. In fact, senior Okinawan and other Karate teachers have advocated kata-centered Karate for many years. Unfortunately, when kata-centered Karate is mentioned, it generally refers to just that, the constant repetition of the solo kata!

Many styles claim a connection with the Shaolin Temple, or use material derived from its practices. Such schools—and there are many of them—usually regard themselves as traditional. Some distance themselves from Zen, but continue to use traditional forms and etiquette based on it. Others are still inappropriately associated with militarism, yet largely untested. Traditional styles often pay considerable attention to lineage and sometimes teach or encourage the study of martial arts history.

---

[11] As far as I know, this book is not available any longer. This information came from a magazine article by Graham Noble, "The First Karate Books," *F.A.I*, no. 90, 1995, p. 20.

Often less interested in lineage or history, modern Kung Fu and Karate styles offer collections of variations, interpretations, and what their followers believe to be new, improved, and up-to-date techniques loosely based along established lines. Modern styles seldom embrace militarism. They sometimes forego the traditional Kung Fu costume or the white Karate uniform (*do-gi*), a garment styled on Tang-dynasty Chinese clothing, and wear brightly colored outfits or tee shirts instead. They often emphasize kicking techniques, commonly use protective equipment in light sparring or free fighting, and also engage in full contact matches. The followers of these modern styles appear to have more freedom than those adhering to tradition.

It is sometimes assumed that styles just grow or mutate to fit new circumstances, and that new or modern styles represent present-day requirements. To some extent, this is true, particularly where sport and entertainment are concerned. Indeed, market forces have had considerable impact and some modern schools have enormous worldwide followings.

Modern styles often imitate traditional styles by using forms, but these forms tend to be flamboyant and demonstrative, and are becoming increasingly spectacular and movie-like. Some claim, in mitigation, that the traditional forms are just representations of fighting experiences that can and should be reinvented or updated to suit modern environments and circumstances. If, on the one hand, the quest is for entertainment, this may be true. If, on the other hand, the quest is for self-defense, it is not. Moreover, it must be borne in mind that such alterations may ultimately deprive future generations of the received wisdom of the ancients, if the antique forms are either abolished or replaced by spectacles designed to thrill the public, or reworked to represent hypothetical skirmishes.

In the following sections, and again in chapter 8, we will see that this thinking stems from a failure to understand the original purpose for practice, the connection with Zen, and the construction of an authentic form.

Applications and Self-Defense: Unraveling the Difference

Modern and traditional Karate styles consist, in the main, of a miscellaneous collection of antique, modified, and modern forms, a series of basics and various sparring drills, and whatever a given instructor teaches as self-defense. These practices are usually considered complimentary. In reality, however, they are completely different from each other. They belong to separate and largely irreconcilable categories, and exist in four distinct formats requiring specific, and often conflicting, body habits. What's the point of working to keep your rear heel down in a traditional reverse punch (opposite-hand-and-leg punch), only to be encouraged to raise it for a street-defense application? What's the point of practicing to keep your back straight in kata, only to bend it while ducking, bobbing and weaving during sparring? Why not train for solo movement the same way you would for application? These may seem like minor points, but both these examples require the acquisition and use of two different and potentially conflicting neural-pathway programs—two habits.

In the mid 1980s I remember meeting a gentleman who was working the door at an international media function for martial arts film stars. That evening, I was one of two bodyguards minding a Kung Fu master. The gentleman minding the door was large, thick-set, and a very tough customer. In his mid 40s, he was a very experienced martial artist who had created some kata in collaboration with a famous but nonconformist Japanese Karate teacher. As we talked, he offered to demonstrate some *real* kata. I accepted his offer.

He made a traditional bow before performing a kata that consisted of a furious and frenzied series of short, sharp, and extremely violent shadow-boxing techniques, included ducking, bobbing, and weaving, and sparring-type footwork punctuated by an occasional "toe-punt" kick and accompanied by what sounded like obscenities. At one point, I distinctly recognized a headlock position, followed swiftly by a punch to where the head of the imaginary opponent would be. No boxer (who wanted to last more than one round) would fight, or even train, like that (i.e., without a warm-up). Nonetheless, it was an impressive display, because his kata emulated his approach to fighting, and vice versa. (You can't warm-up in a streetfight.) The whole performance was concluded with another bow. As the man turned to look at me, I realized that I was not being asked for an opinion, but was having "the truth" demonstrated to me. In a strange way, I was.

The modern dilemma is clear: what works in one format is inapplicable in another. Hence the demands on the antique kata to supply answers to street-defense or free-sparring problems always leads to a deviation from them. This is precisely why the modernists choose to innovate, adapt. and modify. The belief that it's okay to do so is increasing rapidly. Yet the ancient form-based art was not created to be a multi-function art—a guideline for everything from street Karate, to dojo Karate, to free-style or tournament fighting. I hardly need to remind you that this approach is causing the antique forms to be eclipsed and overshadowed, and their true worth to be increasingly misunderstood and undervalued. As a result, although more people now practice arts originating from Shaolin than at any other time, the tradition is actually in decline.

In traditional systems of empty hands, the forms were originally designed to lead the way and define the teaching that would ultimately be expressed in the applications.

> *To study the ways of fish, one must look into the water;*
> *to study the ways of Karate one must look into the kata.*

If the theories behind the forms are incorrect, the practice will be, at best, inconsistent and illogical, and, at worst, contradictory.

Modern styles tend not to bother too much with forms applications. Unfortunately, many so-called traditional styles that claim to do so, do not have a symbiotic relationship with the forms, even though they maintain that the forms are the backbone of their art. Consequently, their sparring or two-man work does not reflect, or make evident, the specific techniques found in their solo forms, and vice versa. A common attitude is that the forms are "just" tradition—weird, old-fashioned, largely ceremonial movements, typically practiced quite separately from the "real stuff," the free fighting or the self-defense.

It should be clear by now that my contention is that the tradition rests in the antique forms rather than in the style, and that these forms contain specific techniques designed to be used under particular circumstances brought to life in the application. Together, the forms and the applications constitute the ancient art in its entirety. By this, I mean that the art originally consisted solely of a limited number of related forms (the warm-up, catalogues, or repertoire) and their specific hands-on applications, expressed largely at close-quarters and in contact, using touch reflexes and producing a spontaneous practice perhaps more like upright wrestling than boxing. (Naifuanchin again provides an excellent example.)

As we will discover in chapters 7 and 12, techniques used under these circumstances rely on the skillful, nonbrutal, but functional, neutralization and immobilization of a training partner's limbs and the control of his posture. In this sense, the proper applications of antique Karate kata should (to some extent) resemble the restraining techniques now commonly associated with Ju-jutsu (see chapter 7).

Okinawan Shorin-ryu Karate (Shuri-te) and other styles inherited a tradition of Naifuanchin being central to practice. The great emphasis placed on it suggests that it is the primary representation of these techniques. Those interested in grappling and subduing techniques, yet lacking the applications to Naifuanchin, have had to "reinvent the wheel," so to speak, without the benefit of the estimable classical Chinese system.

My Master Was . . .

Many Karate traditionalists argue over styles instead of working together to identify, preserve, and promote the antique kata and their proper meanings and applications on which the authority of genuine tradition rests. One current problem is that these "experts" argue over whose version or style should prevail, with the cult of personality frequently adding fuel to the fire—who someone is—carrying more weight than what knowledge they have or what they do.

Does the 18-year-old son of a deceased master have more knowledge and ability than the top students of that master, who, for example, followed their teacher for twenty years or more? And, should the son take over because of his family name? Perhaps he does have considerable knowledge and ability, but commonsense suggests that skill, experience, seniority, competence, and other factors should be paramount.

In my view, partisanship for its own sake is ultimately self-defeating for would-be traditionalists who are in severe danger of becoming, at best, a minority, and, at worst, extinct! Traditionalists would be stronger if they were united. Of course, the problem of defining authentic forms and their applications still remains.

Even though many traditional Shaolin-based Kung Fu and Karate styles are the products of the last fifty or sixty years, they have, to a large extent, preserved and promoted the antique forms. For reasons already stated, however, antique forms are increasingly seen as curious and dated. In recent years, this has contributed to a rejection of the so-called traditional styles and the creation of modern eclectic ones, all in the much-vaunted name of progress.

Many so-called traditional schools are already fragmenting and crumbling, particularly after the deaths of their various founders. Moreover, we are suffering more than ever from the cult of personality and teacher attachment. Spending even a little time in a Buddhist monastery will quickly reveal to anyone how and why Buddhists train to avoid teacher attachment and superficiality by following the teaching—not the teacher.

Teaching, Not Teacher

Following a teacher rather than the teachings (the "way') is a potential pitfall common to all students. In such a situation, students often inherit the teacher's quirks and idiosyncrasies, or use the teacher's faults to justify their own. Thus the teacher's limitations become the students'. If, for example, a teacher is caught with his hand in the till, the student can be devastated and lose the way (give up). Teacher attachment creates followers, not understanding individuals of like mind. It is important to recognize the difference.

To illustrate my point, I include a quotation from the 9th-century Zen master Lin-chi (Rinzai in Japanese). It concerns Zen personalities, but could apply equally well to others.

> Followers, do not take the Buddha as the supreme aim. I personally see him as a privy hole and the Buddhist saints as beings who bind men in chains.[12]

This statement is not intended as an outrageous and disrespectful attack on the historical Buddha and his teachings, or on martial arts and empty-hand teachers. Rather, it should be viewed as a warning against teacher attachment and hero worship.

Hero worship should not be confused with the need for role models. Role models *show* us the way; heroes do it all for us. Following heroes is a type of emotional distraction characteristic of pop culture—the idolization of individuals who can do all the things that we cannot, and who make us wish that we were like them. Hero worship is frequently confused with loyalty, an attribute often encouraged in the practice of martial arts. While loyalty to a teacher and a group is important, loyalty to oneself and the truth is essential. It is advisable for all who are involved in these arts to consider exactly what loyalty they are professing.

Zen and the empty-hand arts are to be experienced (felt) directly by each individual. They do not entail simply being told what to do and abdicating personal responsibility. Traditional wisdom teaching encourages us to nurture the master inside. Zen is concerned (at first) with seeing into the true nature of things and acting accordingly. In receiving instruction, what truly counts is what has been taught and how we apply it, not where it was taught, when it was taught, or even who taught it!

The Popularity of Restructured Shaolin Forms

It cannot be denied that, in the huge country of China, the martial arts gained an early popularity. Yet, as we will see, among styles not influenced by street-vendor Kung Fu (see chapter 9), the Chinese theater, or the popularity of modern Karate, there is a uni-

---

[12] Judith Blackstone and Zoran Josipovic, *Zen for Beginners* (London: Unwin, 1986), p. 154.

formity of style bordering almost on conformity. On examination, and despite superficial differences and emphasis, the forms from each group closely resemble each other in Sanchin-like construction and clearly arise from a common prototype. Examples of these styles and their solo forms can be found in chapter 8, and a prototype form appears in chapter 10. These styles are, as yet, largely uncontaminated by modern notions of self-defense.

I find it difficult to believe that the ancient Hwrang warriors of Korea independently developed choreographed solo sequences (for Tae Kwon Do) virtually identical to those used by the Japanese, Okinawan, or Chinese stylists. I refer here to the original style of Tae Kwon Do founded (or at least promoted) in the 1960s by General Choi. It is alleged that General Choi had previously trained in Japanese Karate (we know his instructor did). This would certainly explain the resemblance between Tae Kwon Do patterns and Shuri-te Karate kata. It seems that the modified versions of Karate kata devised by Anko Itosu in pre-war Okinawa and altered in Japan have found their way

into the modern Tae Kwon Do repertoire, along with an adulterated Naifuanchin kata and other antique kata or restructured Shaolin forms. Paradoxically, however, there still remains a strong tradition in the Far East of not changing forms.

My concern in this is that of the priest for his scripture. Using Naifuanchin again as an example, the form has gone through a series of mutations, depending on which style adopted it. Yet, surely, if its true application had been known to the early founders of these styles, it would have remained technically and functionally unchanged. I, personally, do not wish to distort the genius or lose the experiences of the masters who created the original Naifuanchin. It stands as a record that has preserved immutable truths for centuries. Nor do I think it valid for people to change one of history's messages because they've failed to understand its language. To willfully obscure or degrade a kata and its application is certainly not the act of a responsible person, let alone a

Figure 10. A Naifuanchin lock.

master. I'm not advocating sycophantic worship of masters or a return to a perceived classical or golden age. My intention is far more practical than that.

The arrangement of Naifuanchin is not based on choice, but rather on specific techniques performed in the most efficient way. The sequence or form is what one with the requisite experience and ability would devise. This goes beyond mere notions of style or caprice. The arrangement and order of techniques is, in fact, systematic and progressive, and is logically and functionally based on human anatomy and its physiology (the joint system of the human body). Further, the range of techniques illustrated fully exhausts, in sequence, all the possibilities of the techniques involved. As such, it need never change, unless the human anatomy changes. In short, it is complete, and, contrary to modern practices, has nothing at all to do with blocking, punching, striking, and kicking. Naifuanchin is a masterwork that has endured, in high regard, particularly on Okinawa, despite the loss of its functions or applications.

Forms may be misinterpreted and misrepresented because of broken lineage, imperfect transmission from China, failure to comprehend function, or a blind following of authoritarian, ersatz tradition primarily engaged in promoting simplified Karate for mass consumption. This may explain how a great deal of modern "ballistic" Karate was unwittingly built on the solo sequence Naifuanchin (Naihanchi or Tekki), which, we will later discover, is, in application, unquestionably a catalog of grappling, wrist- and elbow-locking, subduing, and tumbling or throwing techniques from China.

No wonder some creators of modern styles abandoned Naifuanchin. Lacking the proper applications, common sense dictated to them that it would not work as a blocking and striking sequence and, further, that it could not be usefully integrated into sparring. Sadly, they considered it as outmoded and its applications as quaint and naïve. In the context of modern self-defense, it seemed hopelessly ineffective.

Less Can Be More

With home-grown forms now a modern fact and interdisciplinary borrowing common, you may be tempted to ask: "Why does this book confine itself to so few forms, when there are so many to choose from, when contemporary styles practice so many?" Let me explain. In 1900, Karate-ka practiced only a handful of kata (three to five). In the 1920s, Funakoshi wrote that a great expert would not know more than five kata. Indeed, it is a well-known fact that Choki Motobu, a contemporary of Funakoshi, practiced only the Naihanchi (Naifuanchin) kata for many years, as did Funakoshi. It is also common to find traditional southern Chinese Kung Fu styles using only a small number of forms.

A Karate school that practices only three to five kata might these days be considered impoverished. Today, most Karate schools practice anywhere from eight to fifty or more kata! Modern styles, in fact, pick and choose, or invent, kata to create a desired curriculum. This change represents the pursuit of quantity and variety over quality and depth, and an emphasis on using kata for grading requirements (especially for children). The modern focus is on learning the solo sequences and demonstrating them to a required technical standard. There is little or no attention given to integrating applications into practice. Generally, students simply move on to the next form after mastering only the mechanics and order of a given solo sequence, without mastering the applications, which, as we've already learned, modern attitudes and beliefs dismiss as nonspecific and as something that can somehow intuitively be discovered later.

According to Zen thought, the spoken and written word have limitations. In the empty-hand art, the Shaolin monks and nuns ingeniously avoided this limitation by creating physical drills and solo forms that comprise a real and enduring nonverbal tradition. It is, therefore, very difficult to present a tradition that was, for this very reason, never written down. How, then, do we choose? We cannot collect forms just because we like them. Nor can we ascribe multiple functions to the forms.

Unfortunately, some modern Karate and Kung Fu styles do just this. Founders of these styles often claim to have selected the best from each style or approach, but how do they know what is best unless they have a practical and objective yardstick? If they claim as a yardstick that which works in fighting, do they engage in actual combat to test their theories? Many founders of Karate styles and contemporary masters of both Kung Fu and Karate (traditional and modern) have never engaged in actual fighting! And, even if they have, do they continue to engage in real fighting on a regular basis in order to comprehensibly field test their techniques? Did they master an entire style or system before they took its material?

To master a single style (let alone several) in one lifetime is a tall order. Traditionally, the old masters confined themselves to a selected few forms that they utilized exclusively. The simple fact is that many modern styles adopt forms indiscriminately. Some even practice several versions of the same kata, or use Kung Fu forms *and* Karate kata together, combining them in a "boutique" approach to the art.

The Challenge Match in Antiquity

Karate-type techniques have been used both successfully and unsuccessfully in conflicts of many types—including defensive situations, tournaments, and personal "grudge" matches—all over the world. These should in no way be confused with alleged "heroic" Karate challenge matches from a Golden Age of Okinawan Karate somewhere in the dim and misty past. Actually, according to Shoshin Nagamine and others, one of the most notable aspects of Okinawan society is its well-earned reputation for being intensely peaceful.

I am skeptical of these legendary challenge matches in Karate history (or perhaps, more properly, To-te history). In fact, one very famous challenge match between two Okinawan Karate masters was, it turns out, a simple arm-wrestling contest! Another famous duel occurred when a 19th-century Karate master and a "strong man" squared off at a distance and engaged in some grueling eye contact! Our imaginations crave the imagery of legendary battles between heroic figures in the days of yore when enemies were everywhere and a man's life depended on keeping his techniques secret. In fact, however, there are very few records of actual Karate matches in antiquity. Books and films have simply repeated the same limited incidents, involving the same few characters. These incidents appear to have been mostly non-life-threatening contests between youthful hotheads or older men who set questionable examples for impressionable students to follow. Whispered accounts of "real" Karate fights are traditionally part of the assurances some need that Karate "works." Indeed most instructors have been asked at some point (particularly by juniors) whether they have ever had to "use it"!

Gichin Funakoshi, the figurehead and founder of Shotokan Karate, deplored fighting and, along with many other notable teachers, was not known as a man to use his fists. He stressed courtesy instead and collected and taught over fifteen kata. It is inconsistent to promote a kata-centered practice encouraging courtesy and formal movements if your true goal is self-defense or efficiency in a streetfight. Funakoshi taught the standard maxim: *Karate ni sente nashi*—there is no first attack in Karate. This moral principle, which means that one should never strike the first blow, demonstrates the true nature of Karate. Indeed, it is claimed that kata always start with a defensive maneuver—what a potentially expensive limitation in a streetfight!

Funakoshi believed and taught that Karate practice should remove conflict from life and produce the kind of individual who is unlikely to get into trouble. Some modern Karate instructors however, understandably feel forced to contend with new social environments and the dangers (real or otherwise) they present. To do so, they adapt their teaching: "In *traditional* Karate we don't hit first, but, on the streets. . . ." This leaves a student in a kind of moral vacuum, and we know how nature hates a vacuum! When we encounter the "hard man" (see page 40) however, we will see that he suffers from no such moral dilemma.

It is not my intention here to attack established styles. My goal is simply to put the Shaolin tradition into proper perspective and bring attention back to where I feel it belongs—to the preservation and dissemination of Zen wordless gesture through traditional forms and, most importantly, their applications. Such practice promotes skill with dignity and humanity. It promotes self-control, the very antithesis of the violence that some people think Kung Fu or Karate cultivates. Fortunately there are still those who reject violence and uphold the traditional methods manifest in the forms.

At the risk of sounding nostalgic, I suggest that the antique forms engender a degree of trustworthiness, certainty, and reliability. In this context, the timeless teachings of the masters are preferable to the satin-clad egotism of the modern performer, or the dehumanizing exhibitions of those obsessed with the grossest kinds of urban violence.

Street Defense and the Forms

At the core of any practice is the *idea*, the reason, for practice. This reason must be serviced by the appropriate material. For example, kata practice is inappropriate training for a boxer. Likewise, it can only improve the high-jump performance of an athlete very indirectly, while high-jump training contributes little toward pushing-hands skills. The forms were devised to produce a spiritual warrior, not a physical superman.

As we have seen, the Shaolin art, in being mistaken for a combat method, suffered inappropriate revisions. It was militarized (even in China), and mixed with boxing techniques in the West and Kendo tactics and combat distances in Japan. Boxing and

Kendo seek to maximize ballistic force—never the object of the Shaolin art (see chapter 7). Similarly European and American bare-knuckle fights and genuine wrestling bouts, though often dismissed as barbaric, were doubtless effective, and were historically far more visible and well-documented than contemporaneous Karate contests.

In urban violence, imposing physique, intimidation tactics, vicious aggression, and speed are mandatory, along with downright cunning, brutality, and the cultivation of natural instincts for survival. These characteristics have always been present in the profile of the "hard man," regardless of culture! These attitudes and actions are learned *in situ*—that is, by observation, emulation and actual participation, and not by practicing forms in a sports hall. Such tactics and methods are free from etiquette and moral, intellectual, social, or philosophical restrictions. That is partly why they work, and precisely why there is nothing noble or culturally satisfying about them. Although many modernists seek to emulate them, the devotees of such ignoble tactics are often perceived as the (potential) enemy by many traditional martial artists. Be that as it may, such tactics cannot profitably be recorded in a form. They have no connection whatsoever with the Zen Shaolin tradition and should not be confused with it.

More Can Be Less

The "hard men" who, in all probability, would not take organized forms-based Kung Fu or Karate very seriously, seldom put pen to paper to tell us, but I suspect it is no coincidence that modern styles pursuing functional combat increasingly resemble blood-and-guts Thai or Western boxing, which nowadays is often combined with a medley of simulated ear biting, eye gouging, head butting and Judo or Ju-jutsu-like grappling techniques. These styles, although still structured, lack definitive form and consequently are not open, as are Kung Fu and Karate, to improbable exotic theories, fantastical claims, or improbable applications. I would even suggest that the more "formatted" a method becomes, the more theoretical and formal it gets. Thus, collecting more forms means ending up with less practical ability.

This runs contrary to popular opinion, which suggests that the more forms you collect the more tricks or skills you will have at your disposal. This kind of thinking can be a trap. In real fighting, spontaneous adaptability around direct and simple methods rules supreme, not fixed forms and sophisticated strategies that can't easily or practically be combined spontaneously. We will return to this topic in chapters 7, 8, and 13.

The Shaolin Connection to T'ai Chi Ch'uan

Some people prefer Karate, perhaps because of its (supposedly) military format, while others identify with what is generally seen as its extreme opposite, the soft and flowing populist *T'ai Chi Ch'uan* (Chinese, grand ultimate fist) and the teachings of the Chinese Taoists (see chapter 4). It could justifiably be claimed that the technical differences alone lead to the choices made, but one must also consider powerful cultural and marketing influences as well. These influences have had a colossal effect on the belief systems, attitudes, and actions of many thousands of people.

T'ai Chi Ch'uan literature lays its own case for superiority. Traditionally degrading the Shaolin art (from which it grew) as rigid and dependent upon brutal strength, T'ai Chi Ch'uan sought to fill the spiritual gap left when the monastic Shaolin art fragmented into myriad rough village-combat-oriented systems and street vendor Kung Fu. Even though the apparent lofty aims of T'ai Chi Ch'uan practice may seem to fill the gap, however, its aims are much more personal and individual than those of the Mahayana Buddhism from which the Shaolin art sprang.

At first glance it appears that Karate and T'ai Chi Ch'uan are divided by a huge chasm, yet later we will see that Sanchin (Saam-Ching or San-Tzan), a mainstay Karate kata, is primarily a product of the White Crane (Kung Fu) school of Fujian (Fukien) in China (see chapter 10). Sanchin enjoys a prominent position in the Fujianese and other systems. The eight key hand techniques of the Crane style taught by the late Chen Dzwo-Dzen, a Taiwanese Kung Fu teacher, are fundamentally the same as the eight underlying techniques of T'ai Chi Ch'uan.

Horwitz and Kimmelman record that Chang San-Feng, the legendary creator of T'ai Chi Ch'uan, reworked the original forms of Shaolin to create the art.[13] This is further supported by Jou Tsung Hwa, who states that Chang San-Feng allegedly stayed at the Shaolin Temple for ten years and mastered all the Shaolin exercises.[14] In chapter 13, we will investigate the political and cultural motives responsible for the promotion of T'ai Chi Ch'uan in China.

Even if the legends concerning the history of T'ai Chi Ch'uan are inaccurate, historically we do know that it originated in Honan province, where the Shaolin Temple is situated. It is now common knowledge that T'ai Chi Ch'uan was a late development of Honan village boxing, which grew from the Shaolin art, as did key Karate kata. There is, indeed, a common origin for these and other related arts. No matter how indirect the connections have become, the various arts descended from and are related to the original purposes and ideas of the Shaolin order. Metaphorically speaking, the most important teachings lie in the heart of the body upon which the various styles (and cultures) are mere clothing.

The Shaolin tradition itself has suffered severe misrepresentation, mostly at the hands of Chinese (anti-Zen) nationalists, martial arts story-tellers, and writers who seem to have all but forgotten that they were dealing with the home of one of the world's major spiritual traditions, and its teachers and followers.

The Authentic Samurai Tradition

The Samurai tradition of Japan has suffered similar misrepresentation. Ritsuke Otake, a Japanese *sensei* (Japanese, teacher) and principal instructor of the Katori Shinto-ryu, a traditional school of Japanese Budo, asserts that an over-glamorization of the Samurai tradition has taken place, with many deeds and practices being falsely attributed to them. He comments on the uselessness of ritual suicide (*seppuku*, commonly known as

---

[13] Tem Horwitz and Susan Kimmelman, *T'ai Chi Ch'uan: Technique of Power* (London: Rider, 1976), p. 57.
[14] Jou Tsung Hwa, *The Tao of Tai-Chi Chuan* (Boston: Tuttle, 1981), p. 5.

hara kiri—Japanese, belly cut), arguing that by living, a dishonored warrior could attempt to make amends. Otake Sensei does not confuse the practicality and economic sense of retaining the services of highly trained and useful warriors with the value of political death sentences which is what many ritual suicides actually were.

Another example quoted by Otake Sensei concerns the change of targets used in modern Kendo (Japanese, the way of the sword) from the traditional underside of armor to targets on the outside. This is almost a complete reversal of the original practice. In the same way, the empty-hand art has undergone a "reversal" of usage—from not fighting, to fighting.[15]

The Form as Teacher

The original empty-hand concepts are expressed in traditional forms, not words. These forms contain the guiding principles and are the primary teachers, as well as being the art's greatest assets. In authentic versions, they stand as historical and practical records. Thus, the solo, and in some cases two-man, forms can be seen as a language in movement, a living, moving "scripture" left to us by the true masters. They are timeless and do not go out of style. We must follow universal truth, not people or fashions. Likewise, the intention and structure behind the forms are more important than the notions of style or individuals. These physical movements, if left intact, stand the test of time and transcend cultural barriers. This is the art's greatest strength.

In this book, you will be provided with fresh criteria by which the ancient practices of the Shaolin Temple and its developments (and distortions) can be evaluated and their true worth found. It is with this aim in mind that I choose to refer to the philosophy underpinning the authentic teachings expressed in the traditional methods as a "Sacred Science." This Sacred Science does not form the basis for modern free-style or non-Shaolin fighting methods. Ultimately, however, this Sacred Science is not, in essence, culturally attached. It has many expressions.

---

[15] Material comes from a B. B. C. documentary, "Way of the Warrior."

The Sacred Science

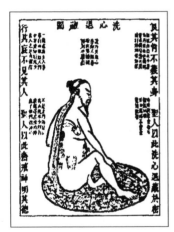

A student asked a Sage,
"What gives life its meaning?"
The Sage answered . . .
"Death, for without it, life loses its meaning."
(ANONYMOUS)

This chapter has been written to illustrate some of the spiritual and philosophical thinking prevalent in China during the development of the empty-hand art. I'm not trying to convert someone or change their spiritual outlook on life. The empty-hand art, as devised in the Shaolin Temple, has its roots in a number of interconnected spiritual systems that influenced the development of a "teaching without words" (Zen Shaolin). These spiritual systems I call, collectively, the Sacred Science. Their presentation is not meant to constitute a belief system, as such, but rather to illustrate the way of thinking that is the foundation of the Shaolin empty-hand art.

Sacred Science is, I believe, a title coined by the French symbolist R. A. Schwaller de Lubicz to denote the teaching of a science of the divine.[1] Such a science does not seek to control or manipulate for material gain, nor does it pursue mechanical innovation for utility or convenience. A working definition of Sacred Science is that it is a timeless and universal[2] science divulged by the ancients, embodying spirituality, cos-

---

[1] R. A. Schwaller de Lubicz, *Sacred Science: The King of Pharaonic Theocracy*, André and Goldian VandenBroek, trs. (Rochester, VT: Inner Traditions, 1982), p. 3.

[2] In using the term "universal," I do not mean to imply that it is a monolithic phenomenon. Sacred Science includes national, regional, and ethnic variations that present themselves with many differences.

mology, theology, living skills, the healing arts, and, in the case of the Shaolin Temple, the empty-hand art. The purpose of such a life science was undoubtedly to raise human consciousness to the highest possible level and to assist in the abolition of suffering.

Sacred Science seeks to uplift individuals (and, ultimately, the whole of creation) by taking them beyond the limits of their own, largely self-imposed, limitations and belief systems. By practicing its teachings, one gains a sense of purpose and identity, and a certainty in the nature of existence, along with a sense of freedom and joy. In Eastern methods, such as Buddhism and Taoism, this freedom frequently includes transcending the very systems that are being studied.

In its final stages, Sacred Science seeks to demonstrate, rather than speculate on, the role of human beings (and indeed all creation) in the scheme of things, and perhaps to reveal the reality of the continuation of consciousness after death—a message that may be vital in the current era of materialism and spiritual uncertainty. Perhaps it is a perfect antidote to the old established, dogmatic, and ill-founded belief system that simply stated says: "You live, you die, and that's it, I don't believe in anything else!"

The teachings of Sacred Science are designed to erase, or at the very least reduce, the fear and doubt associated with the futility of life and the dread of death. Its practitioners learn to master negative instinctual behavior. Are these grandiose claims? We shall see.

Symbolic Coding

Authentic Kung Fu forms and Karate kata follow the traditions of Sacred Science. The initial problem with any Sacred Science is that it is generally coded and expressed symbolically, in ritual, posture, gesture, hieroglyph, or poetic metaphor. This is done, not to mislead, but to contain and preserve. Of course this often makes the science inaccessible to non-initiates who cannot penetrate the coding or symbolism. Why not record the science in plain language? In the case of Zen, its wisdom teachings are clear about the impossibility of actually expressing the way in words.

Words are based on mutual exclusivity and can never be mutually inclusive. The real teaching is beyond duality. Attempting to describe reality (as I am doing now) will always fall short in failing to provide *experience*. This is illustrated by the Taoist sage Chuang Tzu in his parable of the wheelmaker and the duke.

A wheelmaker happens across a duke who is reading. The wheelmaker remonstrates with him about the uselessness of studying the "dregs" and "sediments" of old men. The offended duke bids the wheelmaker to explain himself or die. The wheelmaker (talking about what he knows) suggests that the reality of making wheels doesn't exist in words or explanations, but only in the actual making of wheels. He confesses that he has not even been able to teach his own son, and so continues to make wheels himself, even though he's become old. The duke, realizing the wisdom of the wheelmaker's words, spares him.

The point of any verbal statement can (over time) easily be exaggerated, altered, improperly translated, or taken out of context. The point of any statement can easily be lost by those who want to argue over, for instance, the way the statement was made, who made it, when and where it was made, or the status of the speaker. Indeed, there is a host of possible variables, and any discussion can be conveniently led in a direction that bypasses (deliberately or otherwise) the point being made, until the whole thing becomes an intellectual game, won by the most convincing, popular, or forceful speaker!

Who can describe the taste of a banana to someone who's never seen, let alone tasted, one? Direct pointing to reality, reputedly Bodhi-Dharma's system of teaching, mimics the ancient tradition of revealing and recording wisdom by using symbolic coding, the decipherment and investigation of which precipitates participation and direct experience. This direct pointing to reality has its origin in and is analogous to "wordless gesture," a practice said to have been demonstrated by the Buddha. In fact, we know that wordless gesture has a history longer than Buddhism itself. Yoga traditionally makes use of various hand, arm and body gestures called *mudra* (ritual gesture) and *asana* (posture). These gestures and postures are used to convey a teaching (attitude) without recourse to the spoken or written word. Zen Buddhism has also became well-known for this practice.

No matter how well described, Zen and the empty-hand arts must be experienced (felt) to be fully understood. Being involved in, and not just hearing, thinking or talking about, something is the crucial difference. The true book *Barefoot Zen* is encoded in the mental, physical, and spiritual practices it describes.

History has proven that a teaching preserved in a symbolic format is the most effective and has the best chance of survival. Often, the symbolism employed in Sacred Science is enigmatic or cryptic, even for its initiates. This is a secondary device used by the ancients to promote personal insight. Zen direct pointing (to reality), wordless gesture, and the physical nature of the empty-hand arts explain why there are few early written records of it.[3]

The Old Master's Secrets

In martial arts circles, stories abound regarding the old masters and their secrets. Some of these stories even claim that certain old masters took their secrets to the grave with them. In the teaching of true Sacred Science, however, there are stages of training, but no secrets. Some teachers do use purported secrets to take advantage of the uncertainty experienced by beginners and the confusion sometimes felt by more experienced students. Some, in order to control students, threaten to withhold certain secrets from them. Students then become fearful that they will be left with a half-learned style if they don't toe the line. Can such a method of control be justified? I once heard it explained as just another tool to maintain loyalty, and I was assured it was for the benefit of the students and gave them the opportunity to learn humility. Such a manipulative practice, however, is based on a falsehood. In words allegedly ascribed to the Famous T'ai Chi Ch'uan teacher Chen Man Ching: there are no secrets.

---

[3] Some claim that the old masters were illiterate. This is true only during the period after the decline and fall of the Ming dynasty and the Shaolin Temple (1644–5 onward). When the art reached the Ryukyu Islands (Okinawa), it was taken up principally by illiterate fishermen and farmers.

One of Dr. Chen's senior students even titled a book that way! Lack of understanding also encourages the use of secrets, particularly where the uncertainties experienced by teachers are concerned.

The Shaolin art did not rely on words, but rather on watching, and feeling, and practice. The methodology concerned itself with direct experience through wordless gesture. The beginning point was solo forms. These forms were seldom explained, however. Students, instead, had to absorb the entire ethos, the whole structure that laid the basis for a complete life-style.

Buddha dharma (Buddhist teaching) belongs to everybody, that's the whole idea. It does not belong to individuals; it is not an exclusive club. Dharma is, in the words of the Buddha, "For the benefit of all sentient beings." Imagine, if you will, the frustration on the face of a young novice monk who, unable to answer a certain riddle (Zen Koan), observes the crease of a smile on his teacher's face. "Is the old man holding something back? Is there something he's not telling me? Is there a secret?" he wonders.

The master however, can't tell the young man what he must find out for himself. He must make the experience his own. There is little point in sitting for an exam during which the examiners provide you with a list of the answers. In a proper exam, the answers are not really secret. If you have been faithfully following the curriculum, you will have been given the opportunity to absorb the required knowledge or ability. There is no legitimacy to threats of withholding information.

Some hold that certain techniques are too dangerous to teach. Yet these dangerous techniques always seem to find their way into print or onto film. Titles using the word secret are common. Such "secrets" are, of course no longer secret—if, indeed, they ever had been. Yet people remain interested in the notion of secrets. It has a kind of novelty value that those who approach the Zen Shaolin methods with a combat orientation feel can help to explain some of the complex movements in the forms. Indeed, there is generally only talk about secrets and secret techniques in schools that have set forms. Thai boxers, for instance, rarely talk about secrets. In fact, most secrets turn out to be a combination of common sense and experience.

Alternative Thinking

If you want to understand the forms created by the Buddhist masters, you have to learn to think as they do. The object of the Koan (riddle) is not to encourage clever or amusing answers, but to promote personal insight. Often, the key lies, not in seeking an answer, but in understanding the question.

The object of the Shaolin empty-hand art is not to provide clever answers to actual combat (warfare) problems, but to provide the basis for understanding how to deal with a physical force, without resisting or struggling (aggression) and without giving in and allowing that force to disrupt or hurt you (pacifism). Through such a process of harmonizing, it becomes possible, through the art, to enter the Tao (way of things).

The distinction between what's stated above and actual fighting may be subtle, but it is that very subtlety that makes all the difference. Please bear in mind that a one-millimeter error in a map or compass reading can cause you to stray from an intend-ed destination. The farther you travel on that path, the farther away you get from your intended destination. The warning here is a simple one: If the object (destination) of training is combat efficiency, practicing Shaolin-based forms is inappropriate (as Southeast Asian full-contact and other tournaments effectively demonstrate). You real-ly don't need such a collection of techniques to deal with brawlers. Regarding self-defense, the late, great Wong Shun Leung, a master of Wing Chun Kung Fu, once said to me, "To hell with all that, just hit the guy in the nose!"

The empty-hand art has made a long journey down through the centuries to us, but we don't live in the precincts of the Shaolin Temple, and unfortunately, the Zen mes-sage has become distorted through time and distance. Besides, many of us may have approached the art from the perspective of self-defense anyway. Such a perspective is already wide of the mark. Consequently, when the Shaolin Temple is brought into the equation, we are left to wrestle with the apparent contradiction between Zen and self-defense, or to deny it. Seeking the solution by studying Zen may not help either, because mainstream Zen thought does not appear to be directly linked with the empty-hand arts. Thus, martial arts enthusiasts who try to study Zen philosophy and seated meditation are often unable to reconcile the lofty teachings with the requirements of self-defense, or the methods taught in martial arts classes.

The solution to the problem lies in viewing the empty-hand art from the Shaolin Zen perspective, for the Shaolin approach is distinctive. Although it arose from, and is comparable to, other Buddhist methods, it has its own unique purpose—its own map, if you like. Without a Shaolin Zen understanding, the uninitiated user of Shaolin forms will always be distracted by what looks like a method of fighting, and consequently will be led off the path. Hearing that the empty-hand art is not *for fighting*, but is about *not fighting*, he will be like the uninitiated student who, when asked the famous Koan "What is the sound of one hand clapping?" laughs raucously at the apparently ridicu-lous idea, having taken the riddle at face value. Such a person will (even though he pays lip service to Zen) relentlessly pursue the so-called utility functions of Kung Fu or Karate, but will be no happier than a person trying to milk a bull. He may envisage him-self as a fighter, but, having grown old and gray, what will be left of his fighting days? He will have set out for India but reached America.

Zen teaches that people can become prisoners of their thoughts about the world, especially when direct experience has taken a back seat. In the Zen experience, the wise person, far from being apart from people, is everything that they are and yet more. The masters live in the mundane world, do mundane things, and yet soar to great spiritual heights as well.

Both Zen and Taoism demonstrate a rejection of verbal logic and conventional Western judgmental morality. Thus, there can be no such thing as a Buddhist martial art designed to punish wrong-doers. Later, we will see that, in Buddhism, there are also no notions of a permanent self to defend.

Both Zen and Taoism deal with the refinement of the human mind, body, and spir-it. These refinements, achieved through meditation and life-style, involve letting go and extinguishing (unnecessary) desire, regret, passion, and emotion in order to be one

Figure 11. Aizen Myoo. In the tradition of Japan, this god spans the border of physical and intellectual desire; the transition from indulgence to the wish for true knowledge. Traditionally he is fierce, but compassionate.

with all things. Later, we will see that thoughts are a product of the mind that has them, and not the mind itself. We can learn to be in control of thoughts and feelings, rather than being controlled by them.

In the practice of the empty-hand art, we can learn to rise above fear, violence, and insecurity, as we deal with physical and psychological force, without using aggression or other negative qualities usually associated with encountering such force.

Roots in India

According to R. S. Tripathi, the Dravidian Indians were the original inhabitants of west-ern Asia.[4] They inhabited the region prior to the invasion and settlement by the taller Indo-Europeans, with whom they mixed to produce the Hindu culture. The Dravidians built and inhabited Harrapa and Mohenjo Daro, the two oldest cities in the Indus val-ley, where figurines of men seated in crossed-legged lotus positions have been found, along with symbols of Shiva-Shakti, male-female polar opposites (see figure 12, page 49). This is the earliest evidence found so far of yogic practices, dating back to 3000 B.C.E., a period that corresponds to the first phase of building at Stonehenge in England and the discovery of bronze in Egypt. Others besides the Indo-Europeans learned spir-itual culture from the Dravidians, images of whose multiple-armed deity are well-known throughout the world. Similar images can be seen in cave paintings in old, pre-Indo-European Europe dating back 6000 to 800 B.C.E. (for instance, in Val Camonica, in the Italian Alps.)

Interestingly, a bronze statue of the Sumerian (modern-day Iraq) deity Pazuzu from 1,000 B.C.E. (see figure 13, page 49) has its arms fixed in the *abhaya* and *varada* mudras (Sanchin kata, Section 3, see chapter 10.) Mudras are ritual arm and hand positions tra-ditionally used in Hinduism, esoteric Buddhism, and various Kung Fu forms and Karate kata (see figure 14, page 49). There are many examples of the Buddha and other holy people using mudra.

---

[4] Not to be confused with the Branch Davidians, a modern American cult or sect. RA Un Nefer Amen I, *Metu Neter*, Vol. 1 (Brooklyn: Kamit, 1990), p. 34.

Figure 12. Left: Shiva-Shakti figure. Right: Hindu goddess Kali.

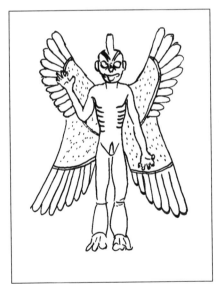

Figure 13. The Sumerian deity
Pazuzu.

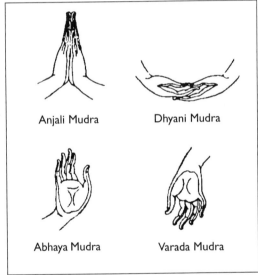

Figure 14. Mudras used in yoga, Buddhism, and
Sanchin kata (see chapter 10).

Other examples of multiple-armed guardian deities include the ancient Egyptian
"Master of animals," the Asian god Shiva, and the goddess Kali (a manifestation of
Shiva), all of which display the characteristics of fierceness and multiple arms (signs of
divinity). Postures and gestures stemming from these ancient cultures can still be seen
in various esoteric spiritual traditions continued up to the present. Tibetan Buddhists

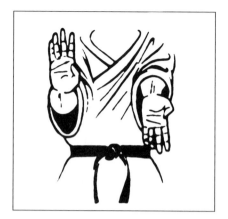

Figure 15. Mawashi uke.

practice a ritual gesture known as "turning the dharma wheel." It is almost identical to the circular hand movements found in section 3 of the Sanchin form. In Japanese Karate, this movement is called *mawashi uke*, or circular block, which terminates in abhaya and varada mudras. The origin of these postures however is, as stated, far more ancient.

Synthesis

Such postures and ritual gestures aid in the process of seeing, experiencing and teaching directly. Seeing directly, from a Zen perspective, helps to reveal the value of integrative thinking, or synthesis, and also reveals the limitations of rationalism.

The non-Zen mind sees a collection of separate things, perhaps by drawing upon exclusive segregative rationality. For instance, such a rationality embraces as fact the existence of several supposedly separate Karate styles, each containing the same or similar kata. Rationality concedes that they may be related, but cannot accept them as part of a generic whole due to the amount of attention paid to externals. This is particularly true if these styles use different national costumes and languages, and claim various national or divine origins or connections with ancient cultures or warrior castes.

The Zen mind, on the other hand, sees *one* thing, in many related and interdependent parts, drawing upon the nonrational, inclusive mind to do so. In other words, the Zen mind dwells on the point(s) of origin and interconnectedness, rather than on the points of emergence or separation. Thus, Zen seeks direct insight into reality. This does not amount to a rejection of diversity, constituent parts, or appearance. The overuse of intellect, the faculty we use to discriminate between things or break them down into their constituent parts, turns readily to chaos. Wisdom can easily become confused with mere opinion, points of view, or a belief in absolute logic or separate independent categories. Without the process of synthesis, a complex, multi-faceted, and once beautiful and useful object is rendered into a pile of useless, but well-classified, dust for the scientist who has insisted on separating the parts from the whole. It is more useful, in the Zen sense, to see the universality of the Tao (way). Without such understanding, the martial artist may, for example, never know of the intimate connections between his art, Buddhist philosophy, Hindu cosmology, and the universal nature of Sacred Science.

A tree severed from its roots will die. Divorced from the Sacred Science, the empty-hand art can, likewise, appear to be an isolated cultural phenomenon, a merely cunning and fiendish way of fighting.

Ritual, Posture, and Gesture

There is a rich tapestry of inspired ritual and symbolic movement in the many Shaolin-based arts. While it is impossible to discover when our ancestors' first engaged in ritual, we can still feel the spiritual impulse that motivated them. Ritual, posture, and gesture are essentially methods of preservation, communication, and demonstration. In the Shaolin tradition, this means forms.

It is interesting to note the mating behavior of the Sterna Hirundo bird. R. A. Schwaller de Lubicz tells us:

> The couple makes its courtship flight, the male bearing a fish in its beak; then the two birds perch. The male offers the fish to the female and then demands its return; mating is not complete until the fish has exchanged beaks several times. The symbolic character of this custom becomes even more evident when one observes this series of gestures performed *without* the fish, showing that the latter does not serve for food![5]

This behavior has clearly evolved into a ritual.

If birds are capable of such ritual behavior, so too are humans. In a highly civilized environment (such as the Shaolin Temple), the series of postures and gestures that made up the Shaolin empty-hand art was utilized as a ritual physical enactment of the drama of life and the conflicts involved, something that the shamans (holy men) from all traditions have practiced for thousands of years. The Shaolin methods were not utilized to cause harm. Nor were they intended as an actual basis for combat effectiveness designed to be used outside the confines of their particular environment. Many people are drawn to the martial arts disciplines because they consist of ritual performances that symbolically deal with fundamental human experiences such as mortality, the quest for control, mystery and power, and the search for identity. Increased fears of street violence and social dissatisfaction sharpen our sense of morality. Through the symbolic enactment of danger in the practice of the fighting traditions we can envision control over fear and unrest.

Animal Images in Kung Fu and Karate

Many Kung Fu and Karate styles have movements named after animals, both mythical and real. Animals such as the snake, crane, dragon, tiger, leopard, and praying mantis feature prominently in the solo forms. Such images are also a feature of many association or club badges.

---

[5] R. A. Schwaller de Lubicz, *Sacred Science*, p. 78.

Many styles have similar names, and the name Shaolin, or Shorin, is quite common. The names of the solo forms in many styles are also similar. In the practice of animal-imitating Kung Fu forms and Karate kata, it is commonly believed that practitioners should seek to emulate the strengths and qualities of a given animal, but this is a failure to understand symbolism. Hand positions, stances, body attitudes, gestures, breathing techniques (Lion breath, etc.) and patterns of movement were named after or identified with animals for symbolic reasons. Often, in the search for utility function, enthusiastic but misguided practitioners attach too much importance to literal translations of poetic symbolism. For example, actual belief in the fierceness of Tiger Claw Kung Fu or Dragon Fist Kung Fu (as opposed to any other style) can lead practitioners astray. I have seen Kung Fu stylists lose full contact bouts to kick boxers despite "supercharging" themselves with animal forms.

What do animals have to do with the Shaolin empty-hand art? We have seen that the use of animal imagery is a part of the Shaolin process of symbolic coding, as it was in the most ancient of times. We can only use this symbolism as guide, however, if we understand it. To do so, a basic working knowledge of the tripartite human brain is required, plus an understanding of the nature of ritual.

Images, Coding, and the Human Brain

Despite lacking modern scientific terminology, the ancients had a profound understanding of the human body, mind, and spirit. This understanding is reflected in their symbolic teaching. In making plain these connections, it also becomes clear just what the physiological basis for the classic three conflicts of Sanchin kata are.

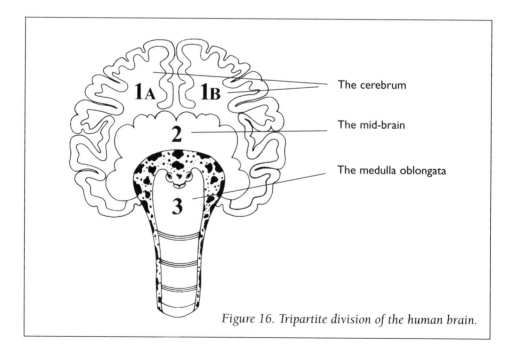

The cerebrum

The mid-brain

The medulla oblongata

Figure 16. Tripartite division of the human brain.

The human brain is divided into four parts at three levels (see figure 16, page 52):

1. The cerebrum (left and right hemispheres, human section of the brain);
2. The mid-brain (mammalian section of the brain);
3. The medulla oblongata (reptilian section of the brain).

Science records that a developing fetus passes through all three stages (amphibian, mammalian, and human) during its gestation in the womb.

The reptilian brain represents all primary urges and is the driving force behind all instinctual behavior. Anatomically, it can be located at the medulla oblongata, the snake-like base of the brain in which resides the reticular activating center, the part responsible for putting us to sleep and waking us up. The reptilian brain is, in the main, a totally self-obsessed, self-preserving, primitive, and reflexive center of being.

It is not difficult to see why the ancients symbolized the reptilian brain as a snake, which is a very basic creature with no arms or legs. It is sinuous, vaguely threatening, and slithers along the ground. It can neither jump nor fly. Further, it has, for countless centuries, been regarded as a physical and spiritual threat to humanity.

The mammalian brain is the caretaker brain. In ancient Hindu beliefs, in dynastic Egyptian religion, and interestingly, in Norse and Scandinavian mythology, these instincts are identified with the nourishing sacred cow (a provider and feeder), as well as with other mammals, such as leopards and tigers. In matters of caring for others, the mammalian brain demonstrates greater or more sophisticated competence than the purely reflexive reptilian brain. Birds, for instance, not being mammals, sometimes ignore chicks that have fallen out of the nest.

The left and right (Yin and Yang) hemispheres of the cerebrum are what make human beings unique. These two hemispheres allow us to fly high with our good thoughts, or soar away with our dreams, goals, motivations, and aspirations. They are symbolized as the crane, or the mythical dragon. In pre-literate shamanic cultures all over the world, cosmologies involving a sacred (world) tree are prevalent. Most place a serpent at the bottom of the tree and an eagle, falcon, crane, or similar bird at the top. Such symbolism is also found in literate cultures.

Yoga depicts the world tree as a human spine (man as microcosm) with seven or more chakras or psychic centers positioned along it. Yogis meditate on these chakras, each of which is associated with various correspondences, to planets, colors, sacred sounds, deities, and animal images. In yogic practice, the serpent Shesha and the bird Garuda are situated in the low belly and on the forehead, respectively. Incidentally, the dynastic Egyptian Pharaoh Tutankhamun was buried with a crown that had a vulture and a cobra attached to it. When the crown was in place, these two creatures, the totemic representatives of Upper and Lower Egypt, would have been positioned over the brow or crown chakras.

As in all careful (cultural) selections of imagery, the use of animal images should be seen as symbolic or totemic, not as a reflection of reality. If you practice empty-hand arts forms without an understanding of these images, they will appear to be very fanciful and exotic, and, to the experienced fighter, quite impractical. You might be disappointed that, for instance, in Tiger boxing, no one growls or has sharp teeth or claws.

What about mythical creatures? Take, for example, dragons. Are we to believe in their actual existence? Will we spend time discussing what they might look like, how big they are, or what they might eat? Have our teachers taught us meaningless fairy tales? Should we search elsewhere for meaning? In Dragon boxing, you may indeed soar up, but your ability to jump up in the air does not improve significantly because of the imagery, nor are you actually able to fly.

Don't try to "go animal." The purpose of such practices, as we will see later, is to control or harmonize with the primitive urges that are sometimes symbolized by animal forms, ultimately allowing you to rise above instinctual or animalistic behavior and master your self.

Practitioners originally work steadily through their own animal natures, investigating and experiencing each in painstaking and methodical practice.

> Not astride any of these (animals) can one reach the un-trodden realm (nirvana), where *a well-disciplined man goes only on his well-tamed (nature), his well-controlled self.*[6]

The traditional legend about the creation of the Wing Chun Kung Fu system provides a classic example of symbolic coding connected with the empty-hand arts. In the traditional tale, told to me by one of my teachers, the creator of Wing Chun Kung Fu was a woman, a Buddhist nun called Ng-Mui (Oong Moy) who decided that the existing Shaolin methods were too rigid and inflexible. One day, she sat and watched a fight between a snake and a crane, and from this observation created Wing Chun Kung Fu.

The significance of this legend is that the creation of this system was based on the control of the reptilian brain (snake) by the higher (crane) functions of human consciousness. Although we may now apply the scientific language of our time, the fact remains that the chosen players in the symbolic story are a Buddhist nun (spiritual aspirant), a snake (a creature very close to the ground), and a crane (a creature that flies).

Likewise, the dragon ridden by the Taoist masters is a combination of a bird and a snake, and represents the resolving of duality. The noble Shaolin masters did not create the empty-hand arts to encourage us to behave like beasts. Without proper guidance, people can be attracted to unwholesome ideas and drawn into bizarre practices, like pounding and crushing the ends of fingers in an attempt to harden them for the practice of Eagle Claw Kung Fu. Clearly the prerequisite for the use of such a weapon is the skill to deliver the blow regardless of the anatomical weapon used. A mind or body capable of understanding and developing such skill would equally be able to improvise a weapon should the need arise (a key, a stone, an item of clothing, etc.), rendering the pounding and disfiguring of the hands unnecessary. Serious warriors have always gone about their business with proper weapons.

> Swans fly in the face of the sun; those who possess psychic powers (Sidhis) go through the air. The wise, having conquered Mara and his hosts, go forth out of this world.[7]

---

[6] *Dhammapada*, Canto XXIII, 323. Italics mine.
[7] *Dhammapada*, Canto XIII, 175.

Freedom to Choose

While recognizing the animal elements in our nature, it is necessary to distinguish clearly between animals and human beings. An animal exists on two instinctual levels of being. The first is its existence as an animate creature, complete with sensory organs, capable of receiving information and stimulation. The second is as the agent of natural and programmed reactions to this stimulation.

Here the animal reality ends. There is simply the animal and its response. Thus, the hunted will run from the immediate danger of the hunter and continue to graze. A human, in a parallel situation, will consider the event, imagine the event, and relive it, while dwelling on the corresponding emotion of fear.

This is because humans live on three levels of being. The first is as an animate being, complete with sensory organs capable of receiving information and stimulation. The second is as the agent of any given reaction to stimulus, both physical and mental. Unlike other animals, however, humans have a third dimension—an ability to be aware of and reflect on the other two processes, a reflecting action of consciousness. This is what gives us free will—the ability to choose to amend our animalistic behavior, or not. Humans have being and response, as well as reflection and choice. Animals have no such choice. They must simply follow their natures. While Zen encourages spontaneity, it does not condone or support thoughtless animalistic behavior, with all the consequences it can bring.

Humans are self-conscious (i.e., conscious of a self). This ability or knowledge is a two-sided gift that immediately creates a condition called duality. On the one hand is the exhilarating feeling of being alive, with its attendant desire to control, judge, and categorize things. On the other hand, we feel pain through the intellectualization of certain experiences, such as disappointment or death. Reflection gives rise to conceptualization, imagination, and the development of conscious strategies for survival. This duality is the starting point for spiritual impulses.

While self-consciousness or self-recognition triggers the spiritual impulse, it also produces the human phenomenon known as ego. Humans are capable of feeling personal insult, based on consideration of position, real or imagined (social position, rank, title, or self-image). This can occur on both a personal and a collective level. Thus, representatives of groups or nations can plan and conduct a war based on ideas or, more properly, ideals. These strategies should not be confused with the authentic empty-hand art, which never draws up plans to destroy people, things, or places. The Shaolin empty-hand art was designed to go beyond thinking and planning, and essentially to serve the spiritual impulse. The masters of the Sacred Science utilized the raw power of the reptilian brain and raised it to a position in which it was placed in the service of the higher, more aware (human), cerebral consciousness. We are not born with self-awareness. This faculty is latent in the infant, developing only as the child develops physically and mentally, and interacts with other beings.

The cerebrum has two hemispheres. Both are vital, although they have completely different functions. The function of the left hemisphere is to separate things, people, and places from the "whole" to which the highest teachings say all things belong or are connected. The right hemisphere of the brain connects all things, places, and people, synthesizing them into that whole of which we are all inescapable parts.

From the left hemisphere comes linear straight-line thinking of the type seen in Cartesian logic. Cold, calculating, and pedantic, it makes individuals of us all. It also fills us with a dreadful sense of separateness, or aloneness. The left hemisphere is information-mad, feeling that all it needs in order to succeed is data. Yet information is not experience (no one ever got fit or lost weight by reading about it). This hemisphere is also the one used to construct strategies and plan war.

From the right hemisphere comes imagination, inspiration, poetry, art, rhythm, intuition, spontaneity and a wonderful sense of interconnectedness. Lao Tze called this interconnectedness the Tao. It is to the right (nonrational) hemisphere of the brain that we must turn in order to access and decipher Lao Tze's work and, indeed, the empty-hand arts. Paradoxically, the right hemisphere seeks to be free from the accumulated clutter of information. It is to this region of the brain that we go when, in a daydream, we seek escape from having to learn or pay attention to a mass of facts or data.

The sages (meditation masters or truth teachers) taught a middle way. They gave practical instruction in how to harmonize both hemispheres of the brain and, in turn, how to synthesize these with the functions of the mid- and reptilian brains. The Eastern masters eventually came to call their discipline yoga. The Shaolin empty-hand art is a lineal descendent of this philosophy.

Trimarga: the Triple Path to Zen

4

T*houghts should be treated like guests*
and desires like little children.
(ANONYMOUS)

Yoga, Buddhism, and the Tao all contributed to the development of Zen. Yoga gave birth to the practices of the Shaolin Temple, where Taoism was blended with Mahayana Buddhism to create Chan (Zen). Specifically, ancient shamanism led to Yoga (Dravidian Indian religion), which in turn contributed to Hinduism, which led to Hinayana Buddhism. Hinayana Buddhism experienced a division with the creation of Mahayana Buddhism, which blended with indigenous Taoism (a lineal descendant of ancient Chinese/Asian shamanism), creating Zen. Collectively, the three make up the Trimarga (Sanskrit, triple path) that leads to the Zen way.

Yoga

According to some sources, the word "yoga" is derived from the Sanskrit root word *yuj*, which means to unite or join. The word referred initially to the need to unify the differing states of consciousness characterized by the four parts of the brain (medulla oblongata, mid-brain, and left and right hemispheres of the cerebrum). Once this occurs, practitioners can go on to seek a transcendental union with god or the eternal.

When the mind learns to internalize and let go of its "is-ness," delusion and conditionings are stripped away, and the mind, in its natural, unconditioned state, enters into a state of bliss, knowledge, and yoga (union). With prolonged practice, adepts often acquire mystical abilities (siddhis) such as the ability to go for long periods without food or water, or the ability to concentrate powerfully, or to stay awake for long periods of time. Would-be adepts are always advised that to chase these siddhis leads off the path. The same applies to the Shaolin-based empty-hand art—to pursue the art as means of fighting leads off the path.

In the modern era, it's no surprise that ignorance of such a path or purpose leaves us nothing but the pursuit of "fringe benefits" such as self-defense or showmanship. The ancient teachings on transcendence and the techniques of meditation found in yoga formed the basis of the methods divulged by Gautama Buddha in his message to the world. While there are clear doctrinal differences between Hinduism and Buddhism, such as whether there exists any such thing as a permanent self, I have not dealt with them here, as they are outside the scope of this book and can only serve to obfuscate the clear connections between the empty-hand art and wordless gesture, be it Hindu or Buddhist.

Buddhism

Before we look at the basic teachings of Buddhism from the empty-hand art point of view, it is interesting to note that, to be accepted as a Buddhist monk, candidates could, be neither criminals nor soldiers. The use of weapons simply does not agree with the foundation of Buddhism nor any of its legitimate developments. Indeed, for Buddhists who discount the notion of a self separate from other things or beings, the notion of self-defense would be ludicrous. With regard to oral and published claims that the Shaolin order devised the martial arts to protect their treasure or defend themselves while traveling, a quote from the British Museum's *Buddhism: Art and Faith* will confirm the true extent of their materialism:

> A monk's duties were his spiritual exercises and the instruction of novices and lay folk. He was permitted to own eight articles; his bowl, three pieces of clothing (an upper and lower garment and a cloak, colored red or yellow), a belt, a razor, a needle and a water filter; to these were added later a garment against the rain, a fan, wooden toothpicks, sandals, a staff and a rosary.[1]

To the modern Western mind, the life-style of a Buddhist monk or nun may seem severe, but that is relative. Prior to the enlightenment of the Buddha, spiritual practices consisted of the most ascetic type, with, for example, mortification of the body through near-starvation, and other austerities. Evidence of these practices can still be seen among the Sadhu priests and other ascetics who still wander across India today.

> Neither nakedness, nor matted locks; neither the application of mud (over the body) nor fasting, lying on the bare earth; neither smearing oneself with soot nor squatting on one's heels can purify a man who has not rid himself of doubt.[2]

---

[1] W. Zwalf, ed., *Buddhism: Art and Faith* (London: British Museum Publications, 1985), p. 12.
[2] *Dhammapada*, Canto X, 141.

The Buddha himself rejected these harsh practices as a way to liberation, and taught instead a "middle way." What follows is a brief synopsis of his basic teachings. These are wisdom teachings rather than commandments, applicable in any culture and any era.

The Four Noble Truths

The Buddhist philosophy is based on a set of four noble truths that, if truly understood, can lead the mind to a state of bliss.

The truth of suffering teaches that everything is suffering—birth, old age, sickness and death, contact with what one dislikes, separation from what one desires, not obtaining what one wishes, and the realization that all things are subject to change.

The truth of the cause of suffering is related to expecting and wanting life to be a certain way. Physical discomfort and suffering are not the same thing. We suffer in the mind, and the mind produces the conditions of life that are unstable and unsatisfactory.

The truth of the end of suffering brings a realization that suffering begins and ends in the mind. (This not to be confused with pain.)

The true way to end suffering consists in living in a harmless way, in the moment, skillfully and fearlessly, as characterized by the eightfold path.

The Eightfold Path

The eightfold path is the way one follows to come to a true understanding of the four noble truths. It includes:

Right Understanding: To understand suffering, its origin, its extinction, and the path that leads to the extinction of suffering; to understand what is wholesome and what is not.

Right Thought: To direct the mind toward benevolence and kindness. To be free from attachment, ill will, views, and opinions.

Right Speech: To abstain from lying, gossiping, and speaking unnecessarily or harshly.

Right Action: To abstain from killing, stealing, and immorality.

Right Livelihood: To maintain one's livelihood without harming any living being.

Right Effort: To make the effort to remain aware and unattached in all circumstances.

Right Mindfulness: To be aware of all that one does in thought, speech, and action.

Right Concentration: To be free of all mental disturbances, such as worry, anxiety, or envy. To be at one with life as it (actually) is.

Hinayana Buddhism

Hinayana is Sanskrit for "small vehicle." It was originally a derogatory term for the conservative, or Theravada, school. Theravada means "teaching of the elders," and the school developed during the period from the death of the Buddha to the end of the first century B.C.E.

According to its adherents, Hinayana Buddhism represents the original, pure teaching of the Buddha, who probably lived between 563 and 483 B.C.E. Born at Kapilavastu (present-day southern Nepal) and named Siddhartha Gautama, the Buddha was a member of the Shakya clan. His father, Suddhodana, was the king of Shakyu state, one of sixteen states into which India was divided during this period. The term *buddha* is not really a name, but rather a title. It comes from the Pali language and means "awakened one." Gautama Buddha was not the first buddha, and, according to tradition he won't be the last. A number of buddhas preceded him, and the Buddha Maitreya is apparently yet to come.

Mahayana Buddhism

Mahayana is Sanskrit for "great vehicle," the inference being that it opens the way for a larger number of people (than the Hinayana), and has the express intention to liberate all beings. The Buddha's original doctrine may appear hard to follow, as it involves withdrawing from the world as a reclusive mendicant (monk) and constantly concentrating on *nirvana* (liberation).

The Mahayana school arose in the first century B.C.E. It was believed that, by placing less emphasis on monasticism, the layperson could also achieve nirvana. Attaining nirvana quickly for oneself, however, was no longer the goal. In fact, this was now considered to be selfish. The aim, instead, was to become a Buddha by first becoming a *Bodhisattva* (one whose essence is enlightenment). The main cut and thrust of this new idea however, was to put others before oneself in order to liberate all beings.

Compassion

Compassion is not an emotion, as such. When active, it is a vital demonstration of the heights human consciousness can reach. Compassion, a key element in most major spiritual traditions, is the linchpin of the teaching of Gautama Buddha. Initially, compassion must be applied to oneself, but, clearly, a person who does not have compassion for others can hardly be expected to have proper compassion for himself. In Buddhism, therefore, one cultivates compassion for all sentient beings, a compassion that cannot be based upon a distinction between other and self. Ego-based self-preoccupation and selfishness are to be reduced, and then avoided. This is why, in reality, there is no such thing as a lone sage. It is also why the Buddha encouraged the creation and maintenance of a spiritual community (*sangha*). It is also why (beyond the commercial reasons) we have empty-hand, Kung Fu, and Karate groups. Ultimately, compassion for others and compassion for self must become the same thing, with the goal of freeing all from karmic rebirth.

Each human creates his own karma, but all karma is linked. Thus we all ride together on the karmic wheel of birth and rebirth.

Karma

Karma is a Sanskrit word with many shades of meaning. It can refer to:

• The chain of cause and effect in the world of morality;

• The sum of all consequences of the actions of an individual in this or previous lives;

• The consequences of mental or physical action;

• Mental or physical actions themselves.

For example, what we do today is the result of what we did yesterday, and what we do tomorrow will be the result of what we do today. This idea has been "met-aphorized" in Christianity as, "As ye sow, so shall ye reap."

Each individual's karma is the result of tendencies and possibilities present in his consciousness. This potential directs the individual's behavior for good or for evil. Every karmic action is the seed of further karma, the fruits of which are reaped in the form of joy or sorrow, accordingly.

Although we all create our own limitations through our past thoughts and actions, having formed these tendencies, we may continue to follow them blindly or alter them (the free will of Christianity). Creating good karma and erasing bad helps loosen karmic bonds and disengages us from the wheel of rebirth and the grip of *Mara* (the symbol of overwhelming human passions that hinder progress on the path of enlightenment). The Buddha's compassionate teaching offers us a means to get off the roundabout, so to speak. This should not be confused, however, with extinction or annihilation. It is concerned, rather, with freedom, the liberation of consciousness, initially birthed as a seed (potential) in the human and subsequently individuated.

From a Buddhist perspective, all life and experience, right up to the present time, exist only as memories! Although, of course, we have to live through the consequences of our previous actions (karma), essentially each present moment is the only reality. Indeed, there is, within the Zen tradition, considerable emphasis placed on launching individuals into the moment! Despite this, each of us must still die, and, according to the Buddhists (among others), our actions determine what happens to us after death. (This is seen in other traditions as a judgment).

Eradicating Negative Karma

Having the ability to choose good or bad is not enough in itself. How many New Year's or other resolutions have we made to give up a habit, or improve behavior, or

enhance some other aspect of our lives, only to find the old habit or behavior returning with a vengeance after a short period of time? Lasting improvement is only to be
found in the participation in, and commitment to spiritual exercises conceived at the
dawn of civilization and refined incessantly ever since.

On an individual basis, the practicality of meditation lies in the fact that, with
enough hard work, you can reprogram your spirit and neutralize your negative karma,
breaking bad habits, modifying behavior, and taking control of fear and your own destiny.

The demons and monsters traditionally depicted in the hells and underworlds of
various cultural traditions are no more than personifications of the deepest and pro-
foundest regrets, doubts, fears and wrong-doings of the conscience/consciousness as it
departs this world. It is with these demons that we do battle during Sanchin (see chapter 10)! One object of this is to consciously eradicate negative karma, now!

One does not need to entertain such beliefs to gain benefit from the practice of
Sanchin, however. It is, after all, not an article of faith, but a matter of direct experience. The Buddha's own admonishment went something like this:

Work out your own salvation!

Examining the Self

If we take away name, career, titles, rank or social position, gender, or marital status, who or what are we? This is one of the fundamental questions and conditions
examined in Buddhist practice. Beyond name, upbringing, and a whole host of shaping
factors, it is easy to see that there is "something" that experiences these experiences. It
is that "something" that enables us to reflect, to be conscious, and to try to know ourselves and others. Perhaps we partake of a very special type of consciousness, a type
that provides us with the freedom to choose, either to remain on the karmic wheel of
life, death, and rebirth, or to achieve liberation.

Physics tells us that matter can't really be created or destroyed. Even if it could, it
would have to be created out of something, and some kind of energy would be needed. It is the common metaphysical belief of many spiritual teachings that consciousness continues after death, and that rebirth is what follows. This does not necessarily
imply that we will be born again as ourselves, but rather that our unresolved tendencies and characteristics (plus our essential aggregates) may be. These are not to be
confused with solely hereditary characteristics. Our consciousness itself must relocate.
In fact, consciousness itself cannot be spatially located, we can only view its effects via
the brain. We cannot talk about how many cubic centiliters of consciousness a person
has. Consciousness seems to be as imminent in nature as fire is in the air. All that is
required to observe its potential is the proper medium—combustible materials in the
case of fire, and a brain and a body in the case of sentient beings. Of course, both need
oxygen.

It may, therefore, be possible to speak of the individual evolution of consciousness.
Indeed, the whole planet in general, and humanity in particular, seeks to become self-
aware. Thus, the cyclic wheel of karmic rebirth grinds on and on. Paradoxically, if we

accept rebirth, upon being reborn, we won't necessarily know ourselves. Mercifully, we can't remember (precisely) who we were before. What remains consistent is the vital sense of individuality that we all insperience/experience. This is the nature of incarnation, and its impression/expression through subjectivity and objectivity. This remains true even when consciousness finds itself in (as) a child, a "new" individual with no previous memory and only embryonic thinking skills. Essentially, only the sense of selfhood moves across incarnations, yet the living out of karma still must be done, and we (collectively or otherwise) have to do it!

Conventional thought often takes cover behind the (left-brain-inspired) veil of skepticism, nihilism, and negativity when dealing with this subject. This persistent habit leads to the well-used cerebral image-idea of death as a "nothing"—as though, at death, a great black curtain descends and that's it. Such thinking insists on the existence of nonexistence, often without proper investigation. The other choices are fundamentalist religion, or rationally justified indifference. It is only through recourse to the tools of Sacred Science, that the world of spirit can be *felt*, by which I mean directly experienced, and nihilism and negation challenged. This experience is beyond thought, argument, or belief. Of course, we must never fall into the trap of negating rationalism, which is, after all, required to consolidate experience and provide a sense of continuity. The process of spiritualization must obviously include thought and memory.

> Live not in the entanglements of outer things, nor in inner feelings of emptiness. Be serene in the oneness of things and [such] erroneous views will disappear . . .[3]

> By self alone is evil done; by self alone is one defiled; by self alone is evil undone [not done]; by self alone is one purified. Purity and impurity depend upon oneself; no one can purify another.[4]

Puja

Puja (Sanskrit, worship or ceremony) is a method employed to eradicate negative karma. It consists of ritual actions. Practicing the empty-hand art is one way of performing puja that uses symbolic postures and hand gestures to create holy space about the worshiper and serves to separate him from the transitory world of the senses. Such a practitioner is called a *pujaka*. Performance of Sanchin form is a classic type of puja.

Mara

Mara is a Sanskrit/Pali word that means literally "murder" or the embodiment of death. Mara is all that hinders us on the path to enlightenment. As lord of the realm of

---

[3] Master Seng-ts'an, Third Patriarch of Zen in J. Blackstone and Z. Josipovic, *Zen for Beginners* (London: Unwin, 1986), p. 38. Brackets mine.
[4] *Dhammapada*, Canto XII, 165

desire, Mara takes on many guises and has many offspring. Three of them—ignorance, fear (worry), and greed—he sometimes sends out in the guise of three of his five daughters, the other two being anger and skeptical doubt.

The Gautama Buddha, during his own quest for enlightenment, was severely tested by Mara, who sent an army of demons to cause fear. They included a spreader of ignorance (lassitude/torpor) and his most beautiful daughter (greed) to distract the Buddha from perfecting the way to liberation, preventing him from showing the way to others.

Gautama Buddha did not fear the demons, who could not find a gap in the perfect emptiness of his defense, or any point at which to engage him. (This relates to pushing hands.) He defeated ignorance by remaining motivated and awake, and by becoming enlightened. Greed turned into an ugly hag in front of the Buddha when she tried to confront him but his enlightenment was too much for her.

In traditional Buddhism, fear, ignorance, and greed can be countered with the triple gem of Buddhism, which consists of:

Buddha: the example of the teacher;
Dharma: the teachings and their applications;
Sangha: the community who support each other in the practice of the teachings.

The function of Mara in Buddhist thought should not be confused with the common notion of the Christian devil, although there are striking parallels (Christ's temptation, for example). In fact, Mara was the catalyst for Gautama's enlightenment. He provided the resistance that led to that enlightenment, and ultimately to the Buddha's development of the doctrine of the middle way. As it is not the Buddhist habit to reject a polar opposite, Mara can most usefully be viewed as a part of the way. When misread, however, this can appear to imply a lack of morals. It can look as if evil is being accepted. Buddhism, however, has a moral code implicit in the four noble truths and the eightfold path (see page 59). The Taoist theory of yin and yang describes two polar opposites, neither of which can function without the other. As in Buddhism, a middle way is sought. This middle way does not imply political expediency or indifference—something of which the Taoists were often accused. The Taoist version of the middle way seeks to harmonize yin and yang and transcend them. This is achieved by entering into a dynamic interactive relationship with nature, uniting heaven and hell, and discovering and following the indwelling divine self, the master within.

Maya

Maya (Sanskrit, deception, illusion) is an agent of Mara. One must be on guard against the many illusions caused by a variety of errors, chief among which is departure from the middle way into extremism. One of the most obvious extremes is pleasure and its pursuit. This can be a difficult concept to understand, as it seems quite natural to desire pleasure. There is, of course, nothing wrong with pleasure itself. The illusion of the possibility of endless pleasure, however, is one of Mara's favorite tricks.

Thus the unwary can be led like a donkey chasing a dangling carrot, with Mara driving the wagon. Such a fool will be led quickly away from reasonable balance and into disaster.

Instead of accepting pleasure when it comes, one may be inclined to attempt its artificial creation, to manufacture it and always have it at hand—planned pleasure, so to speak. How many of us find it difficult to celebrate something according to a calendar date? Sometimes we just don't feel like it. It's difficult to feel good "to order" and we may feel compelled to make ourselves artificially happy. As in any other aspect of life, the artificial is never as satisfying as the real. Artificial pleasure is never as strong as real pleasure. Much artificial pleasure has a grasping kind of violence about it, connected with the drive to succeed, the need to possess, control, or manipulate, to pacify or to satisfy.

When we continually look forward to something, the present moment, vital to mental health, is lost. We become enslaved, controlled by pleasure, and are no longer in control. Nor is there any longer any freedom or peace.

I do not mean to imply that a dull, ascetic, joyless life makes one virtuous. That is no better. For most, this would merely force the issue and cause rebellion in the animal spirit. This can also occur when you are suppressed by religious institutions and the expectations of others. In such a case, the way can be lost. Still others, wallowing in masochistic self-denial, become prone to pride and feelings of superiority, entertaining such notions as, "Look at me, look how virtuous, self-denying, and clean-living I am. You really should try to be more like me, I'm such a good person." This naive attitude can actually deter those who would otherwise embrace the wisdom teachings.

If the resistance isn't there (Mara), the muscle won't grow, so to speak. We must be concerned, however, with the real work, not just cultivate the appearance of working hard. Trying to demonstrate to others that we are trying hard dissipates our focus and diffuses our concentration.

Mara is a master of Maya. In ancient times, Mara was sometimes depicted as a fierce being, with one hundred arms. (I leave it to the reader to work out why.) In practicing the middle way, you become less vulnerable to being controlled by Maya or Mara, and thereby by fear and violence. With a properly structured spiritual system, you can take your destiny into your own hands and gain the means to eradicate negative karma. This is in accord with the most ancient of teachings. The advantage of the empty-hand art lies in its physical nature. Provided the methods are correctly ordered, presented, and adhered to (as was the case in the Shaolin Temple), very little theory or philosophy is actually required.

Through the practice of *physical* Zen (forms, kata, and pushing hands) you can work to become a better person, without even consciously realizing it or having to study lots of theory. The disadvantage of the empty-hand art lies in the fact that, divorced from the Zen principles, it is open to abuse, misinterpretation, and misrepresentation. Under such circumstances, explanation and theory do become necessary, lest the Zen-based art eventually be passed over in favor of distortions.

Taoism

Taoism (pronounced dow/tow-ism) blended with Mahayana Buddhism to form the basis for Zen. It was from Zen that the empty-hand art was devised, as an extension of meditation.

The best-known Taoist teachers are Lao Tze and Chuang Tze. Lao Tze was born in Hu-Hsien, in the state of Ch'u, (present day Honan province) in the sixth century B.C.E. Chuang Tze was born in the fourth century B.C.E., also in what is now Honan province. Their message presents a mystical teaching about the Tao, or the "way," and *Wu-Wei* (unmotivated action).

The original Chinese pictogram for Tao can be read simply as "way." It was in general use as a term to denote moral behavior and general human conduct. The *Tao Te Ching* (The Book of the Way and Its Power), usually attributed to Lao Tze, is the first recorded attempt to give the concept of Tao a profound metaphysical meaning. This book, written in the sixth century B.C.E., consists of eighty-one chapters (9 x 9) of sometimes cryptic and sometimes haunting poetry and prose that prod the reader into a realization of the origin and mutual interdependence of all things and the divine inspiration and purpose behind all things. The *Tao Te Ching* is the canon of Taoism. Part of its value lies in the thought processes needed to read and understand it in the first place. Its verses open one up to the intuitive, and to what C. G. Jung called "the divine and numinous."

For Lao-Tze, the Tao was the ultimate principle. Knowing that it is actually unnamable and beyond description, he was skillful enough not to dogmatize his insight. The very first chapter of the *Tao Te Ching* starts like this:

> The Tao that can be told is not the eternal Tao.
> The name that can be named is not the eternal name.[5]

Compare this with the statement of the sixth-century Zen master, Tao-Fu:

> The truth is above affirmation or negation.[6]

From a Zen point of view, once a concept is made, it is no longer that which it describes. Hence, all concepts are descriptions of reality, and not reality itself.

Chuang Tze's approach was a variation on the theme set out by Lao Tze. He recorded his vision in a collection of works called the *Inner Chapters*. Chuang Tze's attitude toward life was, without doubt, an inspiration to Zen monks hundreds of years later. The following is a quote from the *Inner Chapters*:

> The perfect man uses his mind like a [reflecting] mirror—going after nothing, welcoming nothing, responding, but not storing [grasping]. Therefore he can win out over things and not hurt himself.[7]

---

[5] Lao-Tze, *Tao Te Ching* (London: Penguin, 1985), p. 27.
[6] J. Blackstone and Z. Josipovic, *Zen for Beginners*, p. 35.
[7] Tem Horwitz and Susan Kimmelman, *T'ai Chi Ch'uan: Technique of Power* (London: Rider, 1976), p. 134. Brackets mine.

Chuang Tze's teachings are often simultaneously profound and irreverent, filled with wisdom and humor. They address topics such as greed, ignorance, fear, false modesty, and false piety. Chuang Tze takes particular issue with those who break the laws of nature and the Tao in the name of so-called goodness and virtue. He was no real friend to pomposity and dogma either, and he frequently ridiculed the state and political thinking of the day—particularly Confucianism, of which he was a relentless critic. Confucianism was the adopted state doctrine that reflected the philosophical and socio-political aspects of Chinese culture. Based on the teachings of K'ung(fu)tzu (Confucius, 551-479 B.C.E.), Confucianism had a determining impact on public life in China, Korea, and Japan. A huge socio-political and cultural subject, it must remain beyond the bounds of the present book.

Who Dies?

Struggle as we may, we all die. Yet, what is death to the living? It is no more than an intellectual, conceptual, and emotional idea, connected with the observation or contemplation of mortality. We are afraid—an emotional response. We don't want to lose things, or face our idea of the great nothing, the great zero, the great dread. We don't want to think about it or talk about it, and we certainly don't want to experience it.

We are always in need of, and generally want or desire, something. Even those who don't know what they want have that nagging feeling, "I want something, I don't know what it is, but I want it." In the West, this often gives rise to noise, action, and stress. In Taoism, the practitioner cultivates quiet, non-action (not to be confused with lethargy), and relaxation (not to be confused with leisure or idleness).

Perhaps what we all want is fulfillment. Imagine that you have everything, that nothing is missing. Imagine that you *are* everything, all things in you and you in them. This is to truly be at one with the Tao. Only in this state are you complete. The Taoist path is trod by living vigorously in the moment and practicing acceptance. Here, the Taoist and Buddhist paths conjoin. I also find this truth reflected in the Christian doctrine of love.

Acceptance doesn't mean masochistic pessimism, but rather joyful support of and participation in the great cosmic drama. Perhaps liberation is achieved by the enlightened individual, who, by letting go, "fixes" his transient consciousness, making it imperishable and complete—the Taoist master riding the wind on a dragon, if you will. For the Taoist master who transcends time, the moment is thus eternal. By living in the everlasting moment, he becomes immortal. Modern physicists and psychologists are just beginning to consider that time and space, as we perceive them, may be conceptual constructs based on the limitations of our senses.

Uniting with and becoming one with the Tao cannot be achieved by the use of intellect, thoughts, or even reflection. The adept becomes one with the Tao by realizing (i.e., making real) within himself its unity, simplicity, and emptiness. This requires intuitive understanding. The essential Tao is realized by abiding in silence and letting go, so that limitations and conditions fade until you can recognize your true self and realize the absolute. This is encapsulated in the concept of *Wu-Wei*.

Wu-Wei

Wu-Wei means unmotivated action. It is a concept that stresses a total lack of pre-meditation and intention (not having a strategy or a plan). Wu-Wei is said to be the attitude of a Taoist saint. It depends upon emptiness, which seems to imply nothing or a lack of things—particularly possessions or power. To the Western mind, unfamiliar with Eastern thought, emptiness means desolation, loneliness, or boredom.

The Chinese concept of Wu-Wei cannot be grasped by complicated explanations, because it is something that must be felt or experienced. From the perspective of the empty-hand art, however, the practical application of this philosophy results in several very important benefits:

1. Fear and other unwanted emotions are prevented from interfering with a full range of activities (from daily living to the perfect execution of a technique during empty-hands practice).

2. By being empty, one responds naturally and correctly to what is happening, not to what one thinks will happen. Spontaneity without irresponsibility (in daily life and in empty-hands practice) is the goal.

3. One in harmony with the Tao creates less friction and therefore has a smoother path through life. Water flowing in a river does not compete with anything. Following the "Watercourse Way," physical movements can be kept direct, economical, and practical. Energy wastage can be kept to a minimum, and, in the empty-hand art, the training partner's force can be utilized.

4. One does not need to cultivate aggression or other attitudes that may not be akin to his nature.

5. The proper application of the true spirit of Wu-Wei to daily life will lead to a life in which there is less confrontation. Paradoxically, therefore, the more skillful one becomes in the empty-hand art, the less one gets into situations where confrontation occurs.

Taoism has developed practices to provide direct experience of the way. They are uncannily similar to the meditation techniques used in the Zen school.

Zen

5

To worry in anticipation or to cherish regret for the past are like the reeds that are cut and wither away.[1]

Yesterday has gone, and tomorrow does not exist. (Did it ever?) The only reality we can experience is the now, the eternal present moment.

We all suffer from fear, doubt, and worry. Some of this is the product of our past experience, and some the product of an imagined future. Both have profound influences on us. A major theme of Zen practice is that neither the past nor the future are real. This can seem a little crazy, at first, but, there is a simple model you can adopt to become more comfortable with the notion.

To the left of you is space and to the right of you is space. You exist in the middle. In the same way, we exist between the past and the future. The past and the future are valuable tools for constructing mental and emotional continuity, but they are only conceptual worlds. They are not the vital present moment. Contemplation of the past recalls a whole gamut of previous experiences. Contemplation of the future hinges on uncertainty, but often brings hope. If we continually run the gauntlet between the two, we are absent from the only real experience, the here and now. Acceptance of the present moment is not simply an excuse for immediate gratification and self-indulgence. It is the beginning of "cutting the ties that bind," as one teacher puts it. This requires fearlessly living in the moment. According to Zen thought, existing completely in the

---

[1] Bukkyo Dendo Kyokai, *The Teaching of Buddha* (Tokyo: Buddhist Promoting Foundation, 1979), p. 376.

present moment is the only reality. All spiritual development needs to start from this point. Anything connected with the past or any notions of the future are, when rationalized, merely products of thought, or, more properly, reflection.

The Zen school stresses methods to actualize this understanding and liberate us from illusion, primarily that of seated meditation, the initial object of which is to plunge us into the moment. Gradually, other methods were added (koans and the empty-hand art), but the hallmark of Zen is its unique approach of pointing directly and instantly to reality.

The essence of Zen can be encapsulated in the following four short phrases traditionally attributed to the first patriarch. According to modern scholars, however, they were more probably set down by Master Nan-ch'uan P'u-yuan (Japanese, Nansen Fugan).

It is said Zen is:

1. Special transmission outside the orthodox teachings.

2. Independence from scripture.

3. Immediate pointing to the human heart.

4. A realization of one's true nature and becoming a Buddha.

Despite this brave attempt, the virtually indescribable nature of Zen is what causes Zen masters to utilize Mondo[2] or seek expression in wordless gestures as a means of communicating.

It was the original Zen (Chan) freedom from scripture that allowed it to borrow from esoteric Buddhism, Taoism, and Hinduism. For a teaching that is said not to depend upon orthodoxy or scripture, however, there is probably more material written about Zen than about any other school of meditation. Eventually, Zen itself became "orthodox."

Zen does not deny the usefulness of scripture or the written word. Indeed, it makes great use of the heart and diamond sutras. Paradoxically, only a person who has been through the experiences described in the writings can truly read what is written there. Thus, like empty-hand forms, they act solely as a mnemonic device—a record.

It is not common knowledge that the Shaolin art grew out of Zen wordless gestures. The questions we must ask are how and why did this occur—that is, how did so-called combat skills grow out of meditation, and why?

Meditation was originally designed as a technique to resolve interior and exterior contradictions (duality) and achieve a state of liberation (oneness). Later, we will see that empty-hand skills were developed with similar objectives in mind.

---

[2] Mondo is a question and answer dialog between masters, or between master and student, in which, although words are used, theory and logic are forbidden.

The Shaolin Temple and Chan (Zen)

The Shaolin Temple situated on Mount Sung Shang in Honan Province in China was probably built during the Wei dynasty in the third century C.E. It became primarily a center for the study of Zen (Chan) Buddhism, despite all the fantastic claims made about it.

Buddhism had actually existed in China since the late Han dynasty (C.E. 25–220). It suffered persecution in later years due to its doctrine of retreating out of the world and giving up family commitments, which clashed with the indigenous Confucian ideologies of filial piety and scrupulous attention to family duties. The Zen school flourished, however, due to its unique approach.

Zen downplayed the study of scripture and ritual observance, while stressing (in typical Mahayana fashion) the importance of lay practice. Anyone with sufficient practice could therefore achieve enlightenment, without recourse to endless learning or the need to become a monastic—which of course, allowed, the practitioner continued commitment to family matters.

Zen also embraced and incorporated indigenous Taoist elements that gave Indian Buddhism a distinctly Chinese flavor or feel. Zen devotees practiced seated meditation, being in the moment, and direct pointing to reality. It is recorded that Bodhi-Dharma often pointed to wild animals or natural beauty to directly convey a teaching without using words. How many of us have not felt a tugging somewhere deep when exposed to an ink drawing of a Zen landscape (or any other art form bearing the hallmark of Zen simplicity). For centuries, teachers have used these direct methods of transmitting the concepts of Zen, which are always better felt than discussed. The direct method also reduces the need to engage in endless and often difficult intellectual discussion.

The genuine empty-hand way is one such method of experiencing the Zen concepts. As we saw in chapter 1, seated meditation (zazen) is a completely subjective and personal experience. Begin by assuming one of the prescribed meditational postures, and then forget about your body. Once your body is still, your mind will become the "agent provocateur" by bombarding you with all sorts of thoughts that rattle around in your head like a box of frogs. Remember that during the meditation process, no attempt should be made to reject or repress any thought. Simply let go of it and return your mind to the point of concentration.

As noted earlier, this is a primary practice of Zen Buddhism. This method, however, still remains subjective, personal, and, above all, solo. The ever-innovative Zen school soon devised an additional and alternative method of "moving Zen" suitable for partners.

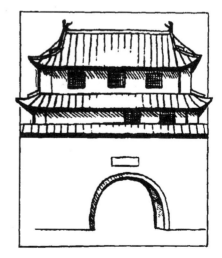

Figure 17. Shaolin Temple.

PART TWO

The Rationale for
the Empty-Hand Arts

The Creation
of the
Empty-Hand Arts

F*all down seven times get up eight.*
—BODHI-DHARMA

Tradition maintains that Bodhi-Dharma, in introducing new methods of meditation at Shaolin, found the resident monks to be physically unable to conduct the practice. He therefore introduced the now famous Eighteen-Monk Boxing Exercises. We are sometimes encouraged to imagine that the empty-hand art grew from these exercises, somehow independently from the rest of Buddhist practice. I would like to take a fresh look at these exercises (see page 176), because, if they are indeed the seeds from which so many arts grew, I think they require conscientious scrutiny. It is of little real importance who introduced the empty-hand art. It may not have been Bodhi-Dharma himself.

We are led to believe that Bodhi-Dharma found the monks physically unfit for the practice of meditation that Buddhism stressed. Even if this were the case, however, why invent a series of eighteen boxing exercises to rectify the situation? Bodhi-Dharma had traveled from India. An obvious and practical solution to the Shaolin monks physical shortcomings would surely have been to teach them some yoga practices that, with an emphasis on breathing, relaxation, and posturing, would have taught all the necessary skills required for seated meditation. In fact, it seems that Eighteen-Monk Boxing was indeed devised as a kind of Chinese yoga—but, as we shall see, a yoga with a difference. In order to understand the true significance of the Eighteen-Monk Boxing Exercises, we must look at them in the context of what Bodhi-Dharma was trying to teach as a whole in meditation.

The rationale for the exercises goes something like this:

1. You are not your thoughts. Thoughts are simply by-products of the mind that has them. Thoughts are mere reflections or demonstrations of our innate consciousness (that is, they help to register and organize consciousness through the will). Yet some thoughts are unwanted and come into the mind unbidden. These thoughts can be likened to forces that attack the mind of the seated meditator.

2. All thought is transient and impermanent (being reactions to our internal and external environments). Therefore, thoughts are experienced, let go of, and dispatched back to where they came from by the meditator.

At the height of the drive among Chinese Buddhists to find new expressions of wordless gesture (probably at some point between 528 and about 900 c.e.), the monks of Shaolin came up with the following question: Why not objectify our subjective experience? Put another way, why not take this practice (meditation) out of the mental dimension, and practice it in the physical dimension? But, how could they achieve this?

Seated meditation starts with a firm posture in which the back is straight. This ensures attentiveness, good blood flow, and good breathing. (Breathing has a direct influence on thought and vice versa—observe how you breathe during an emotionally charged situation). As we have seen, attention is then turned to the point of focus in the meditation—the breath, the posture, a chant, or a mantra (sacred chant). During practice, there is no attempt to repress thoughts or struggle with them. Thoughts simply arise and pass through the mind. If a thought distracts, it must be released so the mind can return to the point of focus.

The monks decided to objectify (externalize) the whole process by substituting thought with force. With arms in contact and bodies positioned in a firm posture (like the horse stance) in which the back is held straight, they pushed one another's arms in various ways. As Buddhist monks and nuns, they had taken vows against struggling and fighting, having chosen to follow the four noble truths and the eightfold path. They could, however, touch or hold and control a physical force (provided by the other) up to the point of resistance, and using a well-centered posture, either "pass" these pushes on or rotate at the waist, yielding to the force and rerouting it, ultimately sending it back to its source in a circular fashion. In this way, they would remain in harmony with the Tao. They developed this insight into a series of movements, or forms, varying the types and amounts of force.

Just as there are many types of thoughts to release during seated meditation, so too there are many types of movements that can be used to redirect force during moving meditation. The results, however, are the same. Students must be "empty" to be effective. If they are not, they are unable to respond spontaneously to force, unable to redirect, and thereby release, it. The trick lay in refining and controlling the (animal) urge to resist.

To reject a force is to struggle and reject the moment, in the process of which you can be hurt. On the other hand, by doing nothing you can also be hurt. The key is to harmonize with the force, reroute it, and return it to the sender.

This practice held the beginnings of what would, in perfected form, become the famous *Tui Shou* or pushing hands that would later be crystallized in choreographed solo sequences known as forms (kata) for symbolic coding, preservation, communication, and demonstration.

The advantages of such a method of moving meditation are clear. Seated meditation is a very personal, subjective experience. Once practitioners adopt the recommended meditational posture, they're on their own. It is virtually impossible for a meditation teacher to gauge students' practice (emptiness), or steer them on the right path, since the teacher has no idea what is going on in the minds of the meditators. (They may be sitting in a perfect meditational posture, but be thinking about food . . . who knows?)

The beauty of the empty-hand practice is that it can be observed and guided. When we engage in practice with a senior, he is not only able to correct the physical details of our practice, but also to monitor the state of mind that governs how we flow from one technique to another, how we absorb, borrow, and return a training partner's force, and how we are able to flow with our partner's movements rather than struggle against them. Using the correct methods, we can cultivate the ability to remain calm and dispassionate under pressure, to transcend fear, violence. and insecurity. Our physical proficiency is a reflection of our state of mind and of our progress along the empty-hand way, a path that goes much further than just the acquisition of fighting skills.

In a sense, the empty-hand art is not for fighting. The so-called fighting skills it encourages are by-products of the skills acquired in mastering ourselves! Serious practitioners of the art obviously do not invest much time and energy preparing for a fight they may never have. Besides, learning to fight is treating the symptom, not the disease. Zen philosophy seeks to remove the fear and aggression in the individual, and thus treats the disease directly. In many respects, we face ourselves and not the world. Zen does not seek to encourage violence, either in thought, word, or deed. We must manifest this in our actual practice. When we learn that fighting is an animal instinct and requires no virtue for man, only excessive vice, we understand that to fight is to become an animal. The empty-hand master always appears dignified, upright, and civilized. The epitome of patience and virtue, he is never a thug or a bully, and is most reluctant (outside of the practice hall) to use the very skills for which he is noted.

He who controls his rising anger as a skilled driver curbs a rolling chariot, him I call a true charioteer. Others merely hold the reins.[1]

---

[1] *Dhammapada*, Canto XVI.

Pushing Hands— Tui Shou/Kahkie

B*e as a dragonfly that perches on the top of a stick raised to strike it.*
(CHINESE PROVERB)

It must have been quite a sight to see the flow of techniques between two monks pushing hands. When one unbalanced the other, or caught him "out of the moment" (not concentrating), a lay observer could be forgiven for thinking that the monks were fighting.

They were not. In pushing-hands, force is passed from one to the other simply with a view to testing a state of mind (psychological balance), physical balance, and reflexes.

During practice, exponents avoid struggling with force, harmonizing it instead, with a particular force or series of forces by blending with them, neutralizing them, and returning them.

Pushing-Hands

Pushing-hands has three stages of practice or training: investigation, duality and non-duality.

Investigation, refers, quite literally, to investigating or learning the movements, responses, and procedures of pushing-hands.

Duality, refers to the adoption of separate roles by the pushing-hands exponents. One takes the role of attacker, force-giver, or driver of the action; the other takes the role of defender, receiver, or meditator.

Nonduality, refers to the use of all possible combinations or permutations insti-
gated at random by either of the partners, who have resolved their differences
(duality) poetically. This is called "dancing the cosmic dance of Shakti-Shiva"
(gender/polar opposites in Hindu cosmology). In this practice, there is no
longer the sense of other and self.

The two fundamental actions consist of breaking the training partner's posture through
pushing and pulling. The methods also include: pushing and changing hands, pressing
and trapping hands, escaping hands, rolling arms, gripping hands, grip escapes, leg
traps, leg presses, leg escapes, advancing, retreating, and circle stepping. These are all
practiced in contact with a partner.

The continuous action of pushing-hands is much more than just a separate auxiliary exercise. It is the original medium through which to express the techniques from
traditional forms. This does not imply the use of pre-arranged movement, however.
Pre-arranged movement is controlled by the knowledge of a rehearsed sequence. Far
from launching one into the uncertainty of the "Zen moment" (the whole purpose of
practice), pre-arranged movement restricts you, or ties you to meticulous, slavish, or
machine-like repetition. This provides security for the intellect and the ego, and a visibly "right" way of doing things. But there is no spontaneity in it.

Although a pair can perfect a sequence and demonstrate it skillfully, the movements are built on anticipation and control (knowledge is power)—quite the opposite
of Zen letting go. Physically, a sequence cannot lead to variety, unless both participants change to another rehearsed sequence. Nor is it likely that partners could mix
two or more sequences without pre-arranging or working out which bits to include
and which to leave out. It might be good for demonstration, but it is self-defeating
from a Zen perspective. Such a practice can only produce *Dharana* (see chapter 10),
or simple concentration, the most basic level of Zen meditation. It will not lead any
further than this.

Knowing a sequence is thus analogous to having the exact answers to specific
exam questions, without understanding the answers, the questions, or the subject
proper. If different questions are asked, you will be unable to answer them. It is a mistake to assume that repeatedly playing tunes by ear will lead to being able to read
music. Similarly, it is a mistake to assume that the continual rehearsal of set pieces will
lead to spontaneity.

Repetition is a part of learning to push hands. The movement, however, must consist of the essential responses, and not routine. You must produce the appropriate
counter to a partner's actions spontaneously, without thought or anticipation. This can
only be consistently achieved by using the sense of touch, or more properly, touch
reflexes.

Touch Reflexes

Touch reflexes are primary reflexes. They are faster than visual reflexes. They can be
executed as quickly as taking your hand away from a hot plate. What is interesting from

a Zen perspective is that there is no thinking through or planning such a response. A visual reflex, on the other hand, is a more complex and time-consuming process. First, the eyes see, then they send a message to the brain, which identifies what it has seen. The brain then initiates a response (nervous impulse) that finally starts the muscles. In Kung Fu or Karate, successfully utilizing visual reflexes, depends on good eye-hand coordination, natural athletic ability, and tactics.

Compared with other physical faculties that can decline by up to 90 percent with age, touch reflexes are among the last of our faculties to diminish. This, coupled with the use of forms that operate only within the natural range of movement, means that a high standard of pushing-hands skill can be maintained into old age. The rules of the purely animal kingdom are adapted and transformed by the pushing-hands practitioner, who puts the efficient reptilian reflexes in the service of meditation and self mastery.

Dr. Yang Jwing Ming, a prolific author on Chinese Kung Fu, states:

> In China, every style has pushing hands. . . . It doesn't matter which style. *Firstly you have to get in touch with each other* to learn sensitivity.[1]

During pushing-hands, movement is triggered by contact, not vision. Changes in circumstance are read automatically by the arms, which, acting like the antennae of an insect, remain in contact with the partner's arms and detect every movement.

Variety is introduced as early as possible. For example, when in double-arm contact with a teacher, a student who has learned a simple "cross" grip escape (right wrist gripping right wrist) could have either wrist gripped or even both wrists gripped simultaneously by the teacher without being told, and still respond effectively. The repertoire is gradually increased until the student can deal skillfully with a considerable variety of "intrusions," all woven together in the nonstop flow of pushing hands.

Once students have acquired the skill of reading force, they can freely utilize an assortment of movements from the traditional forms, without pre-arranging them. Note that, in pushing-hands, there are no formal attack-and-counter sequences in which the defender moves too early, yet, out of compliance, the attacker still misses his mark or continues with an already-failing technique.

No Ballistic Movements

There are no ballistic movements (thrusts) in pushing-hands, and it is important to understand why. I have divided the explanation into two parts, the first technical and practical, the second, ethical.

Practical Reasons for Not Using Ballistic Force

Pushing-hands exponents control and monitor each other's limbs by remaining in contact, so that neither has the freedom or the space to launch a ballistic attack. If

---

[1] Yang Jwing Ming, "The Rationale of Chinese Boxing," *Fighting Arts International* (F.A.I. 68, vol. 12, no. 2), p. 48. Italics mine.

either breaks contact to strike, that person instantly becomes vulnerable to attack as well. If this happens, simultaneous exchange of techniques can occur. The thrust of a larger person (in all probability) carries the greater force, which is undesirable from an equality perspective. Also, one has difficulty proving a strike. Such an attack may have to be halted before it reaches its target (to avoid injury), and a training partner may have to accept a theoretical defeat.

If, during practice, one partner loses concentration for a moment, he might be unbalanced, actually and not just theoretically. He might find his arms pinned or cross-tied (a major tactic in the ancient Chinese art). He might find himself continuously kept off balance, his posture broken, or the corner (same-hand same-leg side) lost. He might find he has to tumble out of a subduing technique or be unable to recover balance from a leg trap. All this can actually be accomplished without anyone getting hurt, and without entertaining arguments about whether or not a blow might have landed, what damage it might have done, and all the theoretical problems that dog some modern martial arts.

Legs can also be successfully used without causing injury, if their use is restricted to presses, traps, or tripping actions. With the use of such leg actions, it is imperative that proper consideration be given to individuals thrown off balance. (It may be necessary to help them maintain their balance, or lower them gently to the ground.)

If ballistic force is allowed to come into play, fast "snappy" blows, in which the hand is lashed out and speedily withdrawn, will predominate, simply because they are so difficult to stop. Such techniques are only possible if the arms are left free, untrapped, and unmonitored. Promoting the use of ballistic force will ultimately encourage this type of practice, at the expense of pushing-hands and the application of traditional forms. In fact, this is in part what has happened, and is what has led to the creation of modern freestyle sparring methods. (Old-fashioned styles of ballistic Karate did not withdraw the thrusting hand, thus at least giving the defender a chance to complete a traditional block.) By avoiding the use of ballistic force, it becomes possible to play with force in a genuine and productive way, a way more akin to wrestling than boxing.

To avoid loss of physical balance when being pushed or grappled, use the tight compact movements from Sanchin form, taking care to stay centered on your training partner. To avoid loss of psychological or mental balance, simply let go of fear, anticipation, and other potential or actual distractions.

Using ballistic techniques inhibits this process, leading, as it does, to a fracturing of the silk (see page 85). Furthermore, these techniques can encourage excessive expectations related to self-defense. One must be realistic about what is, after all, moving meditation, however dynamic.

The use of ballistic force in pushing hands is self defeating (self-limiting), inappropriate, and not part of the authentic practice. Finally, the use of ballistic (snappy) force in the air can be damaging to the joints.

The continuous flow of forces during pushing hands exhibits the hallmarks of genuine empty-hand arts—spontaneity and the ability to "borrow" and utilize a training partner's force. If a partner retreats, stick and follow. If a partner advances, stick and retreat, never giving enough space for a strike to be generated, and never desiring to generate a strike of your own.

Ethical Reasons for Not Using Ballistic Force

It is forbidden and inappropriate for a monk or a nun to strike anyone. The action is simply too extreme.[2] Unless you are a monk, a nun, or a Buddhist, this may seem a small point to you. Our subject (Zen Shaolin) is rooted in Zen, and to practice Zen is to cultivate the ability to go beyond set models, such as judgment, rational justification, emotional response, animalistic behavior, or idealistic desire. Instead, those who follow Zen are encouraged to seek and take the middle way.

Please do not make the mistake of thinking that Zen means pacifism, idealism, or any "ism." In its perfect form, Zen is said to be beyond any emotion whatsoever. This can be difficult to understand, because we often consider emotional responses to be quite normal. In matters of conflict, we are often taught to hit back. Hitting back, however, can hardly assist us in the cultivation of the middle way. Nor can passive idealism and quietism.

> To see dualism in life is due to confusion of thought. The enlightened see into the reality of things unhampered by ideas.[3]

To unite heaven and hell (resolve duality), you must reach figuratively between them. This thinking formed the spiritual basis of the Shaolin empty-hand art.

Zen Shaolin—Neither Confrontation nor Surrender

A classic Zen-style conundrum states, *"To fight is a mistake, to give in is also a mistake."*

If force (Mara) is met with force, conflict and chaos ensue. Any individual who responds this way becomes no better than that chaotic force. In emulating Mara, you join his ranks. Thus, even if an immediate opponent (possessed by Mara) is vanquished, if you employ Mara's methods, you too are possessed.

If force is left alone to "do its own thing," it may destroy the potential for liberation (Mara attacking the Buddha) and overcome the passive idealist, just as surely as it will overcome the ignorant and those who have sunk into the world of illusion. Such people also join the ranks of Mara.

> When you try to stop activity in order to achieve passivity your very efforts fill you with activity. *As long as you remain in one extreme or the other you will never know oneness.*[4]

What then is the solution? In the empty hand arts, it is found in the adoption of methods that spring from and demonstrate the middle way.

The existence and effect of the two extremes should be recognized, but not embraced or rejected. By employing curling, flowing, circular patterns that merge and

[2] The famous stories of the ninth-century Zen patriarch Lin-Chi I-Hsuan (Rinzai) using fists and a stick to strike students, are largely allegorical.
[3] Master Hui-neng, Sixth Patriarch of Zen, in Judith Blackstone and Zoran Josipovic, *Zen for Beginners* (London: Unwin, 1986), p. 45.
[4] Master Seng-ts'an, Third Patriarch of Zen, in J. Blackstone and Z. Josipovic, *Zen for Beginners*, p. 38. Italics mine.

join with, but redirect and order, chaotic force, pushing-hands exponents emuate the action and nonaction of the Tao (way) and shape chaos into order. In a sense, the practice is about being, not doing. By its very nature, this cannot include the use of brutal or ballistic force. Finally, using ballistic force in pushing hands prevents you from practicing at the level of non duality.

Hard (Go) and Soft (Ju)

Go and *Ju* are the Okinawan/Japanese terms for "hard" and "soft." In the context of the martial arts, they are used to describe physical attitudes in combat. These terms are also employed to denote style. For many years, people have argued about the strengths and weaknesses of the "hard external" style/s and the "soft, internal" style/s. These two approaches are considered to be diametrically opposed, with the so-called hard (external) school characterized mainly by strength, speed, and power, and the so-called soft (internal) school stressing softness, pliability, yielding, and the use of *qi* (internal energy). Some styles claim to include both, assuming that if one partner is hard, the other is soft, and vice versa. A paradox indeed! The real reasoning behind Go and Ju is explained in the section on borrowing force (see below). The question of hard and soft disappears, however, if you do not generate or use your own power, but learn to blend with and use a supplied force.

External and Internal

Regardless of style, and putting all mystical or unprovable claims aside, the production and use of ballistic force consists of its generation and transmission from one partner to the other, and amounts to the same thing in all styles, regardless of method. Therefore, movements that are born of self-manufactured power (triggered by a conscious desire to hit) should be considered as external, regardless of style.

Automatic bodily responses (prompted by contact) that borrow and return a given force should be considered as internal regardless of style. Such responses, having been programmed into the body and internalized, occur only as reflex responses and virtually without cognizance.

Borrowing Force

Borrowing a training partner's force can best be achieved by adhering to the four keys or principles of applied Sanchin, known as: float, sink, swallow, and spit.

Float (Pu) can be compared to the resistance created by a buoyant object floating in water. It relates to the natural tactile resilience of the body (through the arms) in intercepting force. This amounts almost to a resistance, as the body detects and instantly protects, the arms not being overwhelmed and caving in at the instant of contact. When float becomes a potential struggle (this may be in a fraction of an instant), it discharges its load and changes to sink. Keeping good Sanchin and observing this rule ensures that you respond only to genuine force and are not disturbed by fake or insubstantial pushes or pulls.

Sink (T'm) can be compared to the floating object retaining its mass, but suddenly and completely losing its buoyancy. In practice, you let go, causing the force-giver to fall into the resultant void and perhaps lose balance, depending on skill.

Swallow (Tun) is well named, after the muscular action of swallowing, which is enhanced by gravity. In the same way, the body muscles are used during swallow to assist the force (and its giver) past the point of no return. Agreeing with the direction of the force encourages either a complete loss of balance (after sink) or a retreat (usually in the opposite direction). It is this retreat that sets up the best possible conditions for spit.

Spit (Toh) can be likened to forcefully spitting out a table-tennis ball. The ball volleys out with force, because it is under (air) pressure. Similarly, spit occurs when your momentary opposition becomes agreement with your training partner's force (direction). Thus, even in retreat, your own force seems enhanced.

A somewhat crude, but useful, explanation for float, sink, swallow, and spit follows.

The Inward-Opening Door

Imagine yourself with your shoulder pressed close to a door that opens (inward) toward you. Some man is pressing the door to get in and you are preventing him (float). He begins to push harder. Perhaps he is stronger than you. It doesn't matter. Calmly, you let the force build up, and, at a judicious moment (at the point when it becomes a struggle for you), you suddenly let the force go, slipping to the hinge side of the door (sink). As the other person comes crashing through, you, well-placed behind, give him a push (swallow). As your partner struggles to save what's left of his balance and throws all effort into reversing direction, you are there once again to (bodily) agree with the direction of force, sending the person back out through the door (spit).

It is easy to see that float (Pu) corresponds to go (hard/resist) and sink (T'm) correspond to ju (yield/soft). The task of a practitioner is to blend the two. The easiest way to do this is to study the point of transition, the point at which you are required to let go. Practicing slowly and smoothly is the most effective way to develop skill. Eventually, speeds can be varied . A force may be let go of in a fraction of a second, or retained, depending upon its type, direction, and speed. Once skill is obtained in moving smoothly through all the stages (blending the hard with the soft), you will be able to develop a skill known as keeping silk.

Keeping Silk

Traditionally, the quality of force used between skillful pushing-hands exponents is referred to as "silk." This describes the evenness of tension that must be maintained when spinning silk. If the tension varies, the thread will snap, the spinning will stop and start, and the finished silk will be lumpy and weak. If the thread tension is smoothly maintained, however, the spinning will be continuous and the silk will be fine, even, and strong. The degree of silk exhibited by pushing-hands exponents demonstrates their ability to blend the hard with the soft. It shows how skillful they are in utilizing energy (*jin*) and spirit (*shin*).

If a skilled pushing-hands exponent is grabbed during practice while maintaining or re-establishing leverage, the grab would be smoothly disengaged using a technique that agreed with the direction of the grip force. Pushing hands would then be resumed, without the silk being broken. This is accomplished without panic or the use of sudden, jerky, or aggressive movements.

Combat Methods Can Reduce Skill

Pushing hands requires mutual cooperation or it will break down. Imagine if you were to play tennis with someone who refused to return your serve, or even your return of serve, and completely ignored the white lines. You'd probably win, but what kind of game would it be, and what would you learn?

To practice pushing hands profitably, both people need to be skillful (particularly the force-giver). They must also keep within the confines (format) of pushing-hands. Without a clear understanding of format, the practice can degenerate into a shoving match that eventually becomes a crude wrestling contest. In such matches, the techniques from the forms cannot be utilized (as the correct circumstances/situations don't occur). Fighters ultimately emerge from their exertions with their hair and tempers ruffled and their faces red, having learned nothing. No wonder the old masters were reserved when it came to dealing with young men who wanted to rough-and-tumble. It would be difficult to explain the real value of practice to someone who simply wanted to fight.

Pushing-Hands Techniques

Pushing-hands is practiced with the arms in contact. (See figures 18 and 19 on pages 87 and 88–89.) Movement and force are detected through touch, and action is determined according to the magnitude and direction of a supplied force. After detecting a force, cling to it, ride it out, and skillfully redirect it. The motto is: *Stick to the partner's limbs unless your own are trapped; if they are, free them.*

The idea is to control, or "shut off," your partner's arms (control them), gum them up, and prevent (neutralize) forces. Return all forces by either discharging force, with the same hand, turning at the waist and sinking, passing force from one arm to the other (or from hand to leg) and returning it, changing posture, or various combinations of these. The following pushing-hands exercises are drawn from the Zen Shorin-Do system

The "Revolving-Door" Technique
(*Figure 18, page 87*)

A (in black) and B (in white) face each other in interlocked Sanchin stances (top left). Their forearms are in contact at approximately the height of the solar plexus. Both partners maintain sensible leverage and do not let their arms collapse into their chests.

Figure 18. The "revolving-door" technique.

Taking care not to fully extend his arm, A presses smoothly forward toward B's chest with a palm push (see figure 18, top right). B detects the intrusive force and holds it momentarily, before yielding to it by turning at the waist and revolving.

Taking care not to fully extend his arm, B returns the force in a smooth circular flowing action by yielding just enough to neutralize the original push (shown in the center three photos). Utilizing a palm push of his own, B ensures that he does not waste or lose A's force, and that it is A's force that is returned.

In figure 18, bottom, A detects the return force and holds it momentarily before yielding to it by turning at the waist . . . and so the sequence continues (eventually, neither party is clear to whom the force belongs). This is a foundation pushing action, onto which other pushing and changing movements are added.

Pushing-Hands Changes
(*Figure 19, pages 88–89*)

As your expertise grows, you will begin to experience the sheer joy of responding to forces in a hands-on fashion, using traditional techniques automatically and without struggling. At advanced stages, you can even practice while blindfolded.

Figure 19. Pushing-hands changes.

Figure 19. Pushing-hands changes (continued).

Pushing-Hands—Karate's Missing Link

People from different styles can push hands together, without regard to style, if a proper pushing-hands format is used. Many Karate-ka have taken excursions into Tai Chi or Kung Fu, only to find something essentially similar to their own styles.

Although retained in the Karate world principally by Goju-ryu and Uechi-ryu stylists, Kahkie (Car-key ay, Okinawan Hogen dialect, pushing or "sticky" hands) is now demonstrated as crude arm-rubbing exercises between pairs, and substitutes for pushing hands proper. It is commonly only considered as a mere auxiliary exercise. In reality, it should be a fundamental practice for *all* styles that are heir to the principles and techniques once developed in the Shaolin Temple. If you already practice Karate or Kung Fu, you do not have to ignore pushing hands just because it does not appear on your club syllabus.

Karate has its origins in the techniques of Chinese Kung Fu, which was primarily based on pushing-hands. Karate styles appear to be culture-specific, yet the methodology of their kata is distinctly Chinese, even if their modern applications are not.

The Forms—
Their Creation, Purpose,
and Classification

$\mathbf{K}$eep grinding the bar of iron
and a needle will appear.
(CHINESE PROVERB)

Part of the legacy of Shaolin is the invention, or at the very least the continuation, of recording and classifying empty-hand movements in solo and two-person choreographed forms, for practice, preservation, and communication. These forms are, in fact, text books or systems manuals. They are written in the style of Zen wordless gesture, and act as a common link between the Shaolin-based arts, as distinguished from non-Shaolin fighting methods. As stated earlier, these forms, called *quan* (*kuan*) in Chinese and *kata* in Japanese, constitute the backbone of a style or system and have distinctive characteristics.

There are innumerable Kung Fu and Karate styles in existence today, each with its own selection of forms. As we saw in chapter 2, the same forms are often practiced differently, not only among different "styles," but among those who claim to practice the same style as well.

Regrettably, subtle and sophisticated techniques originally cataloging pushing-hand skills, flow drills, yielding responses to pushes, pulls, responses to unbalancing tactics, grip escapes, Chi-Na or Tui-te (grappling, seizing, restraining) joint locking, or subduing, have been reworked. Their applications have been interpreted as "blocks" or "strikes" with little else being considered or demonstrated. As a result, unfortunately, forms are often presented as a variety of mysterious ways to block the ballistic attack of an imaginary enemy (or several imaginary enemies) and strike back. Bent-wrist blocks (most dangerous to the blocker!), dubious strikes using the back of the wrist, puzzling time-consuming two-part blocks, strange blocks using the elbow, and a whole host of improbable movie-like applications and counterattacks are commonly used to explain away the content of the authentic forms.

It is important to make a clear distinction between antique, or key, forms and modern forms. I am not, however, suggesting that we accept a form just because it's old, or reject one because it's new.

New forms were created as "commentaries" on the originals. Still others are, in turn, based on these commentaries. The long-term value of these derivative forms depends on the interpreter's knowledge and ability. This has been the case for generations, leading to an art that has become both diverse and fragmented. New interpretations and variations of the forms continue to appear, and new styles are regularly created. A casual flick through a martial arts magazine will provide a brief glimpse of the number of systems available. Yet, in truth, authentic forms constitute formulae. This is what distinguishes them from confrontation scenarios.

It is advisable to seek out forms that are as original as possible and that have a reasonable history. Such methods constitute the essential ritual and are fundamental to the preservation and transmission of the ancient wisdom and skill. If this history is ignored, or these rituals dismissed, the ancient knowledge will be lost.

There are, of course, many potential and actual presentations of the essential skills, but they will be systematic and cohesive. The various Sanchins—particularly the Goju-ryu, Uechi-ryu and Fujianese (Fukien) Crane and Tiger forms, along with Pak Mei and Wing Chun forms—are excellent examples, as are Naifuanchin and some antique Shuri-te kata. Key, or foundation, kata can be identified by using your own insight and the five criteria provided on page 93. Moreover, these forms will contain more similarities than differences.

Key principles to remember are that, for the forms, function dictates form, and, in application, authentic forms operate by contact reflex and make use of a training partner's force. The movements in the key ancient forms occur in a very specific order. It is vital to understand why. It is also clearly important to know what the form was created for in the first place.

Forms that have recently been created often exhibit combinations of several characteristics:

1. They have been devised or modified from originals, in order to win forms competitions, and therefore have a tendency to be spectacular. This includes modern Wu-Shu.

2. They have been devised or modified from originals to update, expand, or customize a training syllabus, for personal, stylistic, or even national reasons, or to simplify them for children. This can be seen, for instance, in the radical alterations to the Okinawan kata made by mainland Japanese Karate-ka. In some cases their origins have become virtually unrecognizable.

3. They have been devised with (modern) combat or sport in mind, after investigations of the traditional forms led to disappointment with them.

An example of this would be the current split in the world of Tae Kwon Do, the modern (Korean) martial art that stresses the use of high-kicking techniques. These kicks hardly appear in the traditional patterns or forms, which are arguably modified Karate kata in any case. One faction sticks with the traditional (ex-Karate kata) and the other has developed a brand new set of patterns that more accurately reflect the "freestyle" nature of modern Tae Kwon Do sparring.

For the purposes of the book, we need only concern ourselves with those styles that use antique forms originally created in China, or, at the very least, use component parts of forms that were. These forms have a substantial oral and (later) recorded history, and exhibit the hallmark of the Sacred Science. Such forms have many similarities, but the common link between them all is the inspiration and methodology of the Shaolin Temple.

Understanding the Shaolin principles is crucial to a reasonable interpretation of forms based on dignity and nonviolence, even if the form is imperfect. Because of the sheer mass of the subject matter, I have relied on a limited selection of forms to illustrate various points.

Five Criteria of Authenticity

Key, or foundation, forms will meet the following five groups of criteria. Some examples of these traditional forms are shown in figures 20A and 20B (pages 94–95).

> **FIRST CRITERIA**
> A Buddhist or Taoist creator, clear Buddhist origins,
> and esoteric connections.

Wing Chun
(Figure 20A, top)

Wing Chun is a southern Chinese style of Kung Fu supposedly taught to Yim Wing Chun (Cantonese, perpetual springtime) by Nge-Mui, a Buddhist nun and one of the five ancestors who reportedly fled the destruction of the Shaolin Temple. There are several types of Wing Chun. Probably the most popular type is that of the late Hong Kong-based grandmaster Yip Man. Its principle form is *Siu Lim Tao* (Cantonese, small mind way), which contains a set of three repeated movements called *Saam pai fut* (three prayers to Buddha).

Five-Ancestors Boxing
(Figure 20A, center)

The principle form of Five-Ancestors Boxing is Sanchin (Cantonese, three conflicts), which bears an uncanny resemblance to the Wing Chun forms, particularly Wing Chun's "wooden man" techniques.

*Figure 20A. Top: Siu Lim Tao and Cham Kiu (bridge-
seeking form). The second of three solo forms, excluding
Wing Chun's wooden-man form.
Center: Five-Ancestors Boxing.
Bottom: Pak Mei.*

Figure 20B. Top: Lohan Chuan (Quan). Center: Fuchow White Crane. Bottom: Dragon form (sixteen actions).

Pak Mei
(Figure 20A, bottom)

This southern Kung Fu style was allegedly created by a monk, Pak Mei Too Jung. Pak Mei is Cantonese for white eyebrows, pertaining to age and wisdom. Its principle form is Gow Bow Teaw (Cantonese, nine-step push).

Lohan Chuan (Quan)
(Figure 20B, top)

Lohan Chuan (Quan), called "Monk Fist," is another version of Sanchin.

Fuchow White Crane
(Figure 20B, center)

Fuchow White Crane has several versions. Principle forms are based in various versions of Sanchin. Illustrated in Figure 20B (center) are movements from the Babulian form, one that consists of eight consecutive steps, also known as the Happoren form.

Dragon Form
(Figure 20B, bottom)

Dragon form, or "sixteen actions" form. "Dragon" is a generic term that describes several inter-related systems.

SECOND CRITERIA
A Buddhist name, Buddhist titles of postures and gestures, or the employment of esoteric numerology.

The following examples of the names of classical Karate kata will help to demonstrate their Buddhist connections:

Jiin (temple ground)
Jion (temple sound)
Jitte (temple hand)
Shisochin (four-monk conflict)

There are also kata whose names consist of sacred numbers of movements:

Sanchin (three conflicts)
Rokushu (six hands)
Seipai (eighteen hands)
Sanseryu (thirty-six hands)

Neiseishi/Gojushiho (fifty-four steps)

Pechurin/Superinpai (the final one-hundred-and-eight hands)

All the numbers (3, 6, 18, 36, 54) are reductions of the cosmological number, 108. This is the number of beads on a Buddhist rosary, as well as a numerical link to the breath rates used in meditation. I have seen monks who use 27, 54, or 108 beads. Incidentally, the classic yogic (trance) breath rate of 7.5 breaths per minute yields 10,800 breaths per day, a well-known multiple of the sacred number 108 (see page 155 for further discussion of the rhythm of breath). These are key numbers, connected with sacred mathematics, which, when combined with the body geometry of authentic kata, link one firmly to the way.

Unless we are masters of cosmology and the Sacred Science, we cannot devise a true Shaolin form. Indeed, the offerings of people who lack this grounding are usually amalgamations of responses to fight scenarios built around personal fears, experiences, limitations, shortcomings, or something that simply looks or feels good. Such forms will contain examples of the inventor's favorite techniques, yet classical forms are far more profound in construction. The modern forms tend to group techniques of defense and offense into logical sequences, and entire sections are dedicated solely to blocking, punching, striking, or kicking.

Equal numbers of techniques will be practiced on both sides. In other words, all the elbow strikes will be grouped together—say, four for the left and four for the right—and all the punches and kicks will be similarly grouped. The reasoning behind these kinds of forms has little to do with Sacred Science. They are geared, instead, toward a search for utility and are based on individual and limited notions of how self-defense movements should logically be categorized. Yet they are still, in the main, based on exposure to and experience of the antique forms. Grouping techniques this way may be convenient for teaching children and novices, however such inventions should not be presented as true forms. The original forms should be retained. One hallmark of modern forms is their continual alteration or revision, often without explanation. Traditional forms, on the other hand, are formulaic paradigms. True forms are the musical notation and scales of the empty-hand art.

> **THIRD CRITERIA**
> Simplicity of movement, with the form moving mostly
> through one or several simple, straight lines.

The following Karate kata are good examples of this. They are practiced in the (Matsubayashi) Okinawan Shorin-ryu of the late Shoshin Nagamine, one of Okinawa's most respected Karate teachers.

Naifuanchin (Naihanchi/Tekki)

Anaku

Wanhkan (Matsukase)
Rohai (Meikyo)
Wanshu (Empi)
Passai (Bassai)
Gojushiho
Chinto (Gankaku)
Kushanku (Kwanku/Kanku Dai)

FOURTH CRITERIA
The exclusion (or absence) of dodging, ducking, and
weaving, and the sole employment of postures, stances,
positions, and movements that operate only within
the natural range of movement.

Even though kicking techniques seem to be stressed in modern martial arts, they are
not an integral part of traditional key forms.

FIFTH CRITERIA
There will be few (if any) kicks. Where, in authentic forms,
can we find the roundhouse kick, the reverse roundhouse
kick, the back kick? Even the famous side kick is restricted
to a low level in, for example, one traditional Okinawan
kata, the prototype for modern styles. There are no
kicks at all in Sanchin, Naifuanchin, and other
foundational kata, although some styles have introduced
them or have interpreted the leg raises in Naifuanchin
and other kata as kicks or stamps.

Remember, in application, if you do not adopt a supplied force and borrow it, if you are
not receptive to force and do not use hands-on touch (contact) reflexes, it is unlikely
that you will be able to use the techniques in forms without prearranging them.

Karate—Mistaken Notions

There are many claims made concerning the purposes and functions of Karate kata and
Kung Fu forms. They range from the sublime to the ridiculous, and from the credible
to the bizarre.

It would be difficult if not impossible, for example, to identify all the anomalies, discrepancies and inconsistencies in claims that state that Karate kata were designed with all-out combat in mind. Here are just a few:

Multiple Levels of Application

Some Karate teachers claim that there are different levels of practical application for Karate kata, depending upon grade, ability, and willingness to learn. (Perhaps we're back to the "secrets" again?) This has occurred partly because of the difficulties experienced by post-World War II teachers seeking to explain the applications of kata in terms of self-defense.

Such teachers claim that blocks can be strikes and strikes can be blocks, and that kicks can be blocks, although I suppose blocks can't be kicks! They argue that kata techniques have several, even unlimited, applications, each technique allegedly having multiple functions. As we have seen, however, these explanations of kata are generally based on the assumption that all techniques are ballistic (blocks, strikes, thrusts, etc.). Pull-push unbalancing tactics are not properly considered, nor are wrist grappling and reversals. To record them would require very specific movements in a very specific order, yet this is exactly what the fundamental kata contain!

To take a very specific set of movements, laid down in a very specific order with a very specific *embusen* (floor plan or direction) and ask students to make up their own meaning is like saying to a child, "Here is the alphabet, make up your own language!"

With the actual applications missing, modern teachers have given limited guidelines of their own devising. From this, the idea that there are several applications for each movement was born.

I label this the "could be syndrome"—a movement from the kata could be this, or it could be that. If a teacher provides a so-called traditional reason why a particular movement from a kata is done a certain way, and the student comes back with a logical question that the tradition cannot explain, then the teacher can avoid the question by simply saying, "More training, more training." If the student returns with a more logical or practical explanation or application than the one initially provided, the teacher can save face by simply nodding and saying, "Yes, you can do it that way." Claims that the next generation of students will be better than the last naturally occur, as does the belief that the art is advancing.

This kind of thinking agrees well with modern notions of progress, but, in reality, it constitutes a failure to read and understand the records (kata) properly. Such thinking is also leading to a loss of the tradition. Some teachers claim that kata practice simply develops spirit. Full-contact and other fighters develop plenty of spirit, however, without practicing kata.

On the other hand, what if the major antique Karate kata are *not* primarily concerned with blocking, striking, punching, and kicking at all, and, in fact, never were? What if, as I have previously suggested, they have more in common with their Kung Fu parentage?

Some of the comments recently published by senior Karate teachers support this notion. Many of these senior teachers are publicly renouncing the "traditional" applications given to them. In fact, as we have seen, most of these applications are not very traditional at all, having been devised as recently as the end of World War II.

Schoolboy Karate

One of the biggest current complaints is that only "schoolboy Karate" has been taught! Subsequently all sorts of theories and ideas have been advanced as to what the kata are actually for, and why it is that the masters did not know.

I take a simple view on how this state of affairs came about. As regards Kung Fu, I suggest that, in the past, many people in China learned forms, but few learned their meanings. Just as in any process of education, many only learned the elementary skills—in this case, the solo forms. As regards Karate, it must be borne in mind that this art was largely developed by a small number of Okinawan peasants. Some Okinawan notables were involved, but one needs to understand the relative nature of titles, such as *Bushi* (warrior), that were conferred upon some historical Okinawan Karate figures. From the small archipelago of the Ryukyu Islands, the Okinawan version of Chinese Kung Fu proliferated rapidly, accumulating so-called "traditions" as it went. As different styles began to use the same forms in completely different ways, it became and remains the norm for interpretation to take place. In this continuing climate, anyone who dares to suggest that key forms or kata are specific is liable to be labeled as an evangelizing dogmatist. Yet, the evidence indicates that it need not take twenty years to master a kata if you know what it is for! Nor should the applications vary from school to school. Solo kata comprise the "systems manual." In both Zen and Karate, *the real skill is in the application,* not in the mechanical repetition of solo sequences (except where pranayamic breathing is involved; see chapter 10).

Mistaken Notions
(Figures 21 through 25, pages 101–107)

Traditional Karate, it is maintained, is principally a striking art. According to some sources, Ankho Itosu (1832–1916) recorded that hands and feet should be regarded as swords. Others attribute this to Ankho Azato (a contemporary teacher of Funakoshi). Regardless who said it, the fact is that hands and feet are rather blunt! At work here is an impractical association with swordsmanship. Moreover, it is often stated that the student should strive to attain the skill of *ikken hisatsu*—the one-blow finish, or the one hit, one kill principle. This principle, however, reflects an old Samurai sword-fighting ideal, grafted on to empty-hand arts of largely Chinese origin, arts that were originally concerned with "changing hands" (continuous, flowing, defensive responses) and not single committed attacks or counter-attacks.

Such thinking appears, in the past, to have been another attempt to identify empty-hand techniques with Japanese swordsmanship. Presently, it is used as a justification for the obvious lack (in kata) of the sorts of attacking combinations found in other modern styles that are necessary for victory against a strong, highly agile, or at least mobile opponent. Missing are the feints, jabs, and tactics of, for example, boxing. Present are

Figure 21. Top: Solo kata position.
Center: Alleged block in action against a straight punch.
Bottom: A difficult defense!

sequences of so-called blocks or strange two-handed positions, accompanied by time-consuming shifts of position involving full steps and the complete tensing of the body on completion of a technique.

In the hands-on practice of pushing hands, many of the strange two-handed movements referred to in Karate kata as *kamai*, or guard positions, come to life as single and double wrist locks, seizes, counters, crossed-arm ties, arm pins, trapping hands, and a whole host of other techniques that modern Karate no longer has the appropriate format to express!

Two examples will serve to illustrate this. The first is the opening movement from the Shorin-ryu kata, Pasai (see figure 21, page 101). Modern Karate schools refer to this technique as *morote uke* (augmented forearm block). The inference is that the supporting hand reinforces the blocking hand if an attack is too powerful. In conventional Karate terms, if there is no contact with an opponent, why step in such an exotic impractical and unbalanced way? Besides, without having established contact, how would you know that the punch was going to be too strong? Moreover, the footwork makes the technique impractical as a block. It is a wide departure from normal blocking techniques and, if practiced that way, may develop an adverse or conflicting body habit.

Even if you managed to block with such a movement, the technique gives no positional advantage, except for the common and misleading explanation that it would

Figure 22. Solo Pasai postion applied as grappling escapes and performed in contact. This sequence shows the pushing-hands position.

Figure 22. Solo Pasai position continued. This sequence shows the follow through.

break an opponent's arm. It would be easy for the opponent to make a lightning second strike (figure 21, center). You cannot assume that it will be possible to get to the outside of the opponent's arm (elbow) without first being sure that the attack is not a hook punch!

Finally, it's such a complex and committed move when used as a block that a simple feint from an opponent could spell disaster for the defender (figure 21, bottom). Contact and control, on the other hand, would make a big difference.

Figure 22 shows the same techniques applied as grappling escapes and performed in contact. A pushes B, who "takes" the force and captures A's arms in a cross tie. B keeps control of both A's arms and applies the technique by twisting his hips, forming the crossed-leg stance and flowing with A's resistance.

The second example is drawn from the Shorin-ryu kata *Pinan Godan* (*Hein Godan*, in Shotokan). Figure 23 (page 105) shows the solo sequence. Figure 24 (page 104) shows the paired sequence, in which A has his back to B. The usual reason given is that he is busy fighting someone else. A begins to attack B with a straight punch. B supposedly just happens to know that he is being attacked and, presumably gauging the type of attack and the intended target, begins to block. After completing the blocking action, B turns the blocking hand into a kind of "sliding punch." In fact, in the

Figure 23. Pinan Godan—solo kata sequence.

Figure 24. Pinan Godan—alleged kata application.

kata sequence, the performer would be in a superior position and facing the point of contact (the opponent). The defender here, for some inexplicable reason, moves into a weak and vulnerable position, with his back almost turned and his anatomical weapons poorly positioned. The right leg can't kick, because it's weight-bearing; the left leg is too far away, as is the left hand. In this sequence, we can see an attempt to equate the movements with imagined battlefield use.

Figure 25 (on pages 106–107) shows the same techniques again applied as grappling escapes and performed in contact. A pushes B who "turns the corner." B "cross-ties" A's arms (first three photos on page 106). B steps through and firmly locks A's arms. A tries to withdraw. B cross-steps and takes A off balance by causing him to "tread water" (bottom, page 106). If A struggles, B continues with a throwing or tumbling action (photo sequence page 107).

Figure 25. Pinan Godan technique applied as grappling escape and performed in contact.

*Figure 25. Pinan Godan technique applied as grappling escape and
performed in contact (continued).*

Controlling the Arms

The natural control or grasping of the arms developed by the Chinese, used to "shut off" the partner's arms (control them), necessitated the development of counter-strategies, grip reversals, and grip escapes. These are, for the initiated, an obvious theme permeating authentic kata, even if only retained in fragments in restructured kata. Following are some examples of wrist releases drawn from Rokushu (six variations) called Tensho in Goju-ryu Karate.

Rokushu, meaning six variations or six varieties, is a famous form with origins in China. It has been referred to as one of the twin jewels in the crown of Goju-ryu Karate, the other being Sanchin. Historically, Chojun Miyagi, the founder of Goju-ryu Karate, synthesized *Tensho* from Rokushu, probably by reducing the number of steps and repetitions and eliminating the 180 degree turns presumably found in the original form. We know that Miyagi did the same to Sanchin to create an abbreviated kata that remains one of two Sanchins practiced in Goju-ryu today. None of the essential movements in Rokushu are missing from Tensho. The original kata clearly had six key techniques, from which it derived its name, and these six techniques are still extant in the Tensho.

I think Miyagi's motive in eliminating the turns may have been to condense Sanchin and Rokushu kata, perhaps making them easier for beginners to learn. By removing the turns, the teacher can continually face the class. Thus beginners can more easily observe and copy the movements.

In my school, the Tensho is referred to as Rokushu and is practiced complete with the same turns as the Sanchin kata. If you practice the full complement of techniques and turns, starting in a right Sanchin stance and repeating the sequence in mirror image by starting with the left leg forward, you will be practicing the "fifty-four hands," or repetitions, twice, thus completing "one-hundred-and-eight hands."

The applications of the six key techniques of Rokushu (Tensho) are given below. The solo kata sequence is presented for reference only at the end of chapter 10, after an explanation of the foundation kata, Sanchin. I have introduced the applications of the Rokushu kata here, because they will help to illustrate several of the points I have made so far.

Rokushu Hand Positions
(Figures 26 and 27, pages 109–113)

Note that the "clawed" positions of the hands in the Rokushu technique only serve to stretch and expand the wrists to their maximum. Attention should be paid to maximizing wrist-bend, and not to forming the hand positions. If the wrist is fully bent, the hand positions will almost take care of themselves. The claw hands simply assist in the tightening of the tendons to achieve maximum wrist-bend and therefore maximum escape potential; they have no other import.

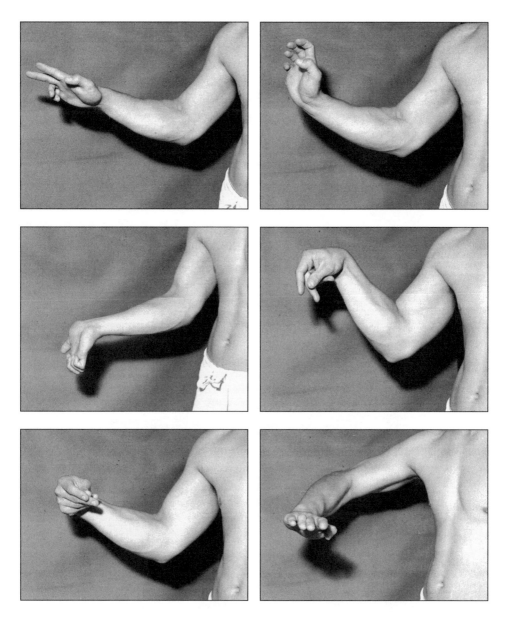

Figure 26. Top left: Snake hand (Shi). Top right: Tiger claw (Hu).
Center left: Leopard claw (Bao). Center right: Standing Dragon hand (Lung).
Bottom left: Laying Dragon hand (Lung). Bottom right: Crane wing (Hoc).

Often, the movements in Rokushu (Tensho) are routinely described as blocks and strikes. The so-called wrist blocks are impractical, however (the wrist peak is such a small area). Anyone even moderately familiar with anatomy and physiology will know that an individual blocking in this way risks fracturing the scaphoid bone, the weakest part of the delicate and complicated wrist joint. As for striking methods, the true form contains none. Encapsulated within this form are techniques I have identified with the classical five animal positions of the Shaolin tradition. They provide systematic, civilized, and non-brutal escapes from wrist grips.

Figure 27 shows the six variations of the grip escapes and "dividing" found in Sanchin kata that gave the form its original name. Note that the Snake is the primary antagonist (grip). Each grip escape works against the weakest part of a partner's grip, the thumb and index finger. This side of the grip also relies, to some extent, on the scaphoid bone in the metacarpals, or wrist joint. Moreover, the position for each grip escape is determined by finding (assuming) a position that puts the partner's wrist (metacarpals) and forearm (ulna and radius) in the weakest positions possible.

The techniques outlined in Figure 27 are practiced and ultimately produced as contact reflexes that conform to and follow the lines of least resistance. They are never part of a plan, and should be produced spontaneously without pre-arrangement. Thus, the technique (escape) applied will depend upon the actual wrist grip felt. All can be combined in smooth sequences.

Figure 27A. Snake Hand—the primary antagonist (grip).

Figure 27B. Tiger Claw grip release, right hand to right hand.

Figure 27C. Leopard Claw grip release, right hand to left hand. (Note: The Leopard Claw and the Crane Wing follow the Standing Dragon and the Laying Dragon respectively; they do so either to free the hand from a persistent grip that slides around the wrist and regrips, or to free the hand from a renewed grip once an initial grip is broken.)

Figure 27D. Standing Dragon grip release, right hand to left hand.

Figure 27E. Standing Dragon
from another view.

Figure 27F. Laying Dragon grip release, left hand to left hand.

Figure 27G. Crane Wing grip release, right hand to right hand.

The Force-Giver Must Be Skillful

The techniques in Rokushu are not defenses against or escapes from static self-defense situations. Just as in pushing hands, the person who applies the grip (force) must do so skillfully. For example, if you grip too tightly when training with a beginner, you will likely cause that beginner to struggle, or fail to execute the technique properly. One of the most common errors in the application of grip escapes is poor elbow position. It is vital in the Laying Dragon technique that the elbow not move away from the body (from the Sanchin position)! All positions must include good leverage, with the elbow acting as a fulcrum. Obviously, this takes time to learn, and no one will be helped by inappropriate gripping. Also, if neither practitioner is properly trained in keeping silk, a grip release will disengage the hand from the grip in an uneven or jerky fashion. This will leave the hands out of contact. The object of these techniques, however, is to escape the grip while keeping the contact, thus making combinations and "play" possible.

A person who smoothly escapes a grip can continue to push hands, taking the grip in stride and preventing any upset to rhythm, timing, and silk. The skillful gripper can also slide the gripping hand around a partner's wrist as the partner begins to escape, thus making him or her go with the changing grip (force). This modifies the escape by feeling (not looking) and moving, for example, from the Standing Dragon to the Leopard Claw. In this way, you can test, or be tested, on the basis of skill (the ability to change) and not on strength.

Unskillful gripping during practice has, in the past, led to the development of brutal tactics designed to facilitate an escape. This has become almost standard in some schools, particularly those seeking utility function. But—and it's a big but—there are no movements in the Rokushu (Tensho) kata for stabbing or striking prior to disengaging from a stubborn grip! I repeat, the techniques in key (authentic) kata do not record or encourage such gross brutalities.

Of course, there are those people who have vise-like grips, from which some people cannot escape. I suspect that the utility-seeking martial artist who encounters them (besides possibly being intimidated) feels that here is a problem that has to be solved in a combative way. In reality, the only problem to be solved is one of communication. The strong gripper should be asked to lighten his grip to let people familiarize themselves with it. The strong gripper should then be encouraged to develop the skill of "testing" the leverage (fulcrum efficiency of the elbow position) and the escape ability, up to the maximum capacity *of each individual*. Sanchin is primary in learning how to regulate or break and control the unbalancing potential of grips or traps. In fact, once you develop genuine skill, you will meet few grips that you cannot reverse or escape. All is done by touch, without thought or aggression and without pre-arrangement.

Contrast this approach with that of those who wish to apply these traditional movements (without pre-arrangement), yet try to do so from no-contact/no-control positions, or who try to use this epigrammatic collection of grip escapes and techniques drawn from other forms as blocks and strikes against punching and kicking attacks.

As previously explained, if you don't control and monitor your training partner's limbs by touch, he or she can move away or change tactics before an intended response can be completed. Failure to do so results in a long-range tactical battle that relies upon a limited range of ballistic techniques (the front, side, and round kicks, and the jabs and reverse punches common to most modern styles). Under these circumstances, neither person is at the right distance or in an appropriate situation to utilize techniques from the traditional forms.

Much modern Karate and Kung Fu free fighting resembles stylized kick boxing. Failure to control a partner's limbs leaves little time for anything else. Even from a combat perspective, however, the hormonal and psychological condition of some people makes them aggressive without necessarily losing efficiency. A strong, fit, and determined young man can do much damage, unless his limbs are entangled and controlled (two arms and one leg). This has been proven both in and out of the arena. For example, boxers will often "hang on," tying up an opponents arms during inside work, particularly when they are tired or losing.

When you try to use techniques from the forms without the vital element of contact you must assume that you will just "know" what movement to make. This is a completely unreliable method, subject to too many variables. Different people have different body rhythms, muscle-twitch quality (some will be faster than others), and degrees of strength. There is no magical technique to evaluate them all. Moreover, a thrusting hand may be a feint that is withdrawn so fast, or included in combinations of such blinding speed, that it becomes impossible to maneuver using the techniques of the forms.

Other, more combat-oriented problems, also remain unresolved in traditional kata. Where, for instance, are the techniques necessary to follow a fallen opponent to the ground and apply an arm lock, choke, strangle, or other restraint? This is done in Judo, Ju-jutsu, and most modern combat styles, and is evident in recently invented forms. Teachers of modern self-defense methods claim that many fights go to grappling and end up on the floor. If you truly believe that Karate kata are about (actual) fighting, can you rely on a supposed ability to render an opponent powerless solely by means of striking?

Pre-Arranged Sparring

When we examine just how many techniques exist in the forms, we can see that we do not want to apply them all against a charging straight punch (Japanese, *oi-tsuki* or *jun-tsuki*). Yet the current modern Karate format relies on this punch in two out of three distinct sparring practices. Literally hundreds of responses are taught to this one punch! The smart attacker is the one who avoids using this punch in the first place! Besides, the punch is begun from a position that is actually out of range. The attack is performed by stepping forward (toward an opponent) with a full step, usually into a front-leg bent stance, and straight punching with the arm on the same side as the forward leg.

This punch is initially employed in pre-arranged sparring, in which the attacker announces the intended target and aims an agreed number of punches at it (usually one, three, or five). The defender moves away while maintaining the original distance and blocks or evades before countering. Such a long-range and committed movement establishes certainty for the defender by providing plenty of time and distance to use a thought-out plan, based on a visual reflex response. If we examine this practice critically, we note that the maintenance of the original relative distances is what keeps the pseudo-attack at bay. The block is almost superficial.

It is often claimed that such a practice is basic, but there is not the slightest scrap of evidence to prove that this contributes in any way to freestyle skill. It only works when the defender knows the intended target *and* the mode of attack. This is why committed tournament fighters seldom bother with traditional Karate or basics! Paradoxically, the *oi-tsuki* full-stepping or chasing punch, so often practiced in pre-arranged sparring is the one punch seldom, if ever, seen in free sparring or tournaments!

A second type of "traditional" sparring consists of the attacker attempting to supply an attack that matches a given defensive maneuver from a kata. Applying kata movements in this way is termed *bunkai* (Japanese, formal application of kata). These bunkai, however, often look as if the attacks were designed to fit the defenses—for example, punching simultaneously with both hands, to justify equally strange double blocks.

This brings to mind the words of a heavyweight boxer with whom I once trained who was ranked number eleven in the U.K. at the time. Having been told by two black belt Karate-ka that Karate kata contained techniques too deadly to be used in the ring, he asked for a demonstration. He found their explanations and demonstrations naive and unrelated to his experiences of real fighting, both in and out of a ring. He suggested that he would gladly "have a go" with them, anytime. Fortunately, they declined. He later told me (still a form fan) that, in Karate kata, the head was too open to fast punching combinations. He asked why the movements were so uneven and why they stopped and started? He regarded kata as exotic, something created by inscrutable people in a strange, far-off land, where they fought politely, having never discovered the head-butt and other brutal tactics. He further added that kata practice might be "traditional," but, to him, the applications were of no recognizable use in the real world—a view echoed by many interested in modern self-defense.

The Myth of the 270-Degree Turn

The Pinan kata of karate, allegedly perfected by the Okinawan Ankho Itosu somewhere between 1905 and 1907, employ 270-degree turns, which are often translated as turns to face and block the attack of another opponent in a multiple-opponent scenario. Why? Even supposing a kata were intended to mimic a fight against multiple opponents, why turn 270 degrees to block the attack of a fresh opponent, when a simple 90-degree turn clockwise would face you in the same direction, and more quickly? Besides, what would the other opponents be doing while you took so much time (in real terms) to turn? Of course, in a symbolic battle, anything is possible.

Actually, standard demonstrations of kata applications are rehearsed and then performed against what often amounts to a passive, or at least stationary, opponent or series of opponents who queue up politely and wait their turn to attack. These techniques are seldom demonstrated as reflexes that conform to and flow with the attacker's resistance and borrow his force in any continuous and productive way. Practice seldom progresses beyond these pre-arranged set pieces, as stylish as they may appear. Heavily orchestrated, they lack the vital (Zen) element of spontaneity and cannot be duplicated in freestyle sparring, the third method we will examine.

Freestyle Sparring

In all instances of sparring, it is the control of distance (Japanese, *ma-ai*) that makes a blocking or evasive action effective. Pre-arranged sparring has a stop-and-start nature in which responses can be pre-determined, but in freestyle sparring, there is no pre-arranging. Consequently, fighters find it impossible to apply kata techniques.

Commonly, both fighters move forward to attack at the same time in freestyle sparring, which causes a simultaneous exchange of techniques (both people hit each other at the same time). This is the chief bane in the life of tournament fighters, referees, and judges. The maintenance of (long) distance makes actual blocking actions appear superfluous.

Much modern Kung Fu uses set pieces and engages in free sparring, which, as I have pointed out, is a modern invention. The situation deteriorates even more when Western-style tactics, such as feinting, ducking, bobbing, and weaving (derived from boxing) are used in sparring. Formal upright and traditional movements become impossible to use against an opponent who utilizes the modern methods. Karate contests have moved away from the straight backs and fixed postures introduced by Japanese teachers. Contestants have become much more mobile. Once Europeans and North Americans got the hang of tournaments, they dominated them, regularly beating the Japanese and other national teams! Improvised slapping deflections have replaced the previously taught two-part blocking actions, and spectacular kicking techniques aimed at the head have become more commonplace. Incidentally, it is my belief that these kicking techniques (not found anywhere in the authentic forms) derive from the Chinese circus.

Naturally, an athletic elite began to excel after the introduction of modern free fighting and tournament techniques, which bear little resemblance to the forms at all. Many teachers of traditional Karate decry free fighting for various reasons, claiming that free fighting distorts proper technique and detracts from the true spirit of Karate as a *budo* (warrior way), reducing it to a sport. Yet many renowned pre- and post-War Karate teachers and founders of styles, including Chojun Miyagi, Hironori Otsuka, and others, experimented with and promoted free fighting of various sorts. I suggest that the main reason for this stemmed from an innate desire to use the techniques of Karate (kata) freely and spontaneously, without the restrictions and limitations of pre-arrangement.

Of course, this can be done if pushing hands is used as the medium, as the Shaolin creators intended. In fact, An'ichi Miyagi, a student of (but no relation to) Chojun Miyagi, tells us that Chojun Miyagi claimed that *Kahkie* (pushing or "sticky" hands) was considered to be the *Jiyu Kumite* (Japanese, meeting hands, or free fighting) of

Goju-ryu.[1] As mentioned earlier in chapter 7, however, the practice of Kahkie is little more than an auxiliary exercise for Karate-ka nowadays.

The Myth of Multiple Opponents

The types of ballistic attacks employed to fit kata movements in modern Karate are contrived. The responses are improbable and impractical, particularly, as previously mentioned, the so-called double blocks, applied against equally improbable double punches (two simultaneous punches). As we have seen, many of the double movements in kata are intended to be solo representations of grappling movements!

Often practiced in threes (like the groupings in Wing Chun and other Kung Fu forms) these so-called blocks are sometimes executed while stepping forward, which, in application, necessitates the opponent stepping back to attack. Sometimes these blocking actions are not even accompanied by a counterattack—as in Bassai/Passai and Chinto Kushanku kata. The usual claim is that blocks can also be attacks. This is the reason often given for the toughening up of arms advocated by some Karate and Kung Fu styles, but it is useful to consider the relative value of such a practice and the body types of individual combatants.

To consider Karate kata as fights against multiple opponents is a mistake, an erroneous conclusion arrived at by assuming that empty-hand forms conform to feudal battle tactics, or are related to (fictitious) accounts concerning the activities of ancient warriors.

Often, students are encouraged to imagine an opponent or opponents during form practice, but this can be no more effective in developing interactive skill than an imaginary dancing partner would be in improving coordination with a real partner. One person cannot fight alone. Technical skills, such as concentration or the development of individual body mechanics, are all that can be practiced alone! The vital skills of coordinating and harmonizing with another person can only be achieved *with* another person. Practical training, therefore, consists of (touch) reflex training between pairs.

The value of the form lies in its formula. It acts as a mnemonic device and serves to train the body and mind to open and maintain neural pathways (to acquire the appropriate actions and body habits). Forms train posture, stance, body geometry, leverage, independent action of the limbs, and refined, economical movement unrelated to feudal battle tactics.

Good (fictitious) examples of the lone warrior surrounded by his enemies can be viewed in several excellent Japanese films starring Toshiro Mifune and directed by Akira Kurosawa. The equivalent Chinese Kung Fu films are well-known. Neither has any relevance to the practice of forms. I suggest that the notion that the kata are representations of fights against multiple opponents originates (or gains wider acceptance) with the quasi-military views and ideals of Itosu and others. Moreover, I believe these are reflected, to some extent, in the creation of the Pinan kata and Itosu's precepts for Karate.

---

[1] There is an article about this in *F.A.I.* 59.

Mark Bishop, an eighth-dan Karate-ka and author, told me that Shinpan Shiroma (a student of Itosu) often admitted to not knowing the technical functions of some movements in Karate kata, and would quite blankly state that Itosu had not known the functions either, merely explaining that they were for show. In my view, the Pinan kata represent part of the original Ryukyu Okinawan contribution to Karate. (Perhaps the Jion, Jiin and Jitte kata can be added to this.)[2] These kata, however, consist mainly of techniques taken from other (Chinese) forms, which is one reason why I don't consider them essential.

Given the fact that Japanese Karate has exerted a major influence on worldwide martial arts markets, and that, in the past, it has always been difficult to get a Chinese Kung Fu master to explain what the forms he teaches are for, it is hardly surprising that some Kung Fu teachers have adopted similar multiple-opponent explanations to account for the pivots, turns, and general changes of direction in their forms. The pivots, turns, and changes of direction in the forms and kata encourage a certain number of repetitions, or are symbolic (see chapter 10). In some cases, they act as movements that throw, lock, trap, or conform to the retreat, advance, or struggle of a single controlled training partner with whom one remains in contact!

The Myth of Systematic Self-Defense

People looking for a systematic or progressive development of attack and defense techniques in the traditional forms will be disappointed. Intelligence alone dictates that the permutations and combinations are too vast to catalog.

If the forms are viewed in this way (as mere examples, rather than formulae), they appear to be illogical and unsystematic. For instance, in Shorin-based Karate, the first time a front kick is performed in a kata, it follows an awkward half turn, and, contrary to basics, is performed with the front leg (as in the Pinan 1 and Heian 2 kata)! This kick has been changed to a side-snap kick in the Shotokan school. It may be suggested that the kata presuppose a familiarity with the front kick stemming from the practice of basic movements repeated in drill fashion (Kihon). We have already discovered, however, that basic drilling—marching up and down the training hall while repeating single or combination techniques—is a modern development. Originally (as in Kung Fu), there were just the kata and their application. Other irregularities include kicking on only one side, or with only one leg, throughout a kata (see Appendix, page 241). Most of the kicks that appear in antique Karate kata started out as simple knee raises, usually used to counterweigh a potential or actual loss of balance.

At the very least, the information given in the Appendix indicates the need for Karate and Kung Fu practitioners to practice the kata and forms on both sides! Such an apparent lack of logical progression and uneven numbers of techniques has provided justification for those who invent their own forms. These forms demonstrate a lack of

---

[2] In Jitte, Jion, and Jiin, because of the arm and body positions, the 270-degree turns strongly resemble throwing actions, somewhat in the manner of *Tai-toshi*, a judo hip throw, executed after the initial gripping of one sleeve and one lapel. After utilizing an opponent's force, he or she is raised onto the toes and thrown by the turning of the body, 180 to 270 degrees.

understanding of the Sacred Science. Yet people who work in this direction often believe they are improving the art!

Moreover, although Karate techniques are classified in three heights (upper, middle and lower), a glance at the full range of kata practiced by most styles reveals that the majority of movements are performed with the hands at shoulder height or below! (The exceptions are the modern Wado-ryu and Kyokushinkai schools.) With a few exceptions, even those techniques that involve the raising of the hands higher than the shoulders terminate at the middle level. This is significant (see page 125)

According to Shoshin Nagamine, in his *Essence of Okinawan Karate-Do*, the famous and somewhat maverick Okinawan Karate-ka, Choki Motobu (a contemporary of Gichin Funakoshi), was in the habit of picking fights in the local red-light district.[3] This resulted in his raising the height of fundamental Karate hand positions (see Naifuanchin, page 182), to protect his head. The changes were reflected in the height of the arm positions in Motobu's kata. I think this amply proves that Orientals aren't "quaint" people who only attack formally with full-stepping punches aimed politely at the chest. Okinawans may have a reputation for peacefulness, but as in all cultures, there is always the exception . . . and Motobu knew where to find one.

Wado-ryu Karate kata place the arms high in comparison to more orthodox styles. It was undoubtedly Motobu, and possibly a Karate-ka named Yasuhiro Konishi, who influenced the founder of Wado-ryu Karate, Hironori Otsuka, a student of both Funakoshi and Motobu. The high positions of the hands in Kyokushinkai Karate may have been influenced by these sources as well. The Kyokushinkai were certainly influenced by the distinctive contact kick-boxing-style sparring they adopted, and this probably was reflected in their kata. Motobu derisively referred to Gichin Funakoshi's Karate as "dancing." Similarly, Masutatsu Oyama, the founder of Kyokushinkai (and a former student of both Funakoshi and Gogen Yamaguchi), once publicly referred to a national Japanese Karate tournament as a dance competition.

Traditional Karate kata contain a message that goes much deeper and is more profound than imaginary fights against multiple opponents or answers to actual self-defense scenarios. When we examine the Sanchin kata, for example, we will see just how profound the legacy of the Shaolin Temple actually is (see chapter 10).

Through physical and symbolic ritual (forms), you can defeat the enemy within. You can also demonstrate, confirm, and enhance your commitment to the way, while eradicating negative karma. You can, time and again, confront Mara in all his guises, daily facing and thwarting negative attitudes and potentially destructive behavior. Moreover, you can feel better for having done so. Practice develops character, fosters patience, and promotes physical and psychological health, coordination, and well-being. The practitioner also gains a sense of worthwhile endeavor from the practice. Fear of, or obsession with, conflict and confrontation can be dealt with successfully where they do the most damage. Confronting fear in this way does not amount to pretending that social conflict does not exist.

In practicing with a partner, you can, by becoming dispassionate, deal with (ritual) physical assault without being affected by lower passions, instincts, and emotions, and

---

[3] Shoshin Nagamine, *The Essence of Okinawan Karate-Do* (Boston: Tuttle, 1976), p. 42.

without judging or becoming aggressive. Again, I suggest that, from a Buddhist perspective, this has a grander and more pressing importance than any immediate needs for self-defense, concerns about imagined scenarios, or regrets about previous encounters.

The Myth of Nerve-Point Strikes

A popular current theory is that kata (including Sanchin) have, as the highest level of application, the purpose of disabling an opponent with paralyzing nerve-point strikes and/or delayed death-touch strikes. Many years ago, an extremely famous Chinese Kung Fu master told me that he'd been "death-touched" in challenge matches so many times that he wondered how he was able to enjoy such vibrant health!

I do not doubt that a strike to a vital point (and there are too many to enumerate or describe here) can produce effects such as loss of consciousness or even death. It is clear that the ancient Zen masters and those who preceded them had a substantial understanding of human anatomy and physiology. It stretches the imagination beyond the bounds of credibility, however, to surmise that the Buddhist masters would construct methods designed to hurt people. From their own perspective, to disable a fellow human being using nerve-point strikes, or to teach others to do so, would incur dreadful karmic penalties. Besides, it would hardly contribute to the liberation of all sentient beings. Some authors have suggested that selective nerve-point strikes can be used ethically (even by Buddhists) to teach transgressors the error of their ways. Such writers, however, are clearly still seeking to assign a secular, utility function to an essentially monastic Buddhist art. A practicing Buddhist would have to become judgmental in deciding whom to punish, or how. Such an attitude is inconsistent and incompatible with Zen thought.

Basic vital points are used with undoubted practical results by self-defense instructors who don't use Zen forms as a base. These vital points include the obvious one: temples, eyes, neck, throat, groin, etc. A new generation of teachers, however, have been busy adding points used in acupuncture and acupressure. Perhaps they hope to support their theories and give them a sense of antiquity and authority by connecting them with the ancient forms. You don't need to study the forms in order to learn how to strike the carotid sinus and other targets used in this type of practice. The charts produced in evidence of this theory are copied from charts used in traditional Chinese medicine. The actual positions of the subtle points vary from person to person, depending upon several factors, including the person's body type, muscle density, state of health, and adipose tissue levels. Even the most skilled acupressurist needs to feel for a point in order to locate it—hardly practical for self-defense.

In mitigation of the nerve-point theory, it has been suggested to me that one need only hit *near* a vital point. The sheer number of suggested vital points implies that a well-delivered blow virtually anywhere will have (some) effect. It has also been suggested that kata sequences record "set-up points" to be struck or gripped in specially recorded sequences. That's fine if you can get someone to stay still long enough! And even this approach requires the initial subjugation of an opponent. If you have skill in subjugation, and can effect it, why do you need to brutalize?

Without doubt, there has been a move toward using the healing techniques for hurting. Moreover, there is evidence that this started in China itself. Enthusiasm for such an approach, however, has little to do with Zen, the ethics of the Shaolin Temple, or the legacy of the techniques handed down in the forms.

While it is possible for myriad explanations to be given for the forms, even the most self-defense-oriented will have to admit that Sanchin, a fundamental form (see chapter 10), is a strange way to start preparing for a no-holds-barred physical confrontation! The most recalcitrant instructors and students of traditional methods of Karate will understandably seek to defend their kata and their belief system(s) if they feel they are under attack. This is understandable, for they have, after all, invested considerable time and effort in them. Perhaps any such defense is the result of intuitive knowledge concerning the value of the tradition and the real worth and underlying purpose of practice. Without the benefit of a clear understanding of the Zen origins, however, and the ennobling purpose of the art (its real power), it is easy to see how practitioners might consider combat to be the bottom-line use for the forms.

Anyone can turn a screwdriver into an offensive weapon. Successive generations, recognizing the limitations of the screwdriver in combat, will adapt it, flattening and sharpening the point and the edges and modifying the handle, until it becomes a knife. I prefer to use the proper tool for the proper job.

Kung Fu—Mistaken Notions

Kung Fu forms, often less problematic than Karate kata (particularly the southern versions), concern themselves with arm trapping, locking, and escaping, practiced largely in contact. The methods employed also include gripping and rolling hands, sticking hands, and continuous action involving the simultaneous use of both hands. Despite this, it took me over seventeen years to admit grudgingly to myself, and with more difficulty to others, that the forms in the Wing Chun Kung Fu system I loved and followed could not supply the answers to modern urban combat problems. I simply didn't want to acknowledge that the Emperor wasn't wearing any clothes! I continue to experience all the consequences of this admission to this day, as it has completely changed my understanding of the Shaolin legacy. As I noted in the Preface, despite all my efforts, and those of my teachers and friends, and despite being subjected to considerable propaganda, I remained unconvinced about the purpose of training in solo forms. I certainly came across more direct and practical methods of practicing fighting.

My peers (and some seniors) derided Thai and Western boxing (and other methods with no forms) as crude, but the majority of them never faced them, and those that did soon changed their minds. They were soundly beaten! Despite this and myriad (unproven) claims concerning Wing Chun, the forms never lost their beauty for me. Incidentally, Kung Fu and Karate students who want to fight against "full contact" or Thai boxers invariably have to emulate them. The more successfully they do so, the better the results they seem to achieve. I have not come across the reverse situation.

Wing Chun, at that time, was often written about and advertised as a street-fighting method. A casual glance at the Wing Chun forms is sufficient, however, to see that they are sedate, upright, and have no ground-holding techniques. Indeed, most of the style's hand and arm techniques are confined to the middle level. Sports science can easily demonstrate that training the arms at one height (for example, at middle level) does not confer immediate skill in using those movements at another height. Different muscles will be used, or the same muscles will be used differently or in differing combinations with others, depending upon the height. All would have to be practiced. Logically, you would expect to find all necessary examples contained in the forms, but they are not! The head was never originally an intended target for the sticking-hands player of Wing Chun (sticking hands is the Wing Chun version of pushing hands).

In terms of modern notions of combat practicality, Wing Chun forms have limited footwork, and, despite claims made by modern teachers, few can apply this system to suit what are considered to be street-fighting conditions without making radical and incongruous revisions or modifications.

Most societies equate the face and head with the personality. It is, therefore, a prime target in civilian fisticuffs. It is the "headquarters," so to speak. Kick boxers do not carry their hands high for stylistic reasons. They do so to prevent themselves from being hit in the head. In a typical Thai or kick-boxing stance, the elbows and forearms protect the ribs and the fists protect the jaw, which is kept well tucked in. Contrast this with the positions found in Wing Chun and other forms. In the modern practice of Wing Chun, there is also considerable emphasis placed on practicing against punches and kicks from a no-contact position. The favored attack is a straight punch (with a front-leg shuffle, rather than a full step).

In the early 1980s, I practiced two separate sets of forms advocated by two of the main worldwide factions into which Wing Chun was then divided. One association kept to the forms taught by Yip Man, the deceased Grandmaster of the style, and the other utilized forms with higher hand positions and more mobility.

The promoter of the new versions of the forms, a former senior student of Yip Man, claimed they were, in fact, the originals, secretly taught to him by Yip Man prior to his death in December 1972. These were *not* the same forms demonstrated to me (in my own living room) by Yip Chun, the eldest son of Yip Man. The senior student continued to claim that the more common Wing Chun forms were, in fact, the modified ones. This claim persisted, despite the existence of 8mm film footage of the deceased Grandmaster performing two of the three forms the way most students of Wing Chun perform them today.

There was worldwide interest in the enhanced mobility and advertised superior efficiency of the "secret" system, now unveiled. Many seminars were given, and private lessons were touted at very high prices. There were claims, counterclaims, and more talk of secrets. Nothing was proven conclusively, except that the senior master, who had an international reputation as an accomplished street fighter (in his 40s at the time), issued a series of public challenges and fared badly as a result.

One day, at a seminar in Cologne, Germany, a 24-year-old student from a rival school answered one of the challenges. The resulting fracas was brief and inconclusive. It consisted of two (presumably adult) men rolling around on the floor, with one (the master) clinging to the other, who was trying hard to punch and elbow him in the head, and partially succeeding.

I was one of the first people in Britain to see the film footage, which, besides disappointing me, supported my developing views that many things Wing Chun practitioners thought would work in real fights did not, and that overall, the movements contained in the Wing Chun forms had little to do with commercial or modern self-defense demands made upon them.

The master failed to turn up for his seminar the following day. He later blamed the fact that he was tripped and swept to the ground while in a clinch on the lack of grip of his Kung Fu slippers.

The young challenger went on to live the life of a triumphant gunslinger. I hope the same thing never happens to him. After the event described, some rejoiced, while others kept silent. Many became disillusioned with the system. I became disillusioned with distorted popular notions of the art. As a result, I intensified my investigation into the Buddhist connections with Kung Fu (principally Crane boxing). Also of immense value to me was relating the postures in the Wing Chun forms to the principles of modern sports science, because all postures, positions, and techniques used in Wing Chun fall within the "natural range of movement."

The Natural Range of Movement

9

T*he gaily decorated royal chariots wear out. So likewise does this body. But the truth of the righteous does not wear out with age.*
—Dhammapada, Canto XI, 151

Buddhists regard the human body as a Dharma vehicle, a tool to help them realize the way. To willfully damage your own Dharma vehicle or that of another is, to Buddhists, as unthinkable as say a motorist stopping his car on the shoulder of a freeway, getting out, and slashing his own tires.

The monks of Shaolin were privy to the wisdom of thousands of years—wisdom connected to the Sacred Science, like that of acupuncture and acupressure (Chinese systems for balancing energy flow within the human body using needles or manipulation), herbal lore, and the traditional skills of the barefoot doctor. The modern (Western) mind is only beginning to come to grips with the brilliance and subtlety of acupuncture, meditation, and a whole range of so-called "holistic" living skills previously viewed with suspicion.

How did the ancients gain this knowledge? Simple. By experimentation. In human history, there have been roughly a hundred thousand generations of hunter-gatherers, and five hundred generations of agriculturists. Compare this to our ten short generations of industrially revolutionized and mere two generations of computer literate people! The ancients knew a thing or two about the human body and mind, without the benefit of the modern pharmacopoeia and the whole host of contemporary scientific terms.

The Monks of Shaolin created their forms while paying attention to the three basic design faults in the human body:

1. The weakness of the back. All authentic forms stress the development and maintenance of a straight back, which also aids proper breathing.

2. The weakness of the inguinal canal and its tendency to herniate, or its associated weakness to cause groin strain.

3. The dangers inherent in the overextension of joints (particularly when weight-bearing) and the abduction of limbs under load (i.e., lifting a weight away from the body). All authentic (pre-Wu-Shu) forms stress the use of safe natural movements incorporating basic stances, in which the practitioner internally rotates the feet and toes, thus protecting the groin, not from attack, but from strain when the rest of the body is loaded with a training partner's force. Good examples of this were illustrated in chapter 8.

Often, the Shaolin tradition is confused with the later theatrical Wu-Shu forms that sprang up out of Chinese opera and "street-vendor" Kung Fu, which consisted of spectacular movements, many of which were outside the natural range of movement. These movements were designed to have the maximum dramatic effect, with the original object of attracting a crowd to which "medicine" could be sold. It was this dramatic Kung Fu that was foisted on the Chinese people by Mao Tse Tung and his cultural revolution. It was promoted as a Chinese national pastime. A national tournament circuit was set up, and the forms inevitably became more exaggerated and spectacular as the postures became even deeper, lower, and more gymnastic.

In these forms, the stress on the joint system of the human body far exceeds the natural range of movement used in the Zen-based forms. This is the type of "Shaolin" Kung Fu that is currently being presented to eager audiences worldwide, by a group of touring "Shaolin Monks" who are, in reality, an export product of the current Chinese regime. What they demonstrate is, essentially, modern Wu-Shu and Chinese circus. There are a small number of genuine monks restored to the Shaolin temple, but, paradoxically, they do not practice the empty-hand arts.

Much of modern Karate has gone down the same road. Fortunately, however, recent research conducted by the new faculties of sport science is at least able to prove that the higher, more natural stances (i.e., those that operate within the natural range of movement) do not cause hyperextension or give rise to the ankle, knee, hip, and back problems that are now plaguing the first and second generations of non-Asian Karate-ka.

As a young man, I was not bothered with, nor did I understand, the dangers of hyperextension. These problems are not as common among the exponents of older schools of Okinawan Karate or Kung Fu styles that utilize shorter stances and that minimize kicking techniques and keep them low. Sports scientist Andrew Comley points out that

> Along-side the kicks and punches, when people see the martial arts for the first time, they are usually captivated by the stances. Whatever the art, weird stances give it mystique. Big, strong stances give it a look of power and immov-

ability. It is the so-called "deep, strong" type of stances that I wish to examine from a viewpoint of sports science (which in all cases, is consistent with Sacred Science).[1]

The Reasoning Behind Wide Stances

If you train in a style that uses wide stances in its basics, you will have been told that they are employed for strengthening the legs and for giving a strong base to techniques. By this, it is believed that a person's Karate ability is enhanced by increased strength in the quadriceps muscles at the front of the thigh from repeatedly standing and moving in stance. Unfortunately, this is largely untrue. To understand this, you must realize that there are two types of strengthening exercise. One is isometric, the other is isotonic.

Isometric exercises are those that strengthen the muscles by holding them in a loaded position for a period of time. An example of this is holding a tin of beans with your arms outstretched in front of you.

Isotonic exercises work the muscles during movement—i.e., the muscle is strengthening through movement of a weight, as in bicep dumbbell curls. Of the two, isotonic exercises are to be preferred, as muscle strength is increased throughout the whole movement, whereas in the isometric exercises, strength is only gained in the position held. Also, and more seriously, people with heart conditions should avoid isometric exercise, as it raises blood pressure and can be dangerous.

If you try to strengthen your legs by maintaining a stance for long periods of time, you are working isometrically, and therefore only gaining strength in that position. This means that any gains made will not enhance movement speed at all. If you are trying to strengthen your legs via a small amount of isotonic movement in the effort of moving forward, back or sideways, I am afraid you have failed again. If you are stepping correctly—i.e., pushing from the back foot—the quadriceps only work when straightening the back leg for the push, pulling it through for straightening the front leg during the last part of the movement (the drive forward). This does not give enough of an overload to increase strength by a great deal.

Finally, as regards leg strengthening, you must ask why you are trying to strengthen your legs in the first place. It is generally accepted that, as a person attains the higher grades, they do not actually use these low stances, but adopt higher versions. These higher stances are more natural (very much like boxing stances). In fact, you have probably been standing in some of them ever since you could walk! With this in mind, why do you need to strengthen your legs for stances that do not need anything more than naturally gained strength?

Undoubtedly, up to a point, the wider the base, the more stable the structure. Handy if you are building a house, not so handy if you are trying to become maneuverable and responsive to force. So why train in wide, low, restricting stances? In other

---

[1] Andrew Comley, in a letter to me, 1986.

words, these two reasons for training in low, deep stances are not enough. This is especially so when you consider that these stances can actually be dangerous for your body.

Low Stances and the Knees

Sadly, the knee joint is one of the most badly designed joints in the body. The fact is that your body weight is loaded onto a joint that consists of only two bones held together by five ligaments and the strength of the surrounding musculature. Unfortunately, this lack of skeletal support leaves the knee vulnerable to injury from movements that twist or overload it. As far as our stances are concerned, research has shown that, for safety, three rules must be followed:

1. Keep you knee over your foot at all times while loaded (i.e., not past your toe).

2. Keep your thigh, lower leg, and foot in line in order to avoid a spiraling twist from the ankle to the hip.

3. Never let the angle behind your knee drop below 90 degrees (see Naifuanchin stance, page 181).

In fact, Reebok, the fitness specialists and major researchers in the sport and health field, says that, while performing "Reebok Step," the knee angle should always exceed 120 degrees under load! This is the same angle employed in the stances of the Sanchin and Naifuanchin kata.

    In general, I am in favor of higher, more natural, stances. All the evidence is against the safety and efficiency of longer, deeper ones. For myself, Kung Fu or Karate should be performed as naturally as possible in order to enhance the whole of your life.

Shaolin White Crane and Sanchin: The Archetypal Solo Form

Steadfast in body and steadfast in mind, whether standing, sitting or lying down, having firmly established mindfulness, one goes beyond the king of death.
—UDANA 6-1

Many venerated Kung Fu and Karate teachers have claimed that an expert practitioner would not know more than three to five forms or kata. Some have even claimed that one is enough!

For both Kung Fu and Karate, there is a form or solo choreographed sequence called Sanchin (three conflicts). Sanchin is the root form for the Naha-based Karate styles such as Goju-ryu (hard/soft school) and Ueichi-ryu (Ueichi-family school), and for most Chinese Crane styles. According to Master Xia Bai Hua of the Beijing Wu-Shu Research Institute in China, Sanchin (also San Chien or San Tzan) is the basic training form for many (if not most) of the Fujianese (Fukien) systems, the most prominent of which is the White Crane school.[1]

In the southern Shaolin Temple Five-Ancestors Boxing, Sanchin is both the preliminary and the advanced training. Indeed, as we saw in chapter 8, the Sanchin form is so similar to other Kung Fu methods (those that operate within the natural range of movement) that I cannot help but agree with Chinese, Okinawan and other teachers who have always claimed that "Sanchin is everything."

---

[1] G. Chaplin, "A Meeting with Master Xia Bai Hua," *Fighting Arts International* (F.A.I. 67, vol. 12, no. 1, 1990), p. 43.

White Crane is a general term used to denote all crane-imitating boxing. Interestingly, in ancient Mediterranean culture, there existed a so-called Crane Dance, said to mimic the courting habits of the crane. The dance consisted of nine steps and one leap (Naha Sanchin generally takes nine forward steps). The dance was also meant to represent the circles made by the crane's coiling and uncoiling (Sanchin Section 3). In Robert Graves' *The White Goddess*, we find the descriptive and poetic lines

> *The crane must aye*
> *Take nine steps ere she flie [fly].*[2]

In classic times, the Month of the Crane was connected with wisdom, an attribute also associated with the color white in esoteric circles. White Crane (*Pak Hoc*, or *Bak Hoc*) also has the associated meaning of wisdom, the wisdom of the Shaolin sages, (short) white hair or beard, and, in the case of one of the alleged five Shaolin ancestors, white eyebrows (*Pak Mei/Bak Mei*) which, as we saw in chapter 8, is also the name of a now-famous Kung Fu style.

Tradition maintains that Sanchin was created by the Shaolin monks. This tradition is supported by Patrick McCarthy and substantiated by many prominent empty-hand art and martial arts practitioners and historians. Dr. Yang Jwing Ming, a martial artist and prolific author, had this to say about the subject:

The earliest reference we can find (for Crane boxing) is the Shaolin.

He goes on to say that even the world-renowned Wing Chun Kung Fu style is just a branch of Crane.

Yong Chun (Wing Chun) also comes from there. This is also part of Crane, a very small branch of White Crane.[3]

There are specific similarities between Sanchin boxing and many closely related systems, including Wing Chun, Pak Mei, Five-Ancestors Kung Fu, Hung Kuen, Hakka Shaolin, Goju-ryu Karate, and Uechi-ryu Karate, once referred to as Pangainoon (Kung Fu).[4] I would say that Crane boxing is the ancestor to them all. The Sanchin form is the archetypal White Crane form and not "just another kata." Practicing and understanding Sanchin can give access to them all!

Sanchin Stance

The *Ishopanishad* tells us that "Physical movements alone are not helpful in themselves, nor does concentration alone bring success. One who combines concentration with physical control achieves success and becomes immortal."[5] Figure 28 on page 135 shows how the Sanchin stance grew out of the cross-legged seated meditation posture. During

---

[2] Robert Graves, *The White Goddess* (London: Faber & Faber, 1961), p. 233. Brackets mine.
[3] Yang Jwing Ming, "Rationale of Chinese Boxing," *F.A.I.* 68, vol. 12, no. 2, 1991, p. 47.
[4] The term "Sanchin boxing" is something of a misnomer and stems from Victorian descriptions of Chinese fisticuffs.
[5] From *Ishopanishad* 9 and 11 from the translation found in *Chakras: Energy Centers of Transformation* by Harish Johari (Rochester, VT: Inner Traditions, 1987).

Figure 28. Cross-legged seated meditation posture and Sanchin stance (side view).

practice of the solo form, the Sanchin stance should be used to acquire and maintain well-grounded and safe body habits. The stance promotes physical and mental stability. Note the triangles made with the feet, legs, back and arm positions. Grip the ground with your feet and let your hips fall naturally backward. Your hips should only be pushed forward during kata practice, and then only in the final phase of each exhalation. When the proper stance is maintained, Sanchin breathing becomes most effective.

Figure 29 (center) shows the natural S curve of the spine. The true straight back is one that conforms to the spine's natural shape. In Sanchin stance, the spine should be

Figure 29. Left: Sanchin stance (front view). Center: Spine's natural "S" curve.
Right: Back position with hips pushed forward.

in the same position it would be in during seated meditation (Zazen). Figure 29 (right) shows the position of the back when the hips are pushed forward at the end of the out-breath.

When using Sanchin stance in training with a partner, it can readily be seen how it provides a sound angled base in which the feet toe inward. This produces good traction making for good stability against pushes and pulls. In the Sanchin stance, the lead foot is toed in on one side of an imaginary triangle. Whenever you shift from one Sanchin stance to the next during practice, feel the ground with your feet. Do not step mechanically, but "read" the terrain with the stepping foot, moving the foot in an arc.

Sanchin Solo Form

The Sanchin form has several different sequences of stepping or moving that are followed by different schools. The essence of all these sequences are the three sections into which the form is usually divided. These three sections are based on specific types of physical movements. Offered here are the *seeds* of Sanchin, based on the trinitarian aspect of Brahma, Vishnu, and Shiva, and on the *Tri-Vikrama* (Sanskrit, triple step).

In Hindu mythology (taken up and utilized by the Chinese), Vishnu traversed the entire universe in three steps: first as a fire god, second as a wind god, and third as the custodian of heaven itself (Vishnu as the Sun/Son God). According to another mythology, these three symbolize the rising, zenith, and setting of the sun. The form utilizes steps and turns based on ritual and mythology in which evil spirits (distractions) are warded off, out and away from the sacred space that the mandala creates. In simple terms, fear, doubt, and other unwanted negatives are abandoned. The final closing step is also part of the opening of the opposite side. If done properly, this brings the hands into the appropriate position to begin the form again on the other side.

Solo Form—Section I
(Figure 30, page 137)

In the first section of Sanchin, you are encouraged to learn and practice how to move one arm independently of the other. The basic geometrical movements used in application during pushing hands are: lead, split, retract, and press.

Assume the attention posture. Stand with your heels together, your back straight, and your hands open at your sides, palms facing inward. Place your feet side by side, bring your hands together in front of your chest, with the fingers pointing upward. Hold this position for a short while. This is the *Anjali Mudra* (formal Buddhist bow or greeting), which is performed as a salutation at the start and end of all forms and when training with a partner.

While inhaling, pivot your hands at the point of contact, and move your elbows outward. Smoothly turn your hands so that the back of your right hand is in the palm of your left, thumb tips touching. Do this while moving your hands to your abdomen.

Figure 30. Solo form, Section 1.

This gesture is the classic *Dhyani Mudra* used in seated meditation. The right hand on top symbolizes enlightenment; the hand resting below symbolizes the world of appearance. The gesture represents overcoming the world of appearance through enlightenment. Keeping your shoulders down, inhale.

Begin to exhale. Keeping your hands in contact, straighten and rotate them and assume the lowered crossed-hands posture: straighten your arms and move your elbows inward. Your palms should remain toward your body as you fully straighten your arms.

Sanchin Section 1—Moving the Right Leg Forward
(Figure 31)

Continue to exhale and begin to step out with your right foot, moving it forward and outward in a clockwise horizontal quarter-circle. Pivot your left foot into position and assume the Sanchin stance. Almost completing the exhalation, form two unbendable arms by moving your still-touching hands slightly forward and turning them in vertical arcs about the elbows to shoulder height, clenching your hands into fists. Your

Figure 31. Sanchin Section 1—Moving the right leg forward.

upper arms should not move. The angle of your elbows should be greater than 90 degrees. Both arms should now be at the same height and in the same position.

Consolidate this position by pushing your hips forward and completing the exhalation. The hip movement helps to push on the diaphragm and expel more air. While inhaling, first let your hips drop back, then, withdraw your left fist to your left side in a straight line. Some styles withdraw the hand in an arc. This is simply a device that ensures that the elbow is kept in and remains in a strong position throughout.

Begin exhaling. Keeping your elbow in, slowly straighten your left arm until it is almost fully extended at the height of the bent elbow. Continue exhaling, and form a left unbendable arm, moving your elbow slightly inward and your fist in an elbow-centered vertical semicircle. The fist travels inward, upward, and outward. Your arms are again at the same height and in the same position.

Sanchin Section I—Moving the Left Leg Forward
(Figure 32, page 140)

Unlock your right foot. By this, I mean place it in a straight line prior to stepping forward. Move your left foot forward in a counterclockwise semicircle. Lock your right foot into position behind it and assume the Sanchin stance. At the end of the step, consolidate the position by pushing your hips forward and completing the exhalation.

While inhaling, first let your hips drop back, then, withdraw your right fist to your right side. Begin exhaling. Keeping your elbow in, slowly straighten your right arm until it is almost fully extended at the height of your bent elbow. Continue exhaling, and form a right unbendable arm. Your fist should travel inward, upward, and outward. Your arms should again be at the same height and in the same position.

Sanchin Section I—Moving the Right Leg Forward
(Figure 33, page 141)

Unlock your left foot, placing it in a straight line prior to stepping forward. Move your right foot forward in a clockwise semicircle. Lock your left foot into position behind it and assume the Sanchin stance. At the end of the step, consolidate the position by pushing your hips forward and completing the exhalation.

While inhaling, first let your hips drop back, then, withdraw your left fist to your left side. Begin exhaling. Keeping your elbow in, slowly straighten your left arm until it is almost fully extended at the height of your bent elbow. Place your left fist under the elbow of your right arm and continue the out-breath. Consolidate the position by pushing your hips forward and completing the exhalation.

Drop your hips back and prepare to turn. In crossing your right leg over in front of your left, take care to measure the distance carefully, so that your feet will be in the proper Sanchin stance after pivoting.

Figure 32. Sanchin Section 1—moving the left leg forward.

Figure 33. Sanchin Section 1—moving the right leg forward.

Sanchin Turn #1—Left Leg Begins Forward
(Figure 34)

Pivoting to face the rear, bring your left hand into the unbendable arm position by moving it in a counterclockwise arc from its position under your right elbow. Do this while simultaneously withdrawing your right arm to your right side in a counterclockwise arc and inhaling.

You will now be in a left-leg-forward Sanchin stance. Begin exhaling. Keeping your elbow in, slowly straighten your right fist until it is almost fully extended at the height of your bent elbow. Continue exhaling and form a right unbendable arm. Your fist should travel inward, upward, and outward. Your arms should again be at the same height and in the same position.

Figure 34. Sanchin turn #1, left leg begins forward.

Sanchin Turn #1—Moving the Right Leg Forward
(Figure 35)

Unlock your left foot, placing it in a straight line prior to stepping forward. Move your right foot forward in a clockwise semicircle. Lock your left foot into position behind it and assume the right-leg-forward Sanchin stance. At the end of the step, consolidate the position by pushing your hips forward and completing the exhalation.

While inhaling, first let your hips drop back as usual, then withdraw your left fist to your left side. Begin exhaling. Keeping your elbow in, slowly straighten your left arm until it is almost fully extended at the height of your bent elbow. Continue exhaling, and form a left unbendable arm. Your fist should travel inward, upward, and outward. Your arms should again be at the same height and in the same position.

Figure 35. Sanchin turn #1, moving the right leg forward.

Sanchin Turn #1—Moving the Left Leg Forward
(Figure 36)

Unlock your right foot, placing it in a straight line prior to stepping forward. Move your left foot forward in a counterclockwise semicircle. Lock your right foot into position behind it and assume the left-side-forward Sanchin stance. At the end of the step, consolidate the position by pushing your hips forward and completing the exhalation.

While inhaling, first let your hips drop back, then withdraw your right fist to your right side. Begin exhaling. Keeping your elbow in, slowly straighten your right arm until it is almost fully extended at the height of your bent elbow. Place your right fist under the elbow of your left arm and continue the out-breath. Consolidate the position by pushing your hips forward and completing the exhalation. Drop the hips back and prepare to turn, this time by crossing your left leg over in front of your right.

Figure 36. Sanchin turn #1, moving the left leg forward.

Sanchin Turn #2—Right Leg Begins Forward
(Figure 37)

You will now be facing in your original direction with your right leg forward. As you pivot, bring your right hand into the unbendable arm position by moving it in a clockwise arc from its position under the left elbow. Do this while simultaneously withdrawing your left arm to your left side and inhaling.

Begin exhaling. Keeping your elbow in, slowly straighten your left fist, until it is almost fully extended at the height of your bent elbow. Continue exhaling, and form a left unbendable arm. Your fist should travel inward, upward, and outward. Your arms should again be at the same height and in the same position.

Figure 37. Sanchin turn #2, right leg begins forward.

Sanchin Turn #2—Moving the Left Leg Forward
(Figure 38, page 146)

Unlock your right foot, placing it in a straight line prior to stepping forward. Move your left foot forward in a counterclockwise semicircle. Lock your right foot into position behind it and assume the Sanchin stance. At the end of the step, consolidate the position by pushing your hips forward and completing the exhalation.

While inhaling, first let your hips drop back, then withdraw your right fist to your right side. Begin exhaling. Keeping your elbow in, slowly straighten your right arm, until it is almost fully extended at the height of the bent elbow. Continue exhaling, and form a right unbendable arm. Your fist should travel inward, upward, and outward. Your arms should again be at the same height and in the same position.

Figure 38. Sanchin turn #2, moving the left leg forward.

Sanchin Turn #2—Moving the Right Leg Forward
(*Figure 39, page 147*)

Unlock your left foot, placing it in a straight line prior to stepping forward. Move your right foot forward in a clockwise semicircle. Lock your left foot into position behind it and assume the Sanchin stance. At the end of the step, consolidate the position by pushing your hips forward and completing the exhalation.

While inhaling, first let your hips drop back, then withdraw your left fist to your left side. Begin exhaling. Keeping your elbow in, slowly straighten your left arm, until it is almost fully extended at the height of the bent elbow. Continue exhaling. Then, opening both hands, place them in the double unbendable arm positions. Your arms should again be at the same height and in the same position, although this time both hands should be open.

Place your palms face downward, elbows extended further to the sides than your hands. Form a right angle at the point where your two hands nearly meet. The elbows are carried higher than the wrists. Consolidate the position by pushing your hips forward and completing the exhalation.

Figure 39. Sanchin turn #2, moving the right leg forward.

Sanchin Solo Form—Section 2
(Figure 40)

In the second section of the form, you are encouraged to move both arms together, with each performing an identical role. The basic geometrical movements are used during pushing hands to counter gripping or pulling attempts. Here the elbow is slightly higher than the wrist as a result of the wrist being pulled, or wedging. Your arms should be held in a diamond-shaped wedge, elbows higher than your wrists, arms triangulated, fingers straight.

While inhaling, first let your hips drop back, then, withdraw both clenched fists to your sides. Begin to breathe out as you slowly straighten both arms, palms down, until they are almost fully extended at the height of the solar plexus. This movement does not constitute a technique in itself. It is practiced merely as a prerequisite to retracting the arms in the next movement.

Retract both hands into the double-wedge positions, with your elbows extended further to the sides than your hands. Form a right angle at the point where your two hands nearly meet. This is practiced to re-establish a palms-down leverage position if your arm is grabbed and straightened during pushing hands. If your arm becomes straight, you can easily be pulled out of stance. It is important here that your elbows be carried higher than your wrists. Consolidate the position by pushing your hips forward and completing the exhalation.

While inhaling, first let your hips drop back, then withdraw both clenched fists to your sides. Begin to breathe out as you slowly straighten both arms, palms down, until they are almost fully extended at the height of the solar plexus *for the second time.* Retract both hands into the double-wedge positions, with the elbows extended further to your

Figure 40. Sanchin solo form, Section 2.
The middle and right movements are repeated three times.

sides than the hands. Form a right angle at the point where your two hands nearly meet. Your elbows should be carried higher than your wrists. Consolidate the position by pushing your hips forward and completing the exhalation. Repeat the sequence in this paragraph one more time so that you have carried it out a total of three times.

Sanchin Solo Form—Section 3
(Figure 41)

In the third section, both arms and a leg are used simultaneously, but performing separate roles, independently, with different timings. The basic geometrical movements in application during pushing hands comprise the movement *Ptoh* (to spit), which is a double-handed grip release and push, the classic *Po-pai* of most southern styles. Classically it is combined with a semi-circular retreat. Letting your hips drop back, place your left open hand palm-down under the elbow of your open right hand, which is held in the unbendable position.

Figure 41. Beginning position for Sanchin solo form, Section 3.

Stepping Back—First Motion
(Figure 42A, page 150)

Unlock your back (left) foot so that it points straight ahead. As you begin to inhale, move your right foot in a counterclockwise semicircle and begin to step back, while bringing your right hand up to a position near the inside of your left shoulder. Lock your left foot.

Keeping your hips back, perform the circular deflection (Turning the Dharma Wheel). Move your left hand across in front of your chest to the left in a vertical counterclockwise arc, with your fingers pointing up. Your left arm should move to the left and back, diagonally across and in front of your body, finishing in a position on your left side, with the fingers pointing down. Simultaneously, slide your right hand across your chest, turning it palm out in the process. Your right hand is now up, your left hand is down. Both hands are in the classic Abhaya and Varada Mudra, the Buddhist gestures of fearlessness and wish-granting, respectively.

Begin to exhale. Extend both hands forward, but do not fully straighten them. Keep your palms and fingers vertical, and your elbows down and tucked in. Consolidate the position by pushing your hips forward as the out-breath is completed.

Figure 42A. Stepping back, first motion.

Stepping Back—Second Motion

(Figure 42B, page 151)

Let your hips drop back as you place your right open-hand palm down under your left elbow. Your left hand should be held open in the unbendable position. Unlock your right (back) leg so that it points straight ahead. As you begin to inhale, move your left foot in a clockwise semi-circle and begin to step back, while bringing your left hand up to a position near the inside of your right shoulder. Lock your right leg.

Keeping your hips back, perform the circular deflection (Turning the Dharma Wheel). Move your right hand across in front of your chest to the right in a vertical

Figure 42B. Stepping back, second motion.

clockwise arc, with the fingers pointing up. Move your right arm to the right and back, diagonally across and in front of your body, finishing in a position on your right side, with your fingers pointing down. Simultaneously slide your left hand across your chest, turning your palm out in the process. Your left hand is now up, and your right hand is down. Both hands are in the classic Abhaya and Varada Mudra. Begin to exhale. Extend both hands forward, but do not fully straighten them. Keep your palms and fingers vertical, with your elbows down and tucked in. Consolidate the position by pushing your hips forward as the out-breath is completed.

Changing Sides
(Figure 43)

Unlock your left leg and begin to bring your right leg next to it. While inhaling, form the Dhyani Mudra, this time with the back of your left hand in the palm of your right, as you finish moving your right foot back, next to your left. Keeping your shoulders down, inhale.

Begin to exhale. Keeping your hands in contact, straighten and rotate them and assume a lowered crossed-hands posture. As you straighten your arms, move your elbows inward. Your palms should remain toward your body as you fully straighten

Figure 43A. Changing sides.

Figure 43B. Sanchin finish.

your arms. Continue to exhale. Step out into a left Sanchin stance and assume the double unbendable arm positions. From there, perform all movements in mirror image for the required number of repetitions.

To complete the form, raise your hands to the height at which Anjali Mudra is performed, while clenching your right hand into a fist covered by your left palm. This gesture is derived from part of the Sanskrit character for "OM." It is a sign of completeness, and ends the form in symbolic nirvana. Finally, finish by performing the Anjali Mudra (salutation, see figure 43B).

Once the mechanics of the form have been mastered, you can go on to build layers of meaning and application into it.

Sanchin Theory

I have divided this discussion of the theory behind the Sanchin form into three broad parts that treat, respectively, its physical, psychological, and esoteric aspects. I have further subdivided the explanation of the esoteric aspects into three parts. In truth, it cannot truly be divided in this way, because each topic depends upon the others. The divisions here are simply a matter of convenience.

Physical Aspects of Sanchin

Sanchin is a whole-body exercise. In the practice of its postures, steps and physical movements, you grip with your feet. The frame made by the stance exercises your ankles, knees, thighs, and buttocks. Providing there is no undue tension in the performance of the form, the closed movements of Section 1 keep your shoulders low and exercise your lattisimus dorsi (muscles at the side of the body), chest, back, and upper arms. This occurs through three specific classes of basic movements: withdrawing the fist, pressing forward with the fist, and lifting the hand back into Sanchin unbendable-arm position). These movements help in training the rotation of the ulna and radius (the two bones in the forearm) and generally train muscle and sinew. The movements in Section 2 exercise the triceps (muscles under your arm, between the elbow and the armpit) and also the deltoid (shoulder) and pectoral (chest) muscles. Section 3 of Sanchin Kata opens the chest and back muscles, stretching them and the ribcage. Next to be considered is the exercise of the large muscle groups controlling the diaphragm, which are exercised during Sanchin breathing.

Breathing (Pranayama): During Sanchin, your breath is carefully regulated through tension diaphragmatic breathing. This is called *pranayama* in Sanskrit. Pranayama actually means to restrain the prana or vital force (Chinese, *qi*, Japanese, *ki*).

The lungs work on a negative pressure, thus normal breathing takes care of itself. In pranayama, although there is a definite technique for the in breath (letting the belly "pot"), the emphasis is on the out breath. The key lies in a one-to-four breath ratio: one beat for the in breath and four beats for the out breath. Contrary to modern Sanchin breathing practices (oriented toward combat usage), the breath should be regulated, but not held. Pranayama is an ancient yogic practice designed to superoxygenate your brain without making you light-headed.

Breath has a direct relationship to concentration.

> There are two causes that make the mind wander around: Desires/thoughts, the product of latent feelings, and breathing.
>   If one is controlled the other will automatically be also. Of the two, breath should be controlled first.[6]

Physiologically, tension diaphragmatic breathing works because it stimulates the nerves within the muscles called proprioceptors. These, in turn induce a state of alertness in the posterior hypothalamus of the brain.

Besides making you fully awake, correct practice of the Sanchin form allows you to rise above superficial thoughts and emotions (fears, worries, etc.) and enter a state of calm, focused concentration. Meanwhile, your brain waves change from a beta to an alpha frequency. This practice serves to unify the four parts of the brain at its three levels (reptilian, mid-brain, cerebral hemispheres), allowing you to enter into a direct relationship with the Tao. This state of "energized absorption" eventually leads to *samadhi* (Sanskrit, to establish or make firm), a state that lies beyond waking, dreaming, and deep sleep, and in which all mental activity has ceased.

When samadhi appears, there is no distinction between subject and object, other and self. If you get it right, you may enter a state known as "deathlessness," where you exist completely in the moment. This is a superior state of meditation in which, as Zen teachers put it, "Thought abides no-where."

> That state of consciousness in which there are no objects, no passions, no aversions, but there is supreme happiness and superior power is samadhi.[7]

The practice of the Sanchin form provides all the necessary tools and stages to accomplish the goals of yoga, Zen, and Taoism. Through its practice, you are catapulted into a direct relationship with the Tao, which equates to Samadhi. How does Sanchin practice do this? Here is a little pseudo-science for you to contemplate.

Everything has a vibration, a rhythm, and a cycle, including the human body and the breath. The normal breath rate for an adult engaged in light activity is approximately eighteen breaths per minute. Yoga teaches that, at this breathing rate, we are the most externalized and fully subject to the domination of thought, emotion, and the stresses and strains of everyday life. Most understand relaxation theoretically. When attempted, however, relaxation quite often leads to drowsiness and then to sleep. Seldom can we *cause* a state of relaxation coupled with awakeness. We may try to do so by involving ourselves in something and fully concentrating.

---

[6] From Yogakundalyupanishad 1.1-2 from the translation found in *Chakras: Energy Centers of Transformation* by Harish Johari (Rochester, VT: Inner Traditions, 1987).
[7] From Mahopanishad 4.62, from the translation found in *Chakras: Energy Centers of Transformation* by Harish Johari (Rochester, VT: Inner Traditions, 1987).

During heavy concentration, the breath drops to about nine breaths per minute. If we are tired, protracted concentration may then easily become sleepiness, which occurs as result of the reduced oxygen intake.

Normal breath volume for adults is approximately 500 ml of air per breath. During Sanchin, the breath rate is reduced to 7.5 breaths (or less) per minute, but the air intake is increased to 1200 ml per breath, or more. The result is better concentration due to improved oxygenation of the brain. This is not hyperventilation, because, although the rate of air *intake* was increased, the breath rate itself was actually lowered!

Another effect of this type of breathing is the altered state of consciousness it induces, which occurs as a result of being put in harmony with natural forces. There is a 1:4 ratio between the breath and pulse rates, which means 18 breaths are taken for every 72 pulses.

According to the American meditation teacher, the Reverend Straugn, comparing the cyclical values of our respiratory and circulatory systems with that of the solar system yields some very revealing facts. The Earth rotates one degree every four minutes. It is useful to view these minutes as *pulses*, rather than arbitrarily conceived time periods.

A good meditation objective might be to see if the 1:4 ratio between our breathing and pulse rates was determined by the clocking mechanism that controls the Earth's rotation around its axis. Here we can see that harmonizing with the Tao is potentially a physical actuality and not merely a mystical or poetical metaphor.

The process of breathing in pranayama is also known as pot-bellied breathing, which begins in the Tan Tien.[8] The Tan Tien is a point traditionally located in the center, about an inch below the navel. You should breathe from your belly and avoid shallow breathing. It is not the will that controls thought-drift, but rather the mechanism of the breath. If you don't breathe from the Tan Tien, you will regularly find your thoughts drifting all over the place. It is important, in Sanchin breathing, to use the mechanism of the diaphragm. Pushing your hips forward in the Sanchin stance at the end of each out breath presses your abdominal wall against your diaphragm, which drives the breath.

The habit of good breathing needs to be carried over to the pushing-hands practice, but pranayama itself cannot be practiced during pushing hands. Although the breath rate may (will) go up, you must still retain the feeling of being centered in the Tan Tien. You must also retain good spatial awareness. Incidentally, the first time a man was put into orbit, as he spun around in a weightless condition, his exact center of gravity—the point around which he spun—was the Tan Tien.

Psychological Aspects of Sanchin

The name Sanchin, or Three Conflicts, refers to the triplicity of conflicts reflected in for example, the conflict between mind, body, and spirit. In Sanchin, the mind is controlled by the breathing, the body is occupied with movement, and the spirit is har-

---

[8] Pronounced somewhere between Dan Dien and Tan Tien, also called Hara by the Japanese.

nessed as a power source for the whole practice. During practice, you should also be aware of the relationships between all parts of your body. Each muscle and joint must be felt to be working as part of a harmonious whole that drives the movement. The result is a tremendous sense of awareness and well-being that will easily repay those who make the effort to practice it. But this is only the beginning.

Stages of Meditation: The three stages of Sanchin solo practice pertain to the three classic types of meditation:

1. Dharana (Sanskrit, concentration), which is an important prerequisite for the practice of deep meditation. Dharana practice provides an opportunity to improve concentration. It consists simply of concentrating completely on what you are doing. During the learning of Sanchin, the form is performed by mind-memory.

2. Dyhana (Sanskrit, meditation), at which stage the mind enters into meditation proper. There is less mental clamor, and fewer notions of self. Your mind no longer projects its own concepts onto an object of meditation, but instead merges with the object. This level of practice is where the Zen school got its name. (Sanskrit *dyhana* became *chan-na* to the Chinese, which in turn became *Zen-na*, *Zen* in Japanese, now used universally.) During this stage of Sanchin practice, the form is remembered by the body-memory (feelings). You become the form.

3. Samadhi (Sanskrit, establish, make firm) is the supraconscious state. Beyond words and description, this state, where duality and the manifest world no longer exist, is reached through the practice of Dyhana. During this stage, the spirit (in part, the programmed automaton) drives the practice, harnessing, drawing on, and uniting the other two levels or aspects of practice.

Esoteric Aspects of Sanchin

Sanchin is a mandala. A mandala (Sanskrit, arch or circle) is a symbolic representation of cosmic forces in two- or three- dimensional form. Practice of the Sanchin form is, in fact, a physical mandala. Its devotional movements mark out sacred space during its semicircular (arc-shaped) steps and corresponding arm actions. This sacred space, or mandala, creates a specific environment for the manifestation of the deities said to dwell at its center. The actions of the form bring you into contact with the qualities of the deities (symbolized, in Hinduism, as Brahma, Vishnu, Shiva, Creator-Sustainer-Destroyer). As noted, the Sanchin form initially takes three steps forward, symbolically mimicking the heroic three steps to liberation taken by Vishnu. Vishnu is sometimes depicted resting on the serpent Shesha, and at other times riding mounted on the bird Garuda. (Remember the snake and crane story on page 54) The bird Garuda is often depicted in the form of a peacock.[9] The physical steps in the form trace a (serpent-

---

[9] Incidentally, it is common for Karate black belt certificates from Japan and elsewhere to have double peacocks at the top, where their tail feathers cascade down to form part of the border.

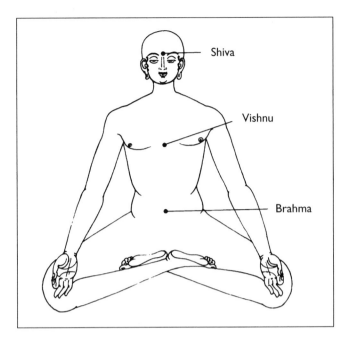

*Figure 44. Yogic diagram showing the traditional placement of
the three deities within the human body.*

shape) mandala on the ground. By combining the physical movements with the breath
and the concentration, the serpent (physical) and the bird (spiritual) are united, and
you can ride the dragon.

As noted earlier, each of the three sections of the Sanchin form can be attributed to
one of the trinity of Hindu deities:

Section 1	Brahma
Section 2	Vishnu
Section 3	Shiva (synthesis of all three)

Through the body, the mind and the spirit can come together.

Sanchin Practice Stage One:
Dharana—Remembering With the Mind

In the following explanation the word "stage" refers to the way the Sanchin form is
practiced. The word "section" refers to one of three sections into which the form is
divided.

The first stage of Sanchin practice consists of a meditation based on intense visualization. This helps to establish an understanding of the symbolism and teaches you
how to think in pictures. The advantages of thinking in pictures are many, not the least

of which is the direct access it gives to the right brain. If we examine the brushed cal-
ligraphy of the Chinese, or the hieroglyphs of the ancient Egyptians, we can see that
both are pictographic in nature. The potency of symbolism to effect real transformation
was, and still is, well-known. To obtain the maximum benefit from a construction such
as Sanchin, you must, quite literally, live the attendant myth. To simply try and live an
entire creation through a destruction-myth cycle is quite a challenge, however, until we
remember that it is not meant to be accomplished intellectually. The cycle of creation,
sustenance, and destruction is something we can feel and of which we can have direct
experience. It is continuous and goes on around us and within us all of the time, as
everything grows, lives, and dies (unless it can free itself from the wheel of rebirth).

Brahma Steps Forward to Create
(Sanchin Section 1)

Brahma creates worlds, people, places, and all things, including duality. He is the
god responsible for the creation of form and name. These forms and names enter our
bodies and minds through the five senses, sometimes referred to in Buddhism as the
five windows (sometimes, five thieves): eyes, ears, nose, tongue, and skin. These five
windows monopolize large amounts of our consciousness, as well as stimulating us.
They also help to create distraction, comparison, fear, envy, and many other conditions.

By controlling the activity of the senses, you become able to direct consciousness
during the stage of Dharana. This stage produces "one-pointedness."

> *The eyes* look straight to the front and slightly down. Vision must be diffused
> (peripheral).
>
> *The ears* must be sealed. If sounds are heard, the distraction that they may pro-
> duce must be dealt with quickly.
>
> *The nose* should be employed in inhalation during the pranayamic breathing.
>
> *The tongue* should be kept pressed to the hard palate of the mouth and the jaw
> left unclenched.
>
> *The skin* should help register spatial awareness. Clothing should be loose and
> comfortable.

Each time you practice Sanchin, you should take (Vishnu's) three heroic steps to liberation, while symbolically and ritually enacting Brahma's creation. As you step out to
form the double unbendable arms, be aware that, in mimicking the act of creation, you
manifest the polar opposites symbolized by the two arms that remain open, equal, and
empty. By exhaling, you find the center.

Having taken your first step and "parted the clouds" to seek the way, you can now
begin to resolve the three conflicts (mind, body, and spirit). After this initial movement,
the rest of Section One consists of three complete arm actions(repeated three times in
those Sanchin forms that have turns). During these actions you create the triune aspects
of all things, with hand and foot in opposition.

When inhaling, draw in vital prana (breath/spirit). Invite it to enter the Tan Tien with the action of your withdrawing hand. When exhaling, feel the vital force (qi) pass through your extending arm and into your fingers. At the completion of Section 1, the qi is raised to the solar plexus (heart/lung) region.

Vishnu Remains Still to Sustain
(Sanchin Section 2)

During the second section, you simulate the role of the sustainer. By this stage, you should begin to experience solid meditation and be firmly in the moment. With your feet firmly planted in the three-pointed stance of Sanchin, hold the ground and retract your hands to the side of your body. Push your hands out before retracting them into the diamond shape, symbol of clarity, endurance, and firmness. Now consolidate your commitment to the path, in the present moment. All forward movement and all duality have ceased and you dwell completely in the eternal moment. Vishnu is a symbol of humanity made perfect, initially by living in the moment, but later through the attainment of liberation. When your hands are returned to your sides, they further accentuate the in breath, which now becomes poetically known as lion breath. This assists the qi to rise to the solar plexus region. The out breath is directed outward from this point.

Shiva Steps Back to Destroy
(Sanchin Section 3)

The final section of Sanchin returns you to the point of departure, destroying ignorance (by turning the Dharma wheel), and invoking all three deities in the process.

On completion of the final movement of Section 2, visualize plunging your arms into the ether (void, space, That Which Is). This causes a flame-red fire to appear. With your arms and environment aflame, begin to turn the Dharma wheel as you step back to the origin (of all things), ready to begin the Brahma cycle again, or end in a symbolic nirvana. This action symbolically counters the actions of Mara and completely cleanses your mandala and your being, as the cohorts of Mara flee. Your qi is raised to your brow, where tradition tells us the third eye manifests between the eyebrows. This symbolism deals with a third and unifying eye, the eye that resolves the dual picture of two eyes. The third eye, in reality, is inward-looking. In Hindu (as in dynastic Egyptian) mythology, it is sometimes depicted as a cobra that rears up on the brow of the person now become deity. (This does not mean being god, but rather being as godlike as possible.)

Shiva is the deity governing this section of Sanchin. Yet, in the action known as the Turning of the Dharma Wheel (*San Sau*, three hands in Chinese, *Mawashi uke* in Japanese), this is, in actuality, a balance between all three deities.[10]

---

[10] These deities are described in the *Puranas* (Sanskrit, ancient narratives) which are divided into eighteen parts (six for each deity). Although these written accounts only date from the sixth century, they undoubtedly draw upon more ancient, oral traditions.

Shiva destroys all—specifically ignorance (*avidya*) and worldliness. Sanchin Section 3 steps back to the point of origin, before the closing movement ends the form (section), or, more properly, returns the practitioner to the beginning. Shiva is also the one who grants wisdom and compassion. Thus, in application, grips are escaped from and the partner's arms are turned, rotated, or spun, and the force returned to the point of origin. Compare these principles to the basic principles in chapter 5.

◆　◆　◆

Stage one of the Sanchin form is about learning and practicing concentration. Initially, you allow your consciousness the time and space to concentrate on or think about what it is doing. With the feeling of the flow of qi permeating every action, you may practice concentration by rallying attention around a set of key images or feelings, such as:

Sanchin Section 1

1. The unfolding of creation (Brahma) and the manifestation of duality; the first of Vishnu's three heroic steps to liberation. Breathe out, symbolically pushing the breath out to the edge of the universe (cosmic breath).

2. Hand and foot in opposition; the second of Vishnu's three heroic steps to liberation. Draw qi into the Tan Tien on the in-breath. Breathe out, symbolically pushing the breath out to the edge of the universe.

3. Hand and foot in opposition; the third of Vishnu's three heroic steps to liberation. Draw qi into the Tan Tien on the in-breath. Breathe out, symbolically pushing the breath out to the edge of the universe.

Sanchin Section 2

4. Pushing the hands out equally and symbolically sending the breath to the edge of the universe, draw them back into the diamond position of consolidation, rootedness, clarity, and strength. Pull the qi upward during the in-breath, and feel it radiate out from the solar plexus on the out breath. Repeat three times.

Sanchin Section 3

5. Turning of the Dharma Wheel and the symbolic destruction of fears, doubts, insecurities, and a whole host of ills promoted by Mara. You may wish to visualize/feel the opening of the third eye, which should have the feeling of shining a torch or a light inside.

Sanchin Practice Stage Two:
Dyhana—Remembering with the Body

Stage Two (all sections) concerns itself with a deeper state of meditation than the concentration required during Stage One. Once a person has truly learned to turn the third eye inward, there is no longer any need to sequence or order thoughts during this level of the form. You no longer think about what you are doing, feeling, or see-ing. Rather you become these objects by merging with them, through practice. (This means repetition!)

The second stage involves no visualization or philosophy as such, but relies instead on the mechanics and practice of pranayama. Thus you remember with your *body*. Return to Stage One occasionally, for a refresher.

Sanchin Practice Stage Three: Samadhi—Remembering with the Spirit

The third stage is achieved by protracted practice of the previous two stages. At the third stage, the spirit (automaton) takes what is learned by the mind and felt by the body and, coordinating them, commits the complete being to practice. All three stages are in reality one.

On a utility basis, Sanchin, of course, forms a skeleton or framework for pushing hands. The three different classes of movement found in the form teach the fundamen-tal co-ordination skills required to push hands skillfully—for example, the ability to use both hands simultaneously yet independently is vital. The Sanchin form allows you to master the basic co-ordination skills systematically (see figure 45, pages 162–163).

1. The ability to move one hand independent of and from the other.

2. The ability to move both hands together, performing the same role.

3. The ability to simultaneously move both hands and a leg independent of and from each other, and performing separate roles.

Sanchin Application

Sanchin applications are structured according to the two fundamental combinations of arm positions: crossed or parallel, either palm up or palm down, when they are gripped. Figure 45 shown the applications specific to each section of Sanchin.

1. Your arms are cross-tied and trapped in the classic Chin-Na arm-tie. (In this case, it is irrevelant whether the palms are up or down.)

2. Your palm-up (bent) parallel arms are gripped, and your posture is threatened by a "pull."

3. Your parallel arms (straight) are gripped at the wrists.

All responses in Sanchin application are against double persistent grips.

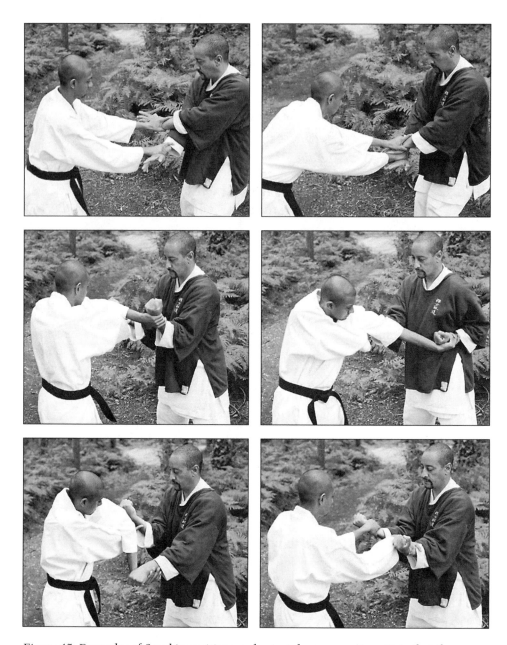

Figure 45. Examples of Sanchin positions and principles in operation. Note that the person who grips tries his best to continue to grip, resist, and divide.

Figure 45. Examples of Sanchin positions (continued).

Solo Sequence of Rokushu

Figures 46 through 50 (pages 165–169) are a photo sequence supplied for reference only. Please note that the turns in the form are not illustrated, being the same as the Sanchin turns. Similarly, the form opens like the Sanchin form (see figures 41 and 42, pages 149–151) and is closed in the same way as Section 3 of Sanchin (see figure 46, page 165). The traditional "clawed" positions are performed as shown in figure 47A and B (see pages 166–167).

Next, perform a Sanchin step and form double unbendable arms (see figure 48, page 167). Then repeat the entire sequence with your left hand and with your left leg forward. After completion of the Crane's Wing with your left hand, chamber your right hand, step forward with your right leg, and form double unbendable arms. Then follow through the form as shown in figure 49 (page 168).

Perform a Sanchin turn and repeat the entire sequence—left hand first, with left foot forward then right hand with right foot forward, then both hands together with the left foot forward, finishing with the left leg forward. Perform a Sanchin turn, ending in a right Sanchin stance. Repeat the entire sequence again, as shown in figures 46 through 50 (pages 165–169), right hand first with right leg forward, then left hand with left leg forward, then both hands with right leg forward. Close the side by stepping back with your left leg and Turning the Dharma Wheel (Sanchin Section 3), then stepping back with your right leg and Turning the Dharma Wheel. To complete a balanced kata, return your hands to Dhyani mudra, change sides and perform the whole kata in mirror image.

A Note on Rokushu Application

In application, Rokushu is designed to facilitate escapes from single arm/wrist grips. Sanchin and Naifuanchin applications deal with double-arm techniques (crossed and un-crossed). Double-arm movements occur in Rokushu solo form simply as a means to prevent or correct a potential "body bias" (a raised or advanced shoulder, or twisted posture) that can occur when techniques for a single arm are practiced.

Figure 46. Rokushu solo form, Section 1.

Figure 47A. Traditional Rokushu "clawed" positions.
A, B: Snake Hand. C, D, E: Tiger Hand. F, G, H, I: Leopard Hand.

Figure 47B. Traditional Rokushu "clawed" positions.
A, B: Standing Dragon. C, D: Laying Dragon. E, F: Crane's Wing.

Figure 48. Double unbendable arms.

Figure 49. Rokushu sequences.

Figure 50. Concluding the Rokushu sequence.

Figure 50. Concluding the Rokushu sequence (continued).

Universal Similarities in the Function of Trinity

11

T*he three worlds are conquered by him who has mastered posture.*[1]

There are many dimensions to the function of trinity. It can be physical, psychological, or spiritual. Trinity is internal, external, hard, soft, fluid, solid, terrestrial, and cosmic. On a universal level, it is all-embracing and all-encompassing. This chapter is offered as a reflection on the universal similarities in the function of trinity, and its relationship to Sanchin.

Sanchin, the primary form of the empty-hand art, Karate, and Kung Fu, can be summarized as the principle of *triplicity* engendering *triangularity*. Physically, triangular positions are the strongest (mechanical) positions of leverage into which you can put the human body (Euclidian solids spring to mind).

Psychologically, most of the imbalances from which humans suffer can be attributed to the conflict existing between the three principal players that express human consciousness (mind, body, and spirit). Sanchin is aptly named and well-aspected to help resolve these three classic conflicts through interaction with the three deities it represents.

Brahma, Vishnu, and Shiva (or whatever you wish to call them) relate mutually with each other, are interchangeable, and do not stand alone. *In fact, the three are one.*

---

[1] From Trishikhibrahmanopanishad mantra section 52, from the translation found in *Chakras: Energy Centers of Transformation* by Harish Johari (Rochester, VT: Inner Traditions, 1987).

The three deities (past, present, and future) coalesce in Section 3 of Sanchin, where both arms and one leg simultaneously describe semi-circles (three in all).

The hands finish with the fingers of the top hand pointing up in the fearlessness gesture (Abhaya Mudra) and the fingers of the bottom hand pointing down in the wish-granting gesture (Varada Mudra). This is an excellent example of the direct application of symbolic ritual action (see figure 51). These balanced (yin/yang) movements mimic those of a multi-armed deity, and can be found in Buddhist, Hindu, and other iconography. These gestures, which may have originated at the dawn of civilization, are still used by teachers today.

Figure 51. Abhaya and Varada Mudras.

Universal Representations
of One, Two, and Three

Symbols and symbolic coding have been potent affectors of consciousness for thousands of years, and will continue to be for many more. The ancient symbols shown in Figures 52 through 54 (pages 172–173) are far more than mere motifs, designs, doodles, or badges. Besides being representations of numbers (possibly the most universal language of all), they convey living, vibrant, and largely timeless principles. Traditional symbols are born simply from stabilizing ways to record and relate phenomena. Neither the signposts nor the vehicle however, must be confused with the destination.

Because Sacred Science rests on observation of consistent and universal principles, it is hardly surprising that the various means of expressing these principles bear uncanny resemblance to each other. For example, the evidence provided below, makes it

Figure 52. One. Top: Single spiral (New-grange, Ireland) Center: The number one. Bottom: Markings from the Tjuringa stone, an Australasian Aboriginal stone.

Figure 53. Two. Top left: Double spiral (New-grange, Ireland). Top right: The number two. Bottom left: Mid-point between the double spiral and Yin/Yang. Bottom right: The yin/yang symbol from China.

Figure 54. Three. Top left: Triple spiral (New-grange, Ireland). Top right: The number three. Bottom left: The Sanskrit (Indian) OM symbol of unity and completeness. Bottom right: The Okinawan triple spiral.

apparent that the yin/yang symbol is not specifically a Chinese invention, and that the triple spiral at New-grange can be found in modified form within Chinese, Okinawan, Japanese, and other cultures. (This is not to say that the New-grange spiral came first.)

Symbols from the Bronze Age tomb in Meath, Ireland (single, double, and triple spirals), aboriginal Australia single and double spirals, Hindu and Buddhist OM signs, Chinese yin/yang symbols, and the Okinawan representation of three are all consistent. Compare them with the three arcs (two arms and one leg) described during Section 3 of Sanchin, which is a postural representation of the same truth—a representation of the fundamental trinity. Collectively, all these symbols help attest to the ubiquitous nature of trinity in the Sacred Science.

The Unification of Trinity

The third factor in a trinity (not necessarily the third in importance) is the unifying function, vital to the establishment of harmony between opposing forces. A mother and daughter share common genes—so do a father and daughter—but the mother and father do not. In three, the two come together—that is the human understanding of family. Look carefully at the construction of the triple spiral to understand this. Pay particular attention to the direction in which the spirals travel!

In Hindu mythology, Brahma is the creator, Shiva the destroyer, and Vishnu the preserver, sustainer, and present moment. Standing between the past and the future, he is the Christ, the Buddha, Krishna, the Prophet, Anglo Saxon Woden, etc. Female equivalents also exist, for example, in the Maid, Mother, and Crone cycle of Indo-European and other traditions.

Identifying function and purpose, however, is more important than arguing dogma, individual personalities, gender, or details of historical periods, or making racial or cultural claims to a monopoly in understanding or revelation. A deity is what a deity does. It is a function within nature. It is also an office, like Mayor, and not a person. Traditionally, in a trinity, the force in the middle, the force between, comprising elements of both poles, is clearly chosen to represent the savior. This savior is the messenger of god, the intermediary, and the teacher. In humans, it is depicted as the heart, mediator between thought and instinct. In the Buddhist trinity, the Buddha (the teacher) expounds the doctrine of the way (Dharma) for and to the people (the Sangha). It is, as ever, a case of (and for) following the middle way. Sanchin is one such way, based on actions, rather than thoughts or words.

The model must be probed, however, and the essence extracted. Wisdom is the key. According to the Zen way, such wisdom is already indwelling in us, thus the path is one of stripping away delusion and not adding elements! Such methods are based on direct experience and personal insight. This must be supported, however, by the received wisdom and teachings of a given tradition.

Decrease little by little, day by day,
and in that manner learn the way.
(ANONYMOUS)

Two-Man Forms and Naifuanchin (Naihanchi)

12

Yield and overcome
Bend and be straight,
Empty and be full . . .
TAO TE CHING, VERSE 22

A two-man form is a set sequence of movements teaching sensitivity to force and specific empty-hand skills. These are performed in a set order, in a practical hands-on fashion, by two people. In southern China to this day, there still exist many two-man forms or drills. The Hsing I (Mind Boxing) school of the late Taiwanese teacher Hung I Hsiang makes use of several of them.

Eighteen-Monk Boxing—The Gate System

The key to understanding the technical construction of authentic empty-hand two-man forms lies in Eighteen-Monk Boxing, or the Eighteen Buddha Hands. These are not techniques, but positions taken relative to the body of a training partner. According to tradition, these positions were expanded into seventy-two "hands," when Jy Yuang, a master monk began to teach at the Shaolin Temple.

Figure 55 (page 176) presents the nine key positions based on three "gates"—outside the left shoulder, in the middle, and outside the right shoulder. Close analysis will show that the figure with the dark hands has its body slanted with its left side continually presented. Its hands are systematically placed in all the positional contact combi-

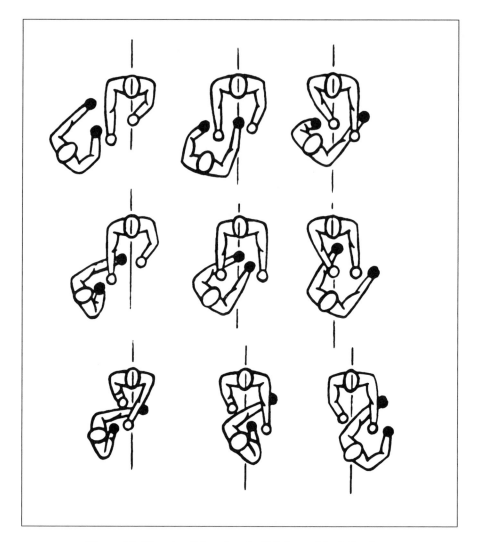

Figure 55. The nine "chambers" of Eighteen-Monk Boxing.

nations possible. If these are then repeated, this time with the body slanted so the right side is continually presented, the total number of positions is eighteen. These eighteen positions indicate all the gates, or contact positions, possible when practicing with a partner. These positions help to classify all the positions that can occur during an exchange of force, whether it be boxing (pushing) or grappling—one hand outside your partner's lead hand, two hands outside the lead hand, one hand in and one out, etc. All grips, pushes, or pulls (or even blows) can be classified, and therefore recorded, using this system.

There are other ways of formulating zones, gates, or positions, based on the three heights or levels—upper, middle, and lower—and the three "guardians" that control contact distance—wrist, elbow, and shoulder. I invite you to find them out for yourself.

Naifuanchin

One recently rediscovered two-man form is Naifuanchin. This solo form has a long history. Before the creation of the Pinan (Heian) kata in 1905 by the Okinawan Ankho Itosu, all Shuri-te and Tomari-te Karate-ka began their training with the Naifuanchin form. Naifuanchin form was traditionally, therefore, the foundation for two of the three major Okinawan Karate strains. In addition, there is a tradition that links Naifuanchin to a Naha branch of Karate known as the Asu that allegedly predates the creation of Goju-ryu.

Naifuanchin is also known in Hogen Okinawan dialect as Naihanchi. Gichin Funakoshi, a student of Itosu, changed the name of the form to Tekki when he exported Karate to the Japanese mainland. The name Naifuanchin translates from the Chinese as "internal divided conflict."

History records that Itosu, whose given name was Yasatsune, was nicknamed "Ankho," or iron horse, a name reportedly stemming from his enthusiasm for and practice of the Naifuanchin form and his ability to root himself firmly in the Naifuanchin stance. Naifuanchin was the basis of the kata-centered Karate taught by Itosu, who, it seems, promoted it as enthusiastically as Higashiona and Miyagi promoted Sanchin. Today, the form is practiced by several million people worldwide.

Naifuanchin was long and erroneously considered a ballistic form. No definitive *bunkai* (applications) have previously been given for Naifuanchin, however, because, clearly, its enigmatic nature has forbidden it. Yet teachers have persistently sought to use this catalog of holding, gripping, twisting, subduing, and rolling or tumbling techniques as a basis for trying to block and counter punches and kicks. They have, as mentioned in chapters 2 and 8, insisted on defining the form according to existing ideas on Budo.

In the early 1990s, I headed a team of researchers at Southampton University (England), where we began serious investigation into the possibilities of the Naifuanchin form being a two-man form of Chinese origin. After approximately two thousand recorded hours, we were delighted to discover that this was indeed the case! The sheer systematic presentation of the form, with its specific, definite, repetitive sequence, built-in variations on a theme, and continual returns to key positions was the foundation for our conclusion.

Though incomplete, our early results were published by Charles E. Tuttle in 1994.[1] We went on to complete our studies at Portsmouth and Oxford Universities. Our discoveries were acknowledged by many leading Karate authorities, individuals and publishing houses. A quote from Patrick McCarthy's European seminar tour confirms this:

> I was fascinated to experience his [Johnson's] theory and application of Naifuanchin. . . . If one was to consider it for what it most likely is, a two-man grappling-hands exercise without worrying about politics, uniform, name,

[1] Nathan Johnson, *Zen Shaolin Karate* (Boston: Tuttle, 1994).

etc., then I believe that Nathan's theory would be widely recognized. In fact, I bet that if an Okinawan master had come forward and introduced that which Nathan has already done, he'd probably have been hailed from the highest sources.[2]

The subtleties of the Naifuanchin form and its application, as well as the spatial limitations of this book, require that I give only a broad explanation of it here. I am pleased, however, to be able to provide enough evidence for the reader to get the gist of the theory, and I am happy to disclose the restored solo form and selected parts of its application for those who want to study or practice it.

Naifuanchin Solo Sequence

The Naifuanchin form differs from other forms in its unique straight-line *embusen* (floor plan).

When the three sections of the form are correctly linked, the resulting sideways movement is considerable. The performer steps neither forward nor backward! There are no 270-degree turns, no pivots, nor any of the usual maneuvers found in other forms. The usual explanation for this sideways movement is that it is useful for fighting on a precipice or narrow ledge with your back to a wall, or, perhaps, on a boat. This explanation owes more to romantic notions of combat than to any reality.

If Naifuanchin were really about fighting in a boat, it would have to have been a very long thin one! The same would apply if the form were concerned with fighting on a ledge. Naifuanchin is also said by some to represent a fight in a narrow alley-way. These are naive and severely limiting interpretations for what is the foundational form of all (so-called) Shorin-ryu Karate.

Despite these and other mistaken beliefs, the standard modern Karate bunkai usually consists of a solo, not a multiple-opponent, scenario, in which the defender blocks (and occasionally counters) various ballistic attacks (usually full stepping punches). In this application, there appears to be no shortage of space. Yet shortage of space was the very reason used to justify the sideways movement of the form in the first place!

According to Choshin Chibana (a student of Itosu), Itosu, who learned Naifuanchin from the ledgendary Sokon "Bushi" Matsumura, also learned Naihanchi (Naifuanchin) from a Chinese man living in Tomari. Kenwa Mabuni (another student of Itosu and founder of Shito-ryu Karate) had a servant, Morihiro Matayoshi, who allegedly taught him a form called Kiba-Dachi-No-Kata (horse stance or Naihanchi kata). Mabuni claimed it was different from the form taught by Itosu. One day, so the story goes, Mabuni showed the form to Itosu who agreed it was indeed the original form (Naifuanchin) that he had studied and later modified.

As we saw in chapter 2, early Okinawan Karate instruction consisted of little more that the constant repetition of forms. *Kumite* (Japanese, meeting hands) was somewhat limited and crude. The pre-arranged and freestyle kumite that exists now is largely the

---

[2] Patrick McCarthy, in a letter to me, 1995.

product of modern mainland Japanese Karate-ka. The level of bunkai (application), as previously discussed, was and is limited mostly to bizarre multiple-opponent scenarios that depend on mechanical stop-start attacks from strange distances.

The Okinawans themselves were apparently given no applications for the solo sequence of Naifuanchin. Neither, it seems, did they do much about this situation until the export of Karate to Japan, when applications were required. We know what these purported applications were, because Gichin Funakoshi published them in his book *Karate Do Kyohan*.[3] Needless to say, they are concerned with notions of blocking and striking. Choki Motobu, another Itosu student, made interesting attempts to unravel the mystery, but, like many subsequent attempts at application, his explanations centered on ballistic techniques that deviated considerably from the exacting requirements of the forms. A proper application does not deviate from the solo form at all!

The original (solo) form steps sideways so many times that it was probably broken down into three parts, or three separate forms because of the demands of space, particularly when practicing indoors. The next three paragraphs are intended primarily for the experienced Karate-ka. They will also be of value, however, to the general reader.

Naifuanchin Part 1 (*sho*) should be performed on one side only. The practitioner then continues with Nafuanchin Part 2 (*ni*) still stepping in the same direction. At the completion of Part 2, the practitioner performs Naifuanchin Part 3 (*san*). The whole sequence is then performed on the opposite side.

One of the most accurate versions of Naifuanchin (Naihanchi) on record is found in *The Essence of Okinawan Karate-Do*, by Shoshin Nagamine. It differs little from the original form presented here. The Shotokan and Wado-ryu versions do differ considerably, but the basic structure is still very much present, although the Wado-ryu school ignores Naihanchi Parts 2 and 3. Wado-ryu also changes the height of the hand positions, but retains the original stance, while Shotokan exaggerates and lowers the stance, but keeps the original height of the hand positions.

Further evidence for Naifuanchin Parts 1, 2, and 3 being one form is found in the fact that Shotokan stylists, who practice Tekki *shodan* (one), *nidan* (two), and *sandan* (three), note that Tekki shodan has a formal opening completely lacking in nidan and sandan. Furthermore, there is confusion among modern Shotokan stylists about the exact sequence of Tekki sandan. Disagreement among senior instructors has resulted in at least two "official" versions.

In this book, the separated parts of Naifuanchin are correctly rejoined. Why? Because the justification for the order of any sequence of movements lies in its function. The proper application of Naifuanchin (Tekki 1, 2, and 3) is a drill consisting of a series of crossed-arm wrestling or grappling movements for two people—one "reverses" a double-arm crossed grip and grips the wrists of the other, dividing his or her arms before leading and keeping him or her off balance by tumbling (rotating) the body, first one way, then the other, using a series of double wrist and elbow locks, and employing two distinct grips. The sequence is a definitive catalog of subduing techniques presented as a classical two-man drill.

---

[3] Gichin Funakoshi, *Karate Do Kyohan* (London: Ward Lock, 1982), pp. 121–143.

A Clenched Fist Does Not Always Signify a Punch

One of the obvious confusing factors in observing the solo sequence is that the fists are clenched throughout most of the form. I think this is what has led to the assumption that the techniques are exotic punches, strikes, and blocks. In fact, the clenched fist traditionally used throughout Naifuanchin indicates something else. The clenched fist in the solo form is a practice in lieu of the double grips that would be applied to a partner's wrists in application. The fist clench employed is not an ordinary fist, although it has been handed down as such throughout recorded Karate history. The fist shown in figure 56 is the traditional Shorin-ryu method. It is found in Naifuanchin and some other forms, but has largely fallen into disuse, although Tsutomu Ohshima, the translator of Gichin Funakoshi's *Karate Do Kyohan*, can be seen employing this fist in the photographs illustrating the three Tekki kata in that book. The fist also appears in a stylized form on the cover of an early Funakoshi publication called *Rentan Goshin Tote-jitsu* and in *Dynamic Karate*, a popular book written by Masatoshi Nakayama, the late chief instructor to the Japan Karate Association.[4]

The Naifuanchin Fist Clench
(Figure 56)

Clench your fist as shown in figure 56 (below), emphasizing the grip of the little, ring, and middle fingers. Keep the first joint of your index finger straight and wrap your thumb around it. The back of your hand should form a straight line with your forearm, and your knuckles should line up with your ulna and radius as shown.

Attempts to use this fist for striking expose you to dislocation of the index-finger base joint. *The fist is only a practice method for gripping.* The anatomy of the human hand is such that the strength of a grip is found in the little, ring, and middle fingers in combination with the thumb, as commonly seen in other arts (the grip used on a Japanese sword, wooden sword, the long or short staff, etc.). There is an anatomical advantage to excluding the index finger from a grip. In the Naifuanchin form, this habit is cultivated by practicing this unique fist clench.

Figure 56. Naifuanchin fist clench.

---

[4] Masatoshi Nakayama, *Dynamic Karate* (London: Ward Lock, 1966), p. 75.

The Naifuanchin Stance

(Figure 57)

The Naifuanchin stance can be quite deep, with maximum knee-bend degrees, but it must not be wide. Your feet should be no more than one-and-a-half shoulder widths apart, your feet should be turned in slightly, and your hips should be back. In some ways, the position should resemble that of a skier, in which the weight can be thrown backward if necessary. There is no mystery or secret involved in this stance. As explained in chapter 2, its proper employment provides traction that prevents the user from being pulled forward. Turning your feet in establishes this balance as well as providing extra traction or grip. The Naifuanchin stance is a classic southern Kung Fu horse-riding stance.

Figure 57. Top: Naifuanchin stance. Bottom: Motobu's Naihanchi stance.

Throwing and Locking

Toshihisa Sofue, a 7th-Dan Shito-ryu Karate-ka who has worked with Patrick
McCarthy, claims that, "Eighty percent of Karate Kata is throwing and locking."[5]
According to Eizo Shimabukuro, a 10th-Dan Okinawan Karate teacher, there are no
blocks in Karate, only striking and locking. This may be true for restructured Okinawan
Kata, but the original Chinese version of Naifuanchin contains no striking or ballistic
movements at all, and, despite popular attempts to suggest so, no pressing or striking
of nerve points either.

Considering the prominence of this form in Shorin-based Karate, the implications
for the meaning of Karate kata in general are immense. Many of the strange two-handed movements, full steps, turns, and what appear to be blocks do make much more
sense as seizing, grasping, two-handed grappling, and throwing movements than they
do as double blocks against improbable double-punch attacks. I suggest that the traditional forms of the Shorin-based styles are grounded, in part, on *Chin-Na* grappling
(Chinese, to seize and grapple). According to Dave Franks (a member of our original
research team):

> Naifuanchin is a continuous grappling sequence. But if you think that perhaps
> because of an unfamiliarity with grappling, that the simple removal of this
> Kata from the training syllabus could leave you Karate reassuringly cocooned
> in the "block and strike" explanations of the remaining Kata and Bunkai, then
> the implications of this far-reaching discovery have not fully struck you, or
> perhaps I should say "grabbed you," yet.
>
> These implications make any such retreat impossible, because
> Naifuanchin, although different in embusen from other Kata, is a cornerstone
> of the Karate introduced to Japan by Gichin Funakoshi who reportedly prac-
> ticed solely this Kata for ten years and, not surprisingly, not only are its tech-
> niques mimicked but its principles are expressed (with variations) in other
> Kata. This however means that at least the awkward/impractical "block and
> strike" explanations need not, indeed should not, be accepted just for the
> want of something better.[6]

Naifuanchin—Civilized Techniques

Naifuanchin consists of pertinent responses and is not a mere routine. Although
the techniques are functional, even utility-based, the practice is one that enhances dignity and avoids brutality or violence.

It is important to remember that the techniques utilized by the locker during
Naifuanchin are "force sensitive," meaning they can be mixed and matched according
to a partner's resistance or change of posture and position, or to match and break his

[5] Kirby Watson, "Shito Ryu Karate Discussions with a Master," *Fighting Arts International* (F.A.I. 78, 1992), p. 50.

[6] My friend, Dave Franks, gave me this material specifically for use in this book.

balance. Naifuanchin is very much a "hands-on" practice. It is important to remember again that its techniques bear absolutely no relationship to modern illogical and unsystematic applications that focus on blocking and striking.

The double/crossed-arm movements comprise the classic application, the single-arm applications are an extrapolation used to demonstrate the similarities between the Naifuanchin "locks" and more common or well-known single-arm locking techniques from other systems.

Naifuanchin Application

The sequence that unfolds in Naifuanchin teaches (in a systematic way) the skills of "leading"—that is, guiding or moving a training partner to the point of loss of balance and then tipping the partner over, causing the him or her to tumble or rotate. As the person being rolled tumbles over and is about to recover balance, the person applying the wrist locks redirects the other, causing the partner to remain on his or her back or to tumble again by applying the appropriate technique to maintain control.

The person being tumbled seeks to roll or rotate safely, and manage a continually off-balance body, which becomes more supple and nimble with practice. Naifuanchin sequence systematically deals with all the basic permutations possible under these circumstances.

In this application, each technique occurs as a result of the previous one—that is, each movement is the result of the one that preceded it. In terms of the partner's responses, the techniques do not deviate from the exacting movements of the form.

Fundamental Grip Reversal
(Figures 58 and 59, pages 184–185)

Double-arm drill applications are generated from the primary position and Naifuanchin grip reversal or initial subduing technique. B reverses A's right-hand grip by "wedging-into" A's right hand and twisting it (somewhat like lowering a motorcycle throttle), while simultaneously trapping the fingers of A's right hand so that he or she can't let go. B also "cross steps" toward A's center, dropping weight into and behind the wedging grip reversal, which now firmly grips and twists. When A resists and pushes against B's top (left) hand, B reverses A's left-hand grip, begins a dividing action, and continues with the classic drill.

For the utility minded, the double wrist/arm locks may appear confusing or complicated. Indeed, you may ask, "Why go to such lengths to create such a sequence?" The two-handed Naifuanchin application is designed to counter the famous Chin-Na crossed-arm tie, reversing it and subduing the user with a progressive series of wrist/arm locks or controls. Naifuanchin form ingeniously records one control for each hand, practiced simultaneously or in close succession. By cataloging cross-arm techniques together, the teaching model (the form) can be made succinct, systematic, and manageable, yet complete. It contains and presents the techniques in the most systematic and unconfusing way possible, providing a solo sequence that acts as a

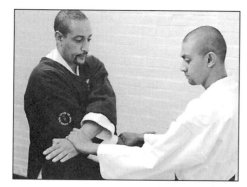

Figure 58. Above: Fundamental grip reversal. Below: Counterwedging grip response.

mnemonic device that can be practiced alone. Unlike other grappling systems, there-fore, there is no need for a written syllabus.

Like Rokushu, Naifuanchin does not present answers to static self-defense situa-tions. Grip reversals are more difficult to catalog than grip escapes, and the practical application of the subduing techniques requires considerably more skill than simple wrist escapes.

In general, subduings are performed by the partner being taken and kept off-balance by having his or her traction (stance or posture) broken through the application of wrist and elbow controls. The subduer utilizes the force from the subdued's attempts to regain traction, that is, get up. Footwork is used to facilitate a tumble or throw.

Categories of Movement

Naifuanchin utilizes two fundamental categories of movements, based on whether a wrist is being twisted with the resulting rotary force moving either clockwise or counterclock-wise, with the elbow being twisted into the center until it can no longer move, or being twisted and locked out. I will term these two categories of positions as "elbow-in" tech-niques, or "elbow-out" techniques (see figure 59). These two fundamental categories of movements can be further subdivided into two types of grips and grip reversals.

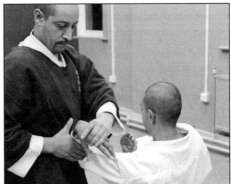

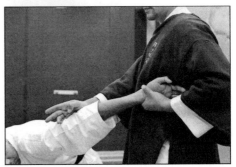

Figure 59. Top: Elbow-in technique.
Bottom: Elbow-out technique.

The two different grip reversals and counter grips have been aptly named "scab-bard" and "sword" grips by Dave Franks, who, as I mentioned earlier, was a member of the original research team that worked on the Naifuanchin project. The scabbard grip refers, not to the way one holds a sword scabbard, but rather to the directional rela-tionship between the hand and the scabbard. The term scabbard grip is used to describe the grip reversal illustrated in figure 60. There are only three subduing or tumbling techniques that can be performed using it.

The trilogy of techniques possible using the scabbard grip is repeated three times in the solo form (and in the two-man drill). Those with experience of the three Naihanchi kata of Shorin-ryu or the three Tekki kata of Shotokan Karate, will see these three techniques repeated in each kata, where, in modern times, they are usu-ally considered as the hook punch, the middle-level forearm block, and the combined lower-level and middle-level forearm block, despite the anomaly of being performed square-on in a horse stance. (The vulnerability of this position is well-known to karate styles that permit kicks to the groin.) In application, these techniques are, as described, the only three tumbling techniques anatomically possible from the sword-scabbard grip.

The Relationship with Pushing Hands

The techniques in Naifuanchin are designed to be used as "side-door" techniques. By side-door techniques, I mean those operated from close quarters and on a training partner's "corner," which is, indeed, the only place from which such techniques can be applied (see figure 55, top left, page 176). This approach requires the use of an oblique or lateral position relative to a training partner. Such a position is designed to limit the partner's use of a free limb, while maximizing your possible use of both hands (and one leg). Such a position also requires contact and is usually preceded by control of the opponent's lead arm. Typical of this "advantageous" position is the position used in Crane-style pushing hands, which is related to *Chin-Na*. As we have seen, pushing hands is used as a base to express the close-quarter techniques found in forms.

Figure 60. Basic scabbard grip.

When used skillfully, the double-hand Naifuanchin subduings completely control the posture and both arms, while any potential single-arm applications would minimize the partner's ability to use his or her free hand, and with posture broken, the partner is forced to either kneel down, sit on the ground, lie prone or supine, or tumble. A training partner can thus be kept relatively restrained.

Scabbard Grip
(Figure 61, pages 187–190)

Figure 61A shows moving into a scabbard grip. A simply grips B's right wrist with a right scabbard grip and stretches B to the side, before turning back and forming the hook-arm position. A simultaneously presses across and slightly down, making sure the arm has the elbow slightly higher than the wrist. This causes B to tumble. The accompanying cross step may facilitate the tumble, but more importantly, prevents B from coming out of the tumble the same way B went in. Thus control is improved. Figure 61A (on page 188) shows two single scabbard-grip tumbling or subduing techniques.

Figure 61B (on page 189) shows the relationship to the double-hands application and the solo form, while figure 61B on page 190 shows them again as singles.

Figure 61A. Moving into a scabbard grip.

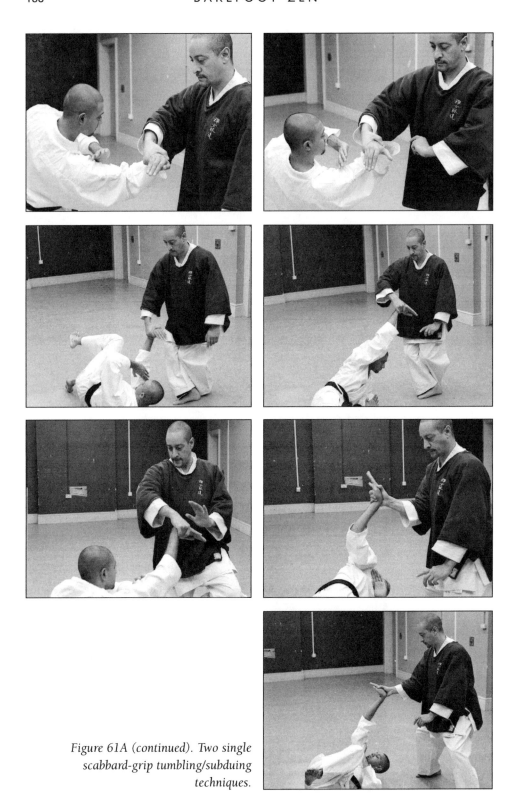

Figure 61A (continued). Two single scabbard-grip tumbling/subduing techniques.

Figure 61B. Relationship to double-hands application and the solo form.

Figure 61B (continued). Relationship between the extrapolated single-hand application and the solo form.

Sword-Grip
(Figure 62, pages 192–194)

The sword grip is shown in figure 62A (top, page 192). The name refers to the way one grips, for instance, a Japanese sword. Despite similarities with a sword grip proper, the main reason for using the term sword grip is to indicate the *directional* relationship between the hands and arms of the person who initially grips and the person who reverses that grip.

The sword grip is the major grip in Naifuanchin application. A series of different subduing or tumbling techniques can be performed using it. The sequence demonstrates consecutive techniques punctuated by the three scabbard grip techniques, which together make a complete series of subduing techniques.

Naifuanchin techniques that flow from the sword grip progressively subdue a partner—the partner is made to sit, or, if necessary, tumble to lie prone or supine, or encouraged to "roll out" or turn over to escape. The person being subdued is, in most techniques, given only one direction in which to escape, based on whether the elbow is in or out. He or she may either remain subdued or roll out of the position, in which case the subduer follows with the next appropriate technique. Figure 62A (bottom) shows the application of the scabbard grip in pushing hands.

To perform the technique, A catches B's wrist with a left-handed sword grip. A twists B's hand, rotating the ulna and radius (forearm) bones to their maximum. If this is done correctly, B will be momentarily immobilized. A then raises the right foot and stamps (*namni ashi*, wave foot), while retracting the left wrist, which still grips B's hand. Twisting his or her hand to be knuckles down, A brings it to the side of the body, ensuring that the elbow is tucked in and the forearm parallel to the floor (classical *hikite*). A may use his or her free hand to "augment" the lock. B begins to recover from the lock, and, following the direction of B's recovery, A applies the next lock, keeping B off balance and subdued. Figure 62B (on page 193) shows the technique in single-hand application; figure 62C (on page 194) shows the technique in double-hands application proper.

Some Naifuanchin wrist controls, based as they are on human anatomy and physiology, can be found in other systems such as Ju-jutsu (soft technique) and Aikido (harmony way)—systems that both stress joint locking. The Naifuanchin catalogue of grappling, subduing, and locking, and of tumbling and throwing techniques, predates both the creation of Ju-jutsu (the Japanese art of locking, throwing, and striking originally derived from Chinese sources) and Aikido (developed from Ju-jutsu). It cannot, therefore, be seen as derivative of them.

In fact, I would go as far as to say that Naifuanchin is the original Chinese catalog for classifying wrist and arm subduing techniques based on human anatomy and its physiology. Perhaps that is why it has survived for so long!

Above: Sword grip.

Below: Application of the sword grip.

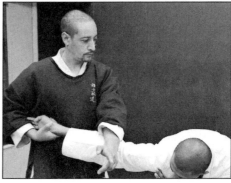

Figure 62A. Single-hand application of sword grip.

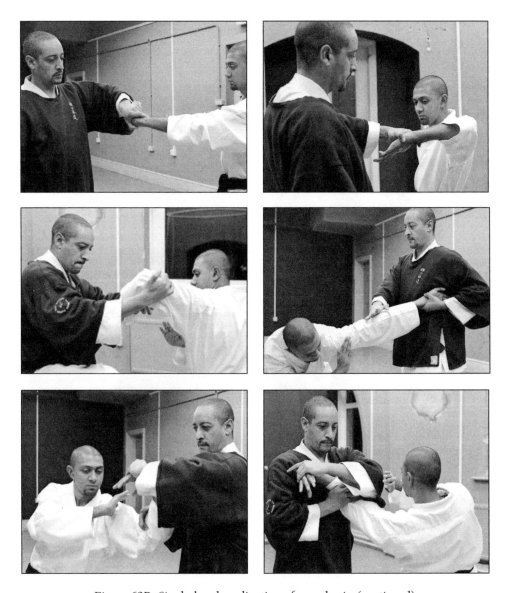

Figure 62B. Single-hand application of sword grip (continued).

Figure 62C. Double-hand application of sword and scabbard grips.

A Little Bit of Evidence

Figure 63 shows the Okinawan Karate-ka Choki Motobu, a contemporary of Gichin Funakoshi, who, according to Shoshin Nagamine, learned the Naifuanchin kata from Kosaku Matsumora (not Sokon Matsumura).[7] Note that Motobu's right fist is centered, an inefficient position, if the position is intended as a block. Also, note that he simply moves his right fist from its lowered position directly to a position beneath the elbow of his left arm, without the left hand being "primed" or "cocked" by the side of the head or higher (preparing to strike) as is done in modern practice. For those who believed that Naifuanchin concerned itself with ballistic techniques, this would not have made much sense. From a ballistic perspective, this movement lacks power and martial application.

---

[7] Other sources state that he also learned from Ankho Itosu, a student of Sokon Matsumura. Like Funakoshi, Motobu held Karate classes at Waseda University, but the club closed after two or three years due to Motobu's emphasis on kumite and the endless repetition of the (solo) Naifuanchin kata, for which there is no evidence he had the proper application. (Photos courtesy Henri Plee and Simon Laily.)

Figure 63. Choki Motobu—Fist-in-the-center position.

Figure 64 (top and center) shows a more functional elbow position for the fist-in-the-center technique demonstrated by Motobu in figure 63. The "roller" or the person tumbled, ends up in the position shown in figure 64 (bottom). Insofar as the double-hand application of this position is concerned, when viewed from the perspective of grappling, its sequence can be clearly seen in the three tumbling techniques utilizing the scabbard grip (see figures 61A and 61B, pages 187–190).

A careful examination of figure 65 (pages 197–198) shows that the elbow is properly positioned higher than the wrist. Students are traditionally taught that the arm must be positioned such that water would run down it from the elbow to the wrist. This instruction is implicit in Gichin Funakoshi's *Karate Do Kyohan*, where it is referred to as the *mizu-nagare* (water-flowing) decline from elbow to wrist.[8] Unfortunately, Funakoshi also designates it as a defense of the solar plexus. Later, this idea was abandoned and the movement was further removed from its proper application by being erroneously cataloged as a hook punch. If you look at the application you will notice that the lock is only made effective by the elbow being positioned higher than the wrist.

---

[8] Funakoshi, *Karate Do Kyohan*, p. 126.

Fist-in-the-center position (double hands).

Fist-in-the-center position (single hand).

Roller, or tumbled, position.

Figure 64.

Figure 65. Mizu-nagare—water-flowing decline from elbow to wrist.

Figure 65. Mizu-nagare (continued)—water-flowing decline from elbow to wrist.

The proper application of executing hiki-te is subtle but specific. It entails withdrawing the clenched fist to your side as you deliver what has mistakenly been considered a hooking punch across the front of your body, while standing in a straddle stance. Although students are taught that the (punching) arm must not go past their opposite shoulder, this is impractical. Anyone who cares to try it (against a punching-bag, for instance) will find that the raised elbow causes a severe loss of power. Moreover, the traditional insistence that practitioners not break or change their stance renders the method totally ineffective as a hook punch. In fact, this combination technique catalogs two techniques, one swiftly following the other. One is a tumbling technique from the sword-handle grip, the other is a tumbling technique from the sword-scabbard grip.

Two-Handed Drill—Sophisticated Techniques

The techniques contained in the Naifuanchin drill are typically Chinese—sophisticated, subtle, and complex. (See figures 66 through 69, pages 200–209.) It must be admitted that successful completion of the two-man two-handed drill requires considerable physical and mental effort. The physical complexity and subtlety is evident in the form, but the mental attitude required for success is not so evident. These qualities, vital for success, make the meaning and applications of Naifuanchin elusive to those whose interest lies in brutality. In order to acquire Naifunchin skills, you must suspend the impulse to win—to defeat, throw, or hurt an opponent. Instead, you must embrace the watercourse way, the path of least resistance, and work not with an opponent, but with a partner.

Initially, the techniques should be practiced very lightly, with particular care for the person being unbalanced, subdued, and tumbled. There is little point in damaging your own or anyone else's wrist joints. You must, therefore, avoid using brute strength and forcing locks on. If you are the one being unbalanced, you must never struggle against the locks or controls being applied to your wrists or elbows. Try to control your tumbling body by remaining relaxed, by rolling or rotating smoothly and close to the ground. There should be as little space as possible between the tumbler's body and the ground during practice. You must flow with the locks and throws, not resisting, but letting go and following the wrist and elbow-led directions gracefully and flexibly, but without being overcompliant or limp.

> Like the ever improbable simultaneous "downward sweeping block" and its complementary "forearm block," these two-handed movements in reality cause an opponent whose crossed arms are controlled by wrist-locks to roll out.
>
> The block/strike Bunkai can now be recognized as choreographed fiction. Similarly, the positions previously explained as X-blocks and augmented blocks/strikes, occur naturally as "tie-up" positions in close quarters encounters where arms are intertwined.
>
> At last these "strange" arm positions, from a whole range of Kata, can be achieved, not just in theory and not just approximately, but in actuality and exactly.
>
> So, if you are a practicing Karate-ka, I urge you not to feel cheated as if you had lost something, because you have in fact gained a great deal: Through the aforementioned and other seemingly obscure positions, whose uses were previously reserved for rehearsed demonstrations of defense against compliant attackers, you can gain an insight into the subtlety and depth of your "Karate," your art.[9]

By always using the form as a guide and seeking to adhere to it as closely as possible, the teachings of the masters will gradually unfold and can be directly experienced. If the techniques are applied properly, the person being subdued can do little more than try to regain his posture. The methods of Naifuanchin comprise a dignified training of the body and mind to acquire the skills of subduing without struggling or using brutality. If you are Kung Fu practitioner, you can easily add Naifuanchin to your repertoire. After all, it is Kung Fu.

Figure 66 summarizes the Naifuanchin solo sequence (see pages 200–204). Figures 67 through 69 show selective comparisons of the solo form and its single- and double-arm applications (see pages 205–209).

---

[9] My colleague, Dave Franks, gave me this material specifically for use in this book.

Figure 66. Summary of Naifuanchin solo sequence.

Figure 66. Summary of Naifuanchin solo sequence (continued).

Figure 66. Summary of Naifuanchin solo sequence (continued).

Figure 66. Summary of Naifuanchin solo sequence (continued).

Figure 66. Summary of Naifuanchin solo sequence (continued).

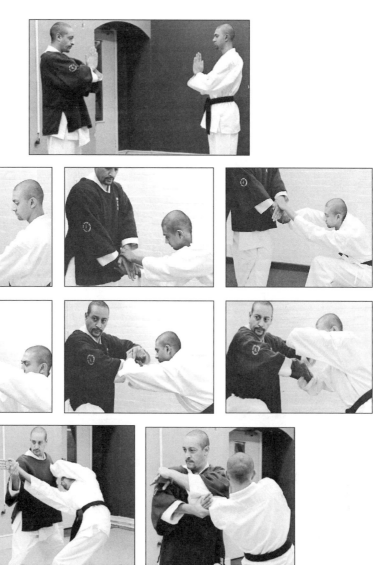

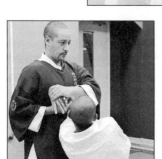

Figure 67. Sequential Naifuanchin double-arm applications.

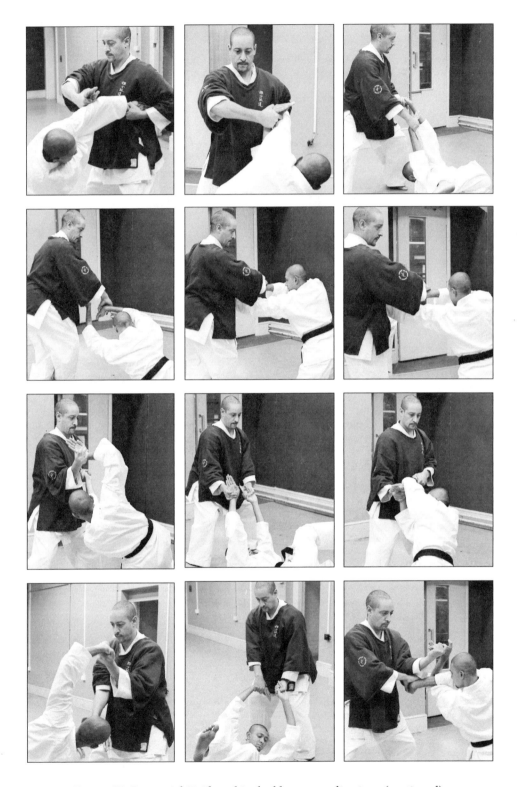

Figure 67. Sequential Naifuanchin double-arm applications (continued).

Figure 67. Sequential Naifuanchin double-arm applications (continued).

Figure 68. Selected comparisons—solo form and double-arm applications.

Figure 69. Selected comparisons—solo form and extrapolated single-arm applications.

PART THREE

A Summary and a Parable
of the Shaolin Temple

The Way Back

It is usually the reply that causes the fight.
(JAPANESE PROVERB)

The Shaolin art is an art of reconciliation—not in terms of compromise or capitulation with an external enemy, but in terms of moving resolutely forward to face your own fears and conquer them. For many centuries, the Shaolin monks were famed for their healing abilities and skillful life-style, particularly during the flourishing era of the Ming dynasty. That they took care of themselves and others during this period is beyond dispute. The reality of skillful living within the confines of a Zen monastery and the celluloid glamour of popular myths and legends have become confused, however, due to many factors.

The Fong Sai Yuk legends date from the fall of the Ming dynasty in 1644. Fong Sai Yuk was the prototype hero for Kung Fu films of the late 1960s on. He was the legendary avenging hero of the Han Chinese struggle against their Manchu oppressors. During the period following the fall of the Ming dynasty and the burning of the Shaolin Temple, previously monastic Kung Fu went public as patriotic societies arose from the ashes of the Manchu destruction of the Shaolin Temple. The fist-in-the-palm Kung Fu salutation (originally, a physical representation of part of the Sanskrit "OM" symbol depicting the Sun and the crescent Moon) was used by the now-warrior-like Kung Fu patriots to declare the overthrow of the Ching (non-native Manchu) dynasty and the restoration of the Ming (the native Han) dynasty.

These patriotic societies, later to become the Triads, still retained flowery names such as "The White Lotus Society," and "The Fists of Harmonious Righteousness."

These names betrayed their original Buddhist philosophic backgrounds. It is no surprise, therefore, to find Kung Fu styles with names like "Perpetual or Beautiful Springtime" (Wing Chun), "Plum Blossom Fist" (Mui Fa Chuan), "White Eyebrows" (Pak Mei), etc.

During this period, and in this political climate, many of the world's Kung Fu styles received their names. In the early 18th century, in the wake of the Manchu conquest, these societies spread various versions of the empty-hand art. Some had traveled as far as the Ryukyu Islands by the mid-18th century, where, as we saw in chapter 2, they became known by various names such as To-de (te), Kenpo (fist art), and eventually Karate.

As the bloody and turbulent history of China unfolded, the empty-hand arts were transformed, and a utility function outside of the original Zen vision was sought. Successive administrations persecuted Buddhism as something alien or foreign. The legacy of the traditional esoteric Zen empty-hand arts began to suffer a decline, becoming a target for rising (Han Chinese) nationalism. The esoteric Zen (Chan) arts were often abolished and forbidden, while their master exponents were persecuted, imprisoned, exiled, or killed. (Hence the instigation of a code of practicing in secret, which persisted even when the art reached the Ryukyu Islands.) In the first instance, the persecution occurred, not because of the esoteric nature of the arts, but because of their supposedly foreign origins. More acceptable to the rising pro-national tide was the emerging art of T'ai Chi Ch'uan, which was hailed as an art of purely Taoist (and therefore indigenous Chinese, as opposed to foreign Buddhist) origins.

The persecution and degradation of the Shaolin way occurred at least three times—the first during the fall of the Ming dynasty in 1644–1645, when the Shaolin Temple was reputedly burned to the ground and all but five survivors lost their lives; the second during the reprisals following the Boxer Rebellion of 1900, and the third during the communist take-over of China (circa 1949–1950) and its aftermath, Mao's Cultural Revolution, in which up to sixteen million people lost their lives at the hands of revolutionary tribunals. Those killed frequently included intellectuals, the educated classes, and, of course, the masters of empty-hand arts. The Chinese authorities tried to ensure (as far as possible) that all the arts with a moral or philosophical undertone that could be used as counterpropaganda were ruthlessly eradicated and replaced with philosophy-free, physically demanding, acrobatic gymnastics (modern Wu-Shu).

In Japan, where there is less urban violence than in the West, attempts to integrate the empty-hand art with the values of Bushido has resulted in the art of Karate becoming a cultural export feigning the dignity and antiquity of Budo. Yet, as we have seen, Japanese Karate is thoroughly modern and in Japan, is considered a "blue-collar" activity, not a noble pursuit.

Terms like "martial arts" don't help when they are applied to arts as different as Karate, T'ai Chi Ch'uan, and kick boxing. Nor is confusion relieved by market forces that demand personal security and self-defense, and look to Kung Fu, Karate and related arts to provide it. The adoption of Kung Fu, Karate, and related arts by the vigilante-minded does nothing to ease the situation either. The ancient and noble empty-hand way is not a preparation for urban street violence. There are more practical and appropriate ways of dealing with such situations, but they are not as aesthetically pleasing or as marketable in the modern world. Real violence never is.

The empty-hand art is not something to be used as a substitute for proper self-esteem. People who use it in that way will always have serious difficulty in extracting themselves from the negative effects of the ego and the ethos of fear and suspicion. Wisdom and living according to the four noble truths and the eightfold path are, on the other hand, deemed meritorious under all circumstances by Buddhists.

The Zen Shaolin approach should not, however, be viewed as pacifism, idealism or a "cop out." Remember, Zen is beyond any "isms." There have always been those who break the social and moral rules of their society. You are not advised, however, to waste time seeking absolute security by devising defense strategies. The empty-hand arts may contribute physically to your dexterity and mentally to your awareness, but please do not dream up endless scenarios with which to punish or frighten yourself, or others. He who is street-wise may be hailed as a success as a fighter, but as a man of the way (Tao), he is a failure. The empty-hand arts can provide a refreshing and liberating attitude of mind that characterizes the original Buddhist vision. But true wisdom only ensues when we understand and practice that wisdom ourselves. It is useless to refrain from something simply because a rule is imposed on us, or because we are afraid of the consequences. We must understand and support the wisdom behind the rule. Spiritual education and the empty-hand way offer solutions that can uplift people through ritual behavior—courtesy, discipline, and the directing, controlling, and refining of individuality through physical, intellectual, and spiritual involvement. This moral cultivation serves a far greater purpose than discriminating against stereotypes and trying to provide solutions to problems reported in newspapers and the media. To utilize aggression (or any emotion) in the empty-hand art is to exclude the Zen mind. When the mind is driven or controlled by an emotive force, it is no longer clear. When your mind is clear of distractions, you achieve *Zanshin* (remaining mind). In that quiet moment of space, of freedom from the consuming flame of pre-occupation with conflict and judgmentalism, it might just be possible to glimpse the Tao. . . or even your own true nature, no longer clad in social armor.

The ethos of the Shaolin Temple was one of harmony through the relentless pursuit of the way (Tao), using Mahayana Buddhism as a vehicle. The empty-hand way was an expression of this, and it was under these conditions that the art grew and flourished. This fact may be unpopular with those who need martial-arts figures to be modern-day heroes, but this is only because the idea of Karate or Kung Fu as a panacea for all evils, a self-defense tool without equal, is so thoroughly ingrained in the minds of millions. This image has, indeed, become an outright impediment to developing the very teachings that the Shaolin art was devised to convey in the first place. In the search for, or the belief in, the illusion of security, people forget that in all other walks of life, cooperation and harmony are of paramount importance.

"The willow tree bends," we are told. The willow tree does not bend itself, however. It is bent by the force of the wind, and springs back as a result of that force. Thus do we train our bodies and minds, by aspiring to be like a perfect mirror for force—not by judging, condemning, or punishing. Rising above our own prejudice, bias, or fear by seeking to become dispassionate during practice, we are neither aggressive nor passive. This is the Shaolin key to mastering the reptilian brain without repressing it, because it is certain we can go nowhere without its strength. A person able to control the reptilian brain can give it wings. Mounted, figuratively, on the dragon that this creates, he or she can ride anywhere, even into heaven itself!

If you practice, or have access to, authentic empty-hand methods, then I say—with regard to the development of modern Kung Fu and Karate Styles—think carefully before you reach for the "magic lamp," should you hear the cry, "New lamps for old, new lamps for old!" For with new lamps, how are we to follow in the footsteps of the Shaolin monks and nuns? The Shaolin way cannot be practiced in words, or by listening to sermons, or by reading and quoting from books. The Zen Shaolin way can only be practiced by deeds. It must be felt, experienced, and lived. Sanchin, approached not as a tool for self-defense, but as a tool for spiritualization, will serve you well.

> *Those who perform meditation for even one session*
> *Destroy innumerable accumulated sins;*
> *How should there be wrong paths for them?*
> *The Paradise of Amida Buddha is not far.*[1]

To enter on the Shaolin path and maintain progress along that path, you must practice Sanchin—a form that claims no utility function beyond sharing the experience with others in pushing hands, a practice in which there is no violence or opinion of the mind, nor distraction of the heart. When I understood this, I was overjoyed. In the words of Robert Smith,

When I began practicing, I did so from scratch; won't you join me?[2]

---

[1] Hakuin, "The Song of Meditation" in *Buddhist Scriptures* (London: Penguin, 1959), p. 134.
[2] Robert Smith, *Pa-Kua Chinese Boxing for Fitness and Self-Defense* (Tokyo: Kodansha, 1967), p. 11.

The Monk

A *Parable of the Shaolin Tradition*

A powerful gust of wind drove the flames higher, as they licked at what was left of the meditation hall. Abbot Chu wanted to cough, but found no air in his lungs. It was ironic. Years of breathing practice and now this. He was trapped, his only consolation, mindfulness. Was it a consolation to be mindful as one burned to death? Hmm . . . philosophizing now? Where was the fear?

A small amount of air entered his lungs and, with it, the smell of burning timber, ancient timber, the very structure of the Temple itself. Close by, a muffled cry followed a thunderous roar, as all around, people were dying. He breathed with difficulty. Past the pain caused by the fallen timber that trapped him, he realized that it didn't matter anyway. The Shaolin Temple was lost.

The old man tried to keep his mind clear and focused on what was left of his breath, but it drifted, back . . . back . . .

◆ ◆ ◆ ◆

"Fighting monks? Bah! Send the lad to an ordinary Madhyamika school!"

Chu's parents were arguing. He glanced up and quickly looked away, as the daggers of his father's gaze swiftly reprimanded him.

"Ask the oracle" said a quiet voice from the corner. "It's the only way to get an answer without making a willful decision and suffering the negative karma from it." The room became silent. Chu's paternal grandfather got up from his seated position and moved to a ledge near the family shrine to cast the I Ching.

It was soon decided. Early the next morning, Chu left for the Shaolin Temple, accompanied by his uncle Chen.

◆   ◆   ◆   ◆

Chu's back ached, and the hemp rope on his sister's carrying bag cut into his shoulder. Despite this, he was excited. He would be the best fighting monk in the whole of China.

The road was wet and it slowed down the journey traditionally taken on foot. He bowed his head in reverence as he passed a village elder. However, after carefully making sure that no one was looking, he screwed up his face at Ming Ye, who was poking her tongue out at him. If he hadn't been fully 12 years of age, he would have pulled her hair.

During the long journey from Szechuan to the misty peaks of Honan province, Chu found that the food, language, customs, people, and villages varied incredibly. In one village, the name of which he couldn't pronounce, he saw two medicine sellers fighting in the street. They growled at each other, leapt high into the air, clashed, and landed. One of them came down with a mock expression of pain on his face, and the other immediately went on the offensive. The action was terrific: kicks, flips, dodges, parries, punches, and counterpunches, all executed with precision and razor-sharp timing. It was amazing that neither of them actually got hurt!

While the fight was in progress, a colleague of the two men (who were obviously partners) sold medicine to the crowd. When the fight was over, Chu ran over to them, pretending not to hear his uncle calling him back.

"How did you kick like that? Where did you learn? How did you know what to do? Are you hurt?" he blurted out. The grizzled man who was the target of the questions merely smiled and winked at the boy before collecting his own share of the medicine money and disappearing into the crowd.

◆   ◆   ◆   ◆

One night, a very tired Chu and his uncle settled into a roadside boarding house. Chu didn't like the look of the landlord, or his drinking companions. Uncle Chen directed him over to the corner of a small and dirty room, and instructed him to unroll his sleeping mat. The floor was filthy and the corner smelled of stale urine and rice wine. Wondering why they were in such a terrible place, he lay down and drifted for a while, before falling into an uneasy sleep.

A crash, followed by thumping noises, woke him only moments later. Hoarse urgent whispers punctuated the silence that followed. Suddenly, rough hands were laid upon him, his head was firmly held back by the hair, and something sharp was pressed against his throat. The alcohol smell on the breath of his assailants made him feel nauseous and he began to struggle. He was trying to recall some of the movements used by the medicine sellers when a blow to the side of his head made him black out.

◆   ◆   ◆   ◆

Ma Tsu shuffled forward again. It was his habit to walk the two miles from his home to the village, using the half-bamboo step from the Lohan style of Kung Fu. The old man's keen ears picked up a rustling sound in the undergrowth to his right. Stopping, he lowered his breath and listened again. To his surprise, he found a partially hidden bundle that proved to be the securely bound body of a small boy. A hemp rope prevented the boy from spitting out the rag that blocked his mouth. Mercifully he was still alive.

Ma Tsu quickly untied the boy and began to examine him. He noted a contusion and some dried blood around a small impact wound on the boy's left temple, but, despite the injury, the boy was fully conscious. The old man quickly treated the wound with some curious dried leaves drawn from an inside pocket.

"Who are you? Where am I? Where is my uncle?" The boy blurted out in a confused rush. The old man, knowing the boy was close to tears, looked away to leave him some dignity.

Sitting, head propped up in his hands, Chu felt deep regret at the loss of his possessions, particularly the ancient family heirlooms destined to be offered to the Sangha at the Shaolin temple. To his annoyance he saw his sister's carrying bag lying on the ground next to him. They hadn't taken that, it had been used to bind and gag him.

Ma Tsu looked toward the boy again. Chu, meeting the old man's calm, steady gaze, saw kindliness and concern in his eyes. Feeling afraid but calm, he was glad that the old man was there. Chu quickly explained who he was, where he had come from, and where he was going. The old man's eyes lit up at the mention of the Shaolin Temple. Moving his hands swiftly through a series of ritual gestures culminating in a formal Buddhist salute, he looked expectedly at Chu, who was fascinated but unable to respond.

"What was that?" Chu asked. The old man shrugged his shoulders and merely inquired whether or not the boy could walk. Soon, they began the short journey to the village.

◆ ◆ ◆ ◆

The tea was refreshing. Chu was sure it was the best he'd ever tasted. Noisily eating a bowl of rice noodles placed in front of him by the surly waiter, he pondered on why the man was so rude.

Feeling lost and homesick, Chu discretely looked at the man called Ma Tsu, who was old and reminded him of his grandfather. The man's clothing was well worn, but clearly of the finest quality. He was of average height, but sat tall and straight. His hands looked strong and his thick forearms were ridged and creased with muscle and sinew. Short-cropped gray hair adorned a well-shaped head, matching his neatly trimmed beard and mustache in color. His almond-shaped eyes sparkled beneath the furrowed ridges of his brow. Sun-bronzed skin gave him a healthy look, and while his overall appearance was rugged, his manner was not coarse and he spoke softly with the accent of an educated man. When the meal was over, Ma Tsu paid for the food and they left the restaurant together.

Chu found the two-mile walk quite an event. He was exhausted, and, for the second time, he feared that the old man was quite mad, walking the way he did. It was a peculiar "shuffle-and-drag" step, with one leg constantly moving ahead. When Ma Tsu had first used the strange step, Chu thought it had been to help him the short distance to the restaurant. He would have been embarrassed if they had met anyone enroute. When he'd asked the old man what he was doing, he had to be content with the muttered reply, "Training."

Chu was pleased when they at last reached the old man's house. It was large and grand with a splendid courtyard—not at all what he'd expected. Ma Tsu pointed out the large water clock, which, it seemed, was a great source of pride and pleasure for him. Showing the boy into one of the rooms off the courtyard, he suggested a rest before supper. Turning on his heels, he strode purposefully away.

In the privacy of his room, the old man picked up a small vial containing an elixir. Steadying his hand, he downed the draught in one gulp. The bitter-sweet taste left a burning sensation in his throat. He ignored it. The elixir made him a man long in years and, for that, he was grateful. He remembered his first meeting with the Taoist hermit of Nine-Cloud Mountain. He'd thought the man's price quite mad, but, thirty years later, he could attest to the truth of the hermit's claims. A swift calculation assured him that he had enough elixir to last him thirty more years.

Leaving the room, he stepped out into the corridor, heading for the kitchen to prepare the food. A short time later he served supper for two. Chu found the food plain but good, and there was plenty of it, although Ma Tsu seemed to eat sparingly. Chu politely refused a lychee offered to him and chose instead a small mandarin orange, which he deftly unpeeled with one hand, making Ma Tsu laugh and inquire where the boy had learned such a trick. A wave of self-pity washed over Chu as he thought of home. Lowering his head, he said nothing.

That night, there was little sleep for him; the strangeness of events and a dull ache from the bruise on his head combined to keep him awake.

The next morning a tired Chu accompanied Ma Tsu to the village. Against his usual habit Ma Tsu decided not to use the Half-Bamboo step and, for once, drew attention to himself and the boy. When they passed old woman Li's house, she laughed so much at the old man's upright walk that she fell off her seat and had to call for assistance. Chu noticed that the woman had tiny feet that must have been bound from childhood. What a curious custom that was!

Enroute to the village, Ma Tsu informed the boy that he would take him to the Shaolin Temple himself, but first he had to take care of some business.

◆ ◆ ◆ ◆

The dragon bird leapt with cockspur in full display and ripped at the underbelly of the tiger bird who had momentarily lost ground. A red crease appeared in the mottled feathers of the tiger bird. The crease turned to a welling-up, and the welling-up turned to a spurt. The tiger bird lashed out, but failed to make contact. The dragon bird changed tactics, pausing for a moment to avoid the desperate reactions of the injured bird. Blood pumped out of the tiger bird's wound and, with it, his life force. The dragon bird instinctively chose the perfect moment to deliver the fatal stroke.

A great shout went up, followed by high-pitched argumentative screaming. Chu felt sick and looked at the old man quizzically. The old man's face was blank.

The birds had been hard baited, and gambling had been fierce that day. It was rumoured that several people had lost water buffalo, bolts of silk, and even fields on the one fight. The uproar made it seem as if man were pitted against man, as beast had been against beast.

"Why are we here?" asked Chu.

Ma Tsu inclined his head to the left and lowered it. Chu followed the direction of the old man's gaze, until his eyes fell upon the surly waiter who had served them their food the previous day. "There are some questions I would like to ask . . . him." Chu was in no doubt as to whom the old man referred.

They moved quickly toward the waiter, who moved just as quickly away. Ma Tsu shouted out a name while motioning to an individual who promptly blocked the path of the fleeing waiter. The waiter turned his head and contorted his face in desperation, as his beady eyes searched hungrily for an escape. Seeing his opportunity, he pushed two disputing people into each other, sucked in his breath, and disappeared during the ensuing commotion.

As the clean air hit his lungs, he congratulated himself on his timely escape from the building. Moving toward the street, he was shocked to hear a voice call his secret name. He turned to gaze at . . . no one! Turning in all directions, he saw . . . no one. Pandemonium reigned in the hall and, over the top of it, *the voice* called again. This time, he located it. Looking up, he saw Ma Tsu, who sat grinning at him from the rooftop of the building.

"A truce, a truce, that's all I want!" he cried. Locust Eater, for that was his secret name, fled for the second time.

Ma Tsu doubled his breath, tightened his lower abdomen, and emitted the spirit shout of the god Kwan Dao. Locust Eater took several more steps before he fell to his knees and looked back with narrow, glazed eyes. Beads of perspiration chased each other down his forehead. His jaw slackened and the color drained from his face. Dread subsiding, he began to feel acutely ashamed of his own cowardice.

◆　◆　◆　◆

Not very far away, another man did his best to run, despite having a smashed leg. The pain was terrible, but not as terrible as the pain that the Society would inflict upon him if they caught him again. Heart pounding, nausea filling his stomach and fast moving upward, Lok found his path blocked, and he crashed to a halt. It was Locust Eater, the waiter. A stab of rage rushed through Lok as he recognized his betrayer. Looking again, he noticed that Locust Eaters' arms were out of sight, which made him look strange and off-balance.

The head of a seasoned-looking man came into view. He had close-cropped gray hair, a steady gaze, and looked strong. Standing directly behind Locust Eater, he appeared to be controlling both of his arms.

Arms flying in the wild abandon of pursuit, two men from the Society, Cheng Bok and Ah Tu, drew to a halt. There, right there, panting on the ground, was Lok Yiu. They had him. But what was Locust Eater doing there, and who was the strange old man holding him so firmly? Cheng Bok decided to issue a challenge.

"Hey old man, what do you think you are up to?" he said. "Get on home, before you get into something you'll regret."

Ma Tsu merely smiled, inclining his head to one side as he did so. Ah Tu decided to follow Cheng Bok's example.

"Get lost gray-head, or we'll . . ."

The roar seemed to be a long way off, until Ah Tu realized that it was right next to him. Galvanized into action, he lunged at the old man who'd emitted the spirit shout. Within the same instant, he was thrown high into the air, so that there was a great deal of space between his body and the ground. Devoid of training in the martial arts, his thin frame hit the ground so hard that the wind was knocked out of him and he was left gasping for air.

Ma Tsu reluctantly released his grip on the cowardly Locust Eater to deal with Cheng Bok, who attacked next. The attack was so feeble, uncoordinated, and amateurish, that Ma Tsu regretted loosing his grip on Locust Eater, who was now trying in vain to flee. A man with a smashed right leg had hold of him and was clinging to him with all his might.

Standing very much to the rear, Chu was baffled by the scene. Thick clouds of dust billowed up, and a melee of bodies moved oddly in the commotion. He saw one man clinging to the waiter they had caught in the gambling hall . . .

The man clinging to the waiter was almost being dragged along, and he saw another fighting painfully for breath. Old Ma Tsu was holding a struggling man. What was going on, and where had all these men come from?

"Keep still everyone, or someone will get hurt." the old man said with quiet authority. Strangely, they complied.

As Chu closed the remaining distance between himself and the confusion, he had a suspicion that the men were his assailants from the boarding house! He was right.

When the confusion was eventually ironed out, it transpired that Lok Yiu was "banker" for the group. He had schemed with Locust Eater to cheat Ah Tu and Cheng Bok out of their share of several recent robberies, including that of Chu, who had been betrayed by his uncle. Locust Eater, however, had disagreed with Lok about the split and had reported him to the local crime syndicate who regulated all crime in the region.

During the confessions, Cheng Bok decided to abandon his colleagues and make a run for it. Incredibly, however, just as he swerved and pushed off with his back leg, Ma Tsu's foot was there to trip him, and, as the man staggered up to continue his attempt at flight, he found himself deftly placed in an arm lock.

Ma Tsu removed the sash from the struggling man's pants and bound his hands neatly behind his back. Lok still had hold of Locust Eater, and Ah Tu stood absolutely still, eyeing Chu suspiciously. Chu moved close enough to smell the alcohol on the man's breath, before the man finally took a step back.

"Where are the gems?" Chu asked, directly. The reply was almost inaudible.

"Speak up!" Boomed the compelling voice of Ma Tsu. The man bowed his head, remained silent for a moment, and then looked up.

◆   ◆   ◆   ◆

Locust Eater, Lok Yiu, Cheng Bok, and Ah Tu felt acutely embarrassed as they were marched trouserless through the village, their hands bound behind their backs with their own sashes. They were delivered into the custody of the local magistrate.

On the way, Ma Tsu extracted information from them concerning Chu's family heirlooms, which included a flawless diamond, a ruby, and an emerald, all of which Ah Tu had confessed to selling to a Japanese pirate-cum-trader. Initially, Ma Tsu disbelieved the man's story—surely they were too far inland for pirate activity. Ah Tu revealed an extensive chain of gangster connections, however, and the astonishing size and structure of the society was corroborated by Cheng Bok.

◆   ◆   ◆   ◆

Three days later, Ma Tsu and Chu stood at the entrance to the ancient Shaolin Temple. The old man put his hand on the boy's shoulder and looked steadily into his eyes. A brief smile creased his lips before he turned and strode away.

Chu stood alone, contemplating the old man's strange decision to go to Japan in search of the gem stones. "Hardly worth risking your life for," he thought.

Standing and facing the great double gates of the famed Temple, he knew he should feel something special, extraordinary even, but he did not. Worse, he felt indifferent, tired, and lonely. Putting down the bag of essentials given to him by Ma Tsu, he rubbed his shoulder, which was sore from the knotted repair to the hemp carrying strap on his sister's bag. Wondering what to do next, he waited and waited, without knowing for what.

Late afternoon drew into early evening and still he waited. Nothing happened and no one came. "Why not bang on the gates?" he reasoned, and yet he didn't. Hearing a sharp sound, he turned to face the road behind him. An old man with a long milky-white beard approached. Dressed in the robes of a monk, he carried a staff. Chu held his breath for a second as the monk advanced toward the gate at a leisurely pace. Surely, here was someone to let him in. He was wrong.

The monk reached the gate and, to the surprise of the young man, completely ignored him. Raising his staff, he gave three sharp bangs on the gate—blows that belied his apparent frailty. One of the gates swung back silently, and a young monk, who was little more than a child, with a squint or a severe cataract in one eye, greeted the old monk deferentially and admitted him before closing the gate in the face of the speechless youngster.

Evening turned into the small hours and Chu lay down to sleep as best he could. It seemed that he had hardly closed his eyes when a gush of water descended upon him, soaking his head, neck, and shoulders.

"You like Yao's piss?" shouted the squinting young man from the top of the high wall.

"Yao always piss nice and clean," he continued, before disappearing.

Feeling humiliated, defiled, even murderous, Chu rushed at the gates and banged them in a frenzy of anger. "That squinty-eyed degenerate is in for a hiding," he thought, "even if I have to disgrace every ancestor that ever lived!"

After several more minutes of banging, all he succeeded in doing was lacerating the knuckles and bruising the edges of both hands. Giving up, he began to brood.

They had to open the gates sooner or later and, when they did, he would be ready; he would be ready!

Two days later, his rations depleted and his resolve weakened, he found himself wondering for the umpteenth time whether anyone (with the exception of the old monk) ever left or entered the place.

On the third day, he discovered quite by accident that the imposing double gate was not an entrance at all. Later, he learned that none but the most senior of monks, the sages themselves, or the divine Emperor, ever used those great double gates, said to be likened to the entrance to heaven itself.

Discovering a track that ran half a league away from the main road and the double gates, and tired but triumphant, he watched the steady flow of human traffic moving along, like so many silent ants, about their mundane terrestrial business. It all seemed so ordinary. There was nothing mythical or spiritual about it at all.

Joining a small procession of monks, he approached a small stone-built arch. His hackles rose and he regretted being last in the line when the squint-eyed youth slammed the small round wooden door shut in his face. A faint voice followed:

"Yao piss plenty every day, better hope he no be sick."

◆ ◆ ◆ ◆

Chu, feeling himself being prodded, looked up through sleep-deprived red-rimmed eyes. A smiling monk was bending over him. Chu smiled back and got up. "At last," he thought. "He seems to be very friendly, for a monk. I should be able to get in now."

The man was dressed in a shabby grey wrap-over. His recently shaved head showed the scalp to be far paler than his face, which was long and thin, and had a sharp, pinched look.

Chu introduced himself, and inquired after the monk's name.

"My name is not important at this point," the man said, mysteriously.

"Will you take me into the monastery?"

"No, my . . . er master has sent me out to give you a . . . task, yes a task, and I am to accompany you."

Chu groaned inwardly, feeling more alone than ever.

"What am I to do?" he asked, his voice hardly able to conceal a note of panic.

"If you want to be a monk, do not talk or ask questions; you are to follow me," the man replied, and strode off. Chu found it strange that the man continued to smile, even though his reply was made in obvious anger.

Yao, who was watching the proceedings from his unofficial post at the top of the wall, scrambled down it and raced madly toward the Dharma hall, his uneven features contorted into a mask that simultaneously registered fear and the sheer effort of his actions.

◆ ◆ ◆ ◆

Ma Tsu sat silent and still on a small and decrepit boat. Fuji San eyed the Chinaman with contempt. "The Chinese are weak and cowardly. No Chinese would be permitted to operate in Japanese waters," he thought.

"You . . . want . . . make pirate?" Fuji San questioned, in heavily accented Cantonese. The man he was addressing remained silent. Fuji San re-phrased the question in Hakka dialect. This time, the man he spoke to nodded his head.

Despite a lifetime of adventure and experience, Ma Tsu felt unwell. He was not used to sea travel. Skillfully concealing his discomfort, he addressed the Japanese who had spoken to him in broken Cantonese.

"I have lands, and know many warlords," he said.

"Good," Fuji, the pirate, replied gruffly.

The small craft hugged the coastal shore, and all Ma Tsu could do was to hope that they would not attempt a serious crossing in such a frail craft.

"We go find another ship. You pay me," was the only information a surly and ripe-smelling sailor would offer, when Ma Tsu questioned him.

"Don't listen to Taira," came a voice that spoke with a smooth and polished Mandarin accent. "He smells like the devil, and his mind is befuddled with sake." Ma Tsu forced an artificial laugh and looked long and hard at the man behind the voice, before speaking.

"Where are we going?"

"To the Ryukyu Islands," replied the tall sallow-looking man in excellent Hakka Chinese that betrayed only a slight foreign accent.

◆ ◆ ◆ ◆

Abbot Chu wanted to cough again, but found even less air in his lungs. He felt the irony of the situation even more. You see, he had himself been trying to light a fire in his cell, and now this!

What misdeeds had been perpetrated to receive such karma? What mishaps or transgressions? They must have been powerful to cause or allow the Temple to burn so. Mara was strong. He contemplated the force of evil and, as if responding to an invocation, Mara, the ancient negative force in the universe, stirred himself, swirled in menacing coils, and answered the old monk by visiting him in a favorite age-old, but effective, guise . . . fear. It started as a faint trickle of nostalgia—nostalgia for his old teachers, Tao Sheng and the venerable Li Tsun Ya, now both long dead. Soon it seemed he would join them. The nostalgia gave way to irritation, as he wrestled with the idea that things didn't have to be like this. Then came the full-blown anger, guilt, and regret. He knew who was to blame.

Mara, uncoiling and spitting fire, redoubled his effort and flew at him again, producing the greatest test of the monk's ebbing life. His guilt and regret turned to open hostility aimed at all those who had wronged him and made his path difficult.

Returning to the memory of his departure from home as a young man, he remembered his uncle, Chen. Why, that scurrilous man was thoroughly dishonest and would be reborn in hell. Ming Ye would be cursed with a thousand rebirths, a thousand tongues, to pay for the offense of the one she had stuck out at him all those years ago. Lok Yiu Min, the man who had attacked him when he was on his way to the Temple, would suffer . . . In considerable physical pain, and watching the tumult of conflict and distortion that was now his thoughts increase in power, it seemed that Mara would overwhelm him.

With a supreme effort, Chu sent his thoughts elsewhere, back again, back . . . back . . . to the time when he had been kidnapped by the rogue monk who hadn't even been a monk anyway.

◆   ◆   ◆   ◆

The man, who had consistently refused to give his name, was involved with the people who had robbed him earlier. As that venture had failed to pay off, Uncle Chen had decided that the family might pay a fine ransom for him. Once again, Chen was wrong. Not that the family wouldn't pay a ransom. The mistake was to rely upon the monk impersonator.

Before they had traveled more than half a league, they were surprised to discover Yao waiting for them at a crossroads. He was accompanied by an ordained monk and a layman. The rogue monk stiffened visibly and went bright red when the ordained monk addressed him. Yao stood there, grinning all the time.

"We will take charge of the young man for you," said the monk. The rogue looked away and replied.

"It's okay, I have to take him to another . . . er temple to see another master . . . my . . . master."

"Which temple would that be?" questioned the monk.

"Er, the White Pagoda shrine," the man replied.

"In that case, you're going the wrong way. Let us escort you," replied the monk. The rogue was silent.

A few hundred yards up the road, he saw his opportunity and fled the party. Yao hooted after him and turned to Chu, beaming.

◆   ◆   ◆   ◆

The memory of Yao's smile distracted the old man, and brought him painfully back to the present. Still trapped in the burning ruin, he began to try and dwell on his successes by remembering a vital time in his life as an adult monk.

He tended to be more eloquent than the other monks. He also found it easier to study and remember the sutras. When the time came for the "choosing," he had arranged by far the most informative and eloquent speech of any monk. After carefully preparing, he retired early to his cell, to be fresh for the morning selections. He wanted to be the new abbot.

The following morning, he awoke with a slight feeling of dizziness and nausea. The worst thing, however, was that he had completely lost his voice. How was he ever going to be able to deliver his lecture?

He remembered walking slowly to the Dharma hall, struggling inwardly with his desire to become the next abbot and patriarch of the whole order. A small voice asked him from inside, "Is that more important than the practice of Dharma itself?" He knew the answer immediately, and, with the answer, came relief. The truth was more important than any position, rank, or title.

That morning, after questioning the other senior monks in open debate, and noticing that Chu hadn't spoken a word, the abbot turned to him and asked him, "What is the essence of Dharma?"

It was the key question that should have prompted Chu to launch into his well-prepared Dharma talk, only he couldn't. Better still, he didn't want to. Believing that he was relinquishing the last and most burning desire he'd ever experienced, he put his palms together in the Anjali Mudra, made the most perfect and empty gesture he had ever made, and left the hall.

The next day, he was summoned into the presence of the abbot, who was departing to become a wandering hermit. It was the same old man who had passed through the gates and ignored him in the road, all those years ago. The same old man who had later explained that being kept waiting, ignored even, was part of the test to find out whether or not a candidate was suitable. Chu looked up at the abbot, who silently handed him the mantle and the bowl of the patriarch.

◆   ◆   ◆   ◆

Tung, the Manchu bannerman, suppressed a tear. It was unseemly for a bannerman to be caught crying, but this was different. He'd joined the bannermen to fight, to win glory for himself and the new emperor, the former Manchu Khan, who had taken the name Shi Tsu. The year 1644 was just drawing to a close, and here he was, picking over the remains of dead bodies in a burned out Buddhist monastery. Things were not good. He felt ashamed. If they killed monks, who was safe?

Pushing aside the charred remains of a young novice, he moved over to what was left of the great shrine room. Sidestepping the burned body of an elderly monk, he entered. A sparkle caught his eye at floor level. Moving over to it, he discovered a half-burned leather pouch that, on investigation, he found contained three large precious stones—one clear, one red, and one green. Contrary to regulations, he pocketed them.

The jewels cost him a hand when he was caught later. The shock of the halberd cut made him see double, but he did not pass out for several minutes—not, in fact, until the incredible blood flow had been staunched with the none-too-speedy application of a tourniquet by a reluctant army medicine man. "Helping a traitor looks badly on one's military record," he remembered hearing the man mutter.

The Manchus advanced on the Southern city of Chia-ting and set it alight. The garrison, who were supporters of the Ming dynasty, surrendered along with the population. On entering the city, the general gave orders that only those wearing the (Manchu) pigtail were to be left alive. Consequently, seventy-eight thousand people were butchered. Tung witnessed all this, because he was still with the bannermen, but only in the lowly position of a cook's second assistant.

It was while serving as such that he made his first contact with the White Lotus Society. They wouldn't grant him full or open membership, because he had been a bannerman and was still in the pay of the Manchus, even if only as a cook's second assistant. They did let him provide them with information, however, something for which he never accepted reward.

Occasionally, he met with members of the Society. During one such meeting, he saw a young man called Fu Hsin. Fu Hsin was what you might call a hothead, but he was interesting from the point of view that he boasted knowledge of the secrets of the now-destroyed Shaolin Temple. When pressed, he readily resorted to a display of Chuan Fa, which he claimed to have "modified" to redress certain weaknesses in the original.

Tung was enthralled by the vibrant display of strange postures and gestures in the young man's performance. The youth had a peculiar habit of snapping every movement so that everything stopped and started. Having been brought up in an environment where physical strength was essential, and the use of Mongolian wrestling and grappling techniques commonplace, Tung doubted the practicality of what he saw, but he liked it nonetheless. When pressed as to how such an art was to be applied, Fu Hsin became secretive, claiming that usage was reserved for his chosen disciples. This amused Tung, because the man was very young to be talking about having disciples. Nevertheless, he decided it might be interesting to seek him out again, in the future.

Fifteen years later, Tung, discharged from duty, was forced to wander around and beg for his living. Finding himself back in Chia-ting, he decided to seek out members of the White Lotus Society. It was then that he came across Fu Hsin again.

He had put on some weight and looked older. Taking on students, he had built a school around himself. He recognized the old cook's assistant by his missing hand, rather than by his face or name. Tung was pleased to receive an invitation to visit the new school, located on the outskirts of the city.

Fu Hsin had prospered indeed. His school was well situated, having a large airy central courtyard with a shaded surround, complete with many storerooms and comfortable living quarters. The local authorities were Ming sympathizers employed by the Manchus, so Fu Hsin had no real problems with them, provided he continued to make regular "contributions" to them.

"Impractical but impressive," thought Tung as he watched two young men who were stripped to the waist and engaged in what was obviously a match of some kind. They circled each other, assuming strange positions as they moved. Then, one unexpectedly leapt at the other with a shout. The other moved away and, with little difficulty, evaded the leaping attack, which Tung thought was rather irresponsible in the first place. The defender after taking evasive action, went on the offensive with a series of quick, unusual, and complicated movements. The bout was inconclusive, but Tung found himself drawn to one of the young men who had used his legs to kick several times. Here was something he could try himself, even with his disability. Thus Tung began to learn a modified version of Chuan Fa from a student of Fu Hsin. He stressed kicking techniques as a result of his disability.

Later, he moved north and took his art with him. He taught over three hundred people during the rest of his life, and his art became known as Northern Leg. It gained great favor with touring opera troups and became a great attraction at nothern festivals.

The School of Fu Hsin continued to flourish, teaching a mixture of Chuan Fa methods derived from the Shaolin empty-hand way, but modified by Fu Hsin, who trained bands of young men to become bodyguards for merchants. These same young men later set themselves up as protection racketeers who had to be paid not to raid the very convoys that they were supposed to protect. Trading information about convoy movements became commonplace, and various factions had to be appeased either with money or goods, or a caravan would be vigorously defended (or not) by the escorts.

◆ ◆ ◆ ◆

Continuing to relive parts of his life, Chu remembered his first encounter with the Mui Fa Jong (The Plum Blossom Piles), of which there were three groups. One group of nine thick upright posts was set into the ground, close enough to step from one to the other, but set at different heights. Another group of twenty-seven was set very high off the ground. A third group of fifty-four stumps was set at several heights, but still close enough for a person to step from one to another.

Chu looked at Yao and wondered what to do. Yao grinned and said, in his heavily accented voice, "Watch Yao, he climb-up . . . you . . . like." He swung himself deftly up onto the group of fifty-four stumps.

For once, there was no grin on his face. His concentration was complete as he moved expertly and spontaneously from stump to stump with consummate skill and grace. When the next stump height required him to descend, he did so effortlessly and in full control of his body. It was remarkable that he did the same thing when the stumps required him to step up as well!

After several minutes of demonstration, Yao descended from the stumps. Chu noticed that, despite the exertion, he was not out of breath.

"What's that for?" asked Chu.

"It . . . like . . . run down hill when legs go very fast. Brain can no keep up with legs. Mind become angry or scared. On stumps we practice move with flow, don't resist, don't plan, don't even think; but, must have big concentration, big, big concentration."

He was grinning again now. Chu thanked him for the explanation and determined to master the Plum Blossom Piles himself. Not wanting Yao to see him fail, he walked away, deciding to tackle them later.

◆ ◆ ◆ ◆

The morning Chuan Fa session was conducted by Tao Sheng. Some of the southern monks referred to Chuan Fa as "Kung Fu," or hard work, but Chu didn't like this name. It seemed too rough. When he'd asked Tao Sheng about it, Tao Sheng just shrugged his shoulders and smiled. Chu liked Tao Sheng, he always thought of him as the monk with the kind face. Tao Sheng had a well-proportioned and solid look about him. His hair was close-cropped, like that of all ordained monks, and his short beard was more gray than black. His eyes were similar in every way to those of Ma Tsu. Indeed Tao Sheng reminded him very much of Ma Tsu. Perhaps that's why he liked him.

The session began with solo-form practice, which was always conducted in the shade of the trees that surrounded the temple. It was believed that the trees would yield up their qi or vital spirit, and that practice in such places was beneficial. Near flowing water was also considered to be a good location, but never near stagnant water, which was considered to cause a negative qi flow, or even a blockage.

With solo-form practice complete, pushing-hands practice began. Chu was doubtful about it. He was still confined to the fixed drills and probably would be for several months to come. He preferred practicing with certain people, those with whom he "got on." Others made him feel irritated and unskillful, and he often tried to avoid them. But teachers Li and Tao Sheng always made him swap partners. He sometimes wondered if they were just getting at him. Later, he knew better.

Tao Sheng's lesson that morning concerned a parable about the difference between heaven and hell. "The main difference" he said, "is this; in hell people starve like hungry ghosts, while in heaven they are well-fed and content. There is abundant food in both heaven and hell; it appears magically as morsels at the end of very long chopsticks. Those in hell starve because they can only conceive of feeding themselves, while those in heaven feed each other! We have the choice to emulate either, and our choice will be reflected in our practices and our lives."

Eight months later, when his basic postures were good enough, Chu began to learn how to practice in "nonduality" during pushing hands. It was rewarding to be able to move and counter with unbalancing forces of his own. He looked forward to learning subduing techniques that would add a greater variety of technique and a new level of subtlety.

During this period, every other day, he learned the Plum Blossom Piles from Yao, whom he now trusted, having been taught that to ask may be a moment's embarrassment, but not to ask was a lifetime's shame. His quest to learn and his search for truth, friendship, and mutuality ruled over his status-consciousness and petty fears. He no longer desired to outrank Yao, whom he had originally reviled for his odd look, his thick accent, and the fact that Yao had been *au fait* with the Temple protocols and the "testing" of novices when he (Chu) had been precisely that, a novice. They became good friends. Yao even took Chu up on the high walls of the Temple, where they both poured a gourd of fresh water over a waiting hopeful camped at the gates, before Yao shouted down to him, "You like Yao's piss?"

◆ ◆ ◆ ◆

Paradoxically, life in the Temple was strict and well ordered, but relaxed. Novices and ordained monks and nuns arose and retired at the same times each day. They woke just before sunrise, and retired just after sunset, taking only one communal meal per day, before noon. In the rainy season, they often meditated during the night and were free to sleep when they chose. The monks and nuns slept apart and led almost separate lives, except when they came together to hear the teachings, for seated meditation, and, of course, to practice breathing techniques, solo forms, and pushing hands.

Chu was disappointed when, one day, he asked an old monk how many real fights he'd had.

"None," replied the old man dismissively.

Chu found no joy anywhere else in the Temple. No one had any stories to tell about real encounters, and no one seemed to care about actual fighting. He tried to tell them about Ma Tsu and all that he had done, but no one seemed to be the slightest bit interested, except one very young novice who hung on Chu's every word. The youth approached his training with renewed vigor and a glint in his eye, after having heard Chu's account of when Ma Tsu apprehended the thieves. Meanwhile, Chu was beginning to wonder of what use all the training was if you never got to test it and find out whether or not it worked.

He also became irritated by the lack of explanation for the solo forms he was studying. Each day he gathered with the others, and they all practiced forms together, but no one ever explained anything. Sometimes, he could see the relationships between certain movements in the forms and the pushing hands he was taught, but it was never explained. He was simply shown what to do once or twice, and then left to get on with it. He decided to seek private audience with Master Tao Sheng. There were too many questions and not enough answers.

◆   ◆   ◆   ◆

"Sit down." Tao Sheng said, slowly. Chu did as he was told. Sitting on the floor of the small standard-sized single monk's cell, he crossed his legs and remained silent. Tao Sheng said nothing either and soon the silence became intolerable. Chu felt that one of them should at least say something. He was just about to speak when Tao Sheng looked directly at him with an expression that said, "Be still and silent."

After what seemed like an eternity, Tao Sheng spoke.

"You have questions concerning Chuan Fa practice?"

Chu winced. Perhaps the master could read minds. He nodded.

"What is the second of the four noble truths?" asked Tao Sheng.

"It concerns the truth of the cause of suffering," replied Chu. "It is related to expecting and wanting life to be a certain way." He paused and looked at Tao Sheng, who said, "Go on."

"Physical discomfort and suffering are not the same thing. We suffer in the mind, and the mind produces the conditions of life which are unstable and unsatisfactory."

"What does that mean?" questioned Tao Sheng.

Chu thought for a moment before shrugging his shoulders in defeat.

"Try to put it in your own words," said Tao Sheng.

Chu thought again.

"I came here to become the best fighting monk in China," he said abruptly. Tao Sheng remained silent.

"I thought that . . ."

"Yes," interrupted Tao Sheng. "You thought!"

Chu looked down at the ground, failing to understand what the master was getting at.

"Did you not want and expect life here to be a certain way?"

"Yes," replied Chu.

"And is it?" questioned Tao Sheng.

"Not really, but I don't blame you for that," Chu added hastily.

"It's not a question of apportioning blame," Tao Sheng said, wisely. "It is a matter of expecting the Shaolin way to be what you want it to be, rather than what it is." Chu looked at him quizzically.

"Perhaps you think that Chuan Fa should be for fighting and that it should have a practical aim based on defeating others, and that the skills that you learn could best be put to use in the service of overcoming social injustices, such as robbery, theft, oppression of the weak, and self-defense."

Chu nodded.

Tao Sheng continued, "Tell me of the second part of the eightfold path."

"It concerns right thought, directing the mind toward benevolence and kindness, the freedom from attachment, ill-will, views, and opinions," said Chu.

"Well," said Tao Sheng, "do you have views and opinions?"

Chu thought for a moment before replying. "Yes, teacher, but how can we live without views or opinions? With respect, even you must have them, views about what we should or should not do?"

Chu found Tao Sheng's smile a relief. The old man spoke slowly and carefully.

"The way cannot be fully expressed in words. Words are based on duality, mutual exclusivity. They can never be mutually inclusive. Give something a name and that name immediately excludes everything else that it does not represent. This is duality. The real teaching is beyond duality, words, form, or even things. It is true that, first, we need right understanding, but this is not a mere opinion or view. Can we have right thought without right understanding? Tell me about the first part of the eightfold path."

"It's about right understanding, and concerns the understanding of suffering, its origin, and the path that leads to its extinction; also to understanding what is wholesome and what is unwholesome," Chu replied.

"Does mere recitation of this teaching give you the power to realize it, to make it real and live it?"

Chu considered for a moment before replying, "No."

"The teaching is not a law. There must be no attempt to force anyone. If we did so, the spirit would rebel against what it sees as a mere view or opinion. So, what can we do to encourage the living of truth and the realization of way?"

Chu shrugged his shoulders again.

"Practice a life-style in which every aspect reflects the teachings of the four noble truths. This is accomplished by the implementation of the eightfold path. We only talk about such things in order to illuminate the way. Do not confuse the words about the way with the way itself. Should we spend endless time worshipping or debating the signpost, or continue on to our destination, our destiny?"

A profound and liberating insight flashed into Chu's mind and he articulated it: "Then Chuan Fa practice is a way beyond words."

"Yes," said Tao Sheng, "and the less said about it the better."

"But surely, teacher, there must be dangers to such a way of teaching."

"Only that of observation without participation, and discussion without practice," said Tao Sheng. "One of the finest ways to effect the transformation of people is to give them exercises, things to do, things in which they can be involved. Thus may they grow without even realizing it! Kung Fu is such a practice. This is why we write the teaching in physical forms that only practice plus knowledge of the key can unravel."

The interview over, Chu returned to his quarters with his mind more at ease.

On another occasion Chu asked Master Li Tsun Ya about the weapons that lined the Eighteen Lohan Hall. "How could Buddhist monks who practiced the perfections of the Tripitaka (the three baskets or original teachings of the Buddha) possibly countenance the use of weapons?"

Master Li smiled and replied: "The so-called weapons that you see lining the Eighteen Lohan Hall are ceremonial staffs, emblems of office similar to the Vajra (thunderbolt scepter) and the Ganta (bell) in the Vajrayana (diamond) tradition of the Tibetans. Our monks manipulate these large ceremonial staffs ritually and symbolically, like a parade master wields a baton. Their use is completely symbolic. The staves are far too cumbersome, hefty, and impractical to be used as actual weapons. Besides, to attempt such a thing would bring disgrace upon us. Would it be a worthy trade, that of living with weapons instead of living the Dharma? These objects are part of the esoteric paraphernalia that we use for the benefit of all sentient beings on and during certain ritual and festival occasions, being used only to chase away the tiresome hordes of Mara."

Chu felt a slight disappointment with this answer. Something in him, perhaps something youthful (he was, after all, only 15) had looked forward to involvement in the secret mystique of twirling those "weapons" around. They looked so powerful and impressive, and it would be so much fun to wield them. He secretly would have loved to look and feel powerful.

His fascination for the ceremonial batons lingered for another year. It wasn't until he was out on a local alms round and healing visit with Master Li that he put aside his fascination with weapons. At a small and cramped house in one of the nearby villages, they tended the festering wounds of a man who had been hacked by a sword. The slashes were deep and, although the blood loss had been stemmed, the wounds were blackening and seeping puss. The man was not very old, perhaps 23 years or so old. Even the skilled Master Li could do very little and, although they returned several times, the multiple infections steadily worsened. All they could do was to administer herbs that reduced the man's terrible suffering. Within three weeks, he was dead. The wail that went up from his wife was the most hideous sound Chu had ever heard. He never considered weapons again.

◆   ◆   ◆   ◆

The woman's scream seemed so close and so real to Abbot Chu that he realized it was similar to the distress screams of the dying, all around him, here, in the present time, where he was trapped and also dying, where he faced the perils of a complete onslaught by doubt, fear, illusion, and guilt, where regret and a whole host of other sorrows and emotions served up by Mara, the evil one, master of delusion and rebirth, inflicted violence on his soul in a final assault.

He drew on the strength of a precedent—the time when he willingly gave way to the circumstances that stopped him from delivering his eloquent speech to become the patriarch. He had practiced acceptance then, and he would practice it now. With this resolve, he put his hands together, made a perfect Anjali Mudra, and died, practicing complete acceptance. He was not reborn, and the present masters claim he never will be, unless it is as the future Buddha Maitreya.

◆   ◆   ◆   ◆

The monk Bak Mei Too Jung rubbed at the tufted hair on his head. Accustomed to shaving his head every third day, the hair irritated him. He was dressed as a peddler, but he had to be careful to whom he spoke, for someone might recognize the tone of an educated man, or worse, an educated Shaolin monk. He was one of five survivors of the burning Temple, and the Manchus were offering rewards for the heads of all of them. He knew that Master Chu had perished. He was given the sad news by Ng Mui, the only nun to escape, and one of the wanted five. He sent her away quickly, surprised that she had taken such a risk to visit him.

Fearing that the death of the master would see the end of Chuan Fa, he resolved to do something about it. He would travel and teach. The only concern he had was how to explain to the lay public exactly what Chuan Fa was.

Bak Mei Too Jung's Chuan Fa was passed on. The system he taught was named Bak Mei (White Eyebrows), after him. It was spread among pronationalist secret societies, where it was used to attract young recruits. Their motto was: Defeat the Ching (dynasty) and restore the Ming.

◆   ◆   ◆   ◆

The nun Ng Mui traveled south to Fut-shan province, where she happened across an old friend and former disciple of the Shaolin way, Yim San Soek. Yim San Soek had been unable to complete his training and was overjoyed to see Ng Mui. He lost no time in requesting that she teach Chuan Fa to his daughter, Yim Wing Chun. Ng Mui agreed. In this way, Ng Mui's Chuan Fa spread throughout Fut-shan through Yim Wing Chun, whose husband and descendants named the art Wing Chun, after her.

◆   ◆   ◆   ◆

Monk Jee Shim Shee, another of the five survivors, was extremely conservative in his approach to Chuan Fa. Keeping intact the methods he had learned at the Shaolin Temple, he secretly spread the Sanchin boxing methods of the traditional Shaolin White Crane. Chuan Fa descendants of his created the Five-Ancestors Boxing in his honor.

◆   ◆   ◆   ◆

Monk Fung Do Tak hid himself with the Taoist recluses, becoming a Taoist himself. Later, he decided to translate the concepts of Chan Chuan Fa into purely Taoist terms. In so doing he created an art that would later influence the developments of T'ai Chi Ch'uan (The Grand Ultimate), Pa Kua (Eight Diagram/directions), and Hsing I (Mind Boxing), none of which demonstrate an authentic history older than the archetypal Crane Boxing of Shaolin.

◆   ◆   ◆   ◆

No records ever appeared concerning the fifth survivor, Mew Hin Too Jung.

◆   ◆   ◆   ◆

Many years later, in a small village in southern China, an old man named Li made his way slowly to a tea shop. There was a public festival and the place was very busy. Noisy patrons were doing their best to attract the attention of the staff. Taking his time, he climbed the stairs to the first floor and, fortunately, found himself a small table in a corner of the room.

Amid the audible hum of the tea-room conversation, the old man became aware of a group of youths who pointed to him before swaggering over.

"Hey," said one of them, "aren't you Yao Li, the Kung Fu man?"

The old man felt like cursing his heritage, all the way back to monk Yao, the Shaolin monk who was his ancestor. If people thought you could fight, your reputation would always provoke envy, fear, or even challenges, yes, even for an old man.

Li shook his head negatively, but the youths came and sat near him anyway. At that point, the tea he'd ordered arrived. One of the youths insisted on pouring it and began to do so. When the cup was full, however, the youth continued to pour, so the tea spilled over onto the table. Li raised his hand to stem the unnecessary flow, and the youth, who had bargained on such an interruption, feigned indignation. Capitalizing on the opportunity, he lashed out at the old man. The blow did not seem to connect squarely. Recoiling, the youth tried again.

The old man rolled with a practiced ease. Keeping calm, he felt no malice for the youth, only disappointment at the reluctance of others to restrain the offender. Rolling his body with the blows while tangling and trapping the youth's limbs, old man Li didn't counter once. In sheer frustration, the youth redoubled his efforts. Seeking to grab the old man and force him down by sheer strength, he lost his balance when the old man's momentary resistance gave way and agreed with the direction of the force. The youth went crashing out of control and into a nearby wall. Such was the force of his attack that the momentum didn't stop there, he bounced off the wall, flipped over, and hit the floor, hard. The other youths did not join in.

His next memory was of old man Li bending over him and tending to his injuries. That day, he was educated. Despite his poor attitude and ill-advised behavior, he was wise enough to understand the lesson. In fact, he became the only student Yao Li would ever take. He was later to name the art taught to him by Li "Drunken Boxing," after the relaxed and seemingly drunken way the old man had moved his body to avoid punishment during their encounter.

◆   ◆   ◆   ◆

It was the year 1806 and summer in Shuri. The Ryukyu Island seabreezes had abated and it was humid. The youth Matsumura hid while watching Sakugawa perform a solo routine of Karate movements. He was enthralled by the performance, which was crisp and well-coordinated, particularly for an old man practicing in such heat.

Sakugawa knew he was being watched, so, as he usually did when he thought he was being watched, he altered a movement here and a movement there, until the kata he had named Kusanku, (Ko So Kun) became quite different from the one taught to him by the kata namesake (more likely a title). He actually enjoyed making the changes, and even considered recording them in a kata of his own.

Tired of the intrusion on his privacy caused by the hidden youth, he paused from his practice, bent down, and picked up a stone, which he threw at the youth hidden in the bush. The stone struck true and sent the youth scampering off with a yell.

Sakugawa laughed before returning to the practice, but the boy was not to be put off so easily. He returned day after day, until Sakugawa was forced to accept him as a student.

Sakugawa spat on the floor before beginning the kata again. It was difficult and he was not sure he'd got it right. Pulling his long shanks into a crouch, he assumed a left cat stance and performed a circular palm-edge press. His mind was distracted by his description of the technique—palm-edge press. That was an uninspiring name. He decided to rename it sword-hand block. Yes, that was much better, much more . . . powerful and practical. As he turned in the opposite direction, he was dismayed to find that his mind had still not settled to the practice. He would have liked to consult the old man, Ko So Kung, but he had gone. Besides, he was probably dead by now.

Ko So Kung had been something of an enigma. He had always claimed to be a diplomat and military man, but while he'd been on Okinawa, he'd never seemed to have any official duties. Besides, he kept very dubious company. Some even said that he was a pirate.

In returning his concentration to the kata, Sakugawa was pleasantly surprised to find that, somehow, his body had remembered the movements. Perhaps he'd been trying too hard.

Finishing the kata, he dusted off his loincloth, walked over to his hakama, dusted that off also, and put it on. Striding off purposefully, he began to apply his mind to finding a name for the kata.

◆　◆　◆　◆

Ko So Kung wasn't dead, but he was close to it. He was resting in a ramshackle beach hut on the Korean peninsula. His health failing him rapidly and his seafaring days over, he turned his mind to the only thing still of consequence to him, Chuan Fa. He had failed to establish or pass on any proper lineage. His sole student had only studied briefly, learning form, but not pushing hands. Besides, he wasn't even Chinese. He deliberately glossed over the fact that he himself was only part Chinese. His father had been half Korean, but he, at least, had been raised as Chinese.

He knew that his great-grandfather three-times removed on his father's side had learned Chuan Fa from a man called Ma Tsu. The story was that the two of them were in dispute over the ownership of some jewels. His great grandfather, although Korean, was tall and thin. He looked Chinese, spoke many dialects and several languages, and had been able to pass the civil service exam. He was working in coastal intelligence, gathering and providing information to the Chinese authorities on smuggling and piracy off the vast Chinese coastline and the Ryukyu Islands.

It was on a pirate boat that he had first met Ma Tsu, who, coincidentally, was also on business for the Chinese authorities. Ma Tsu was a peacekeeper and an expert in civil arrest techniques. He'd posed as a wealthy landowner interested in the transportation of stolen goods and contraband and the lucrative trade between China and Japan. Of course, the two soon recognized each other. They had to take great pains to conceal their affinity. China and Japan had no diplomatic relationship, so all trade needed to be carried out through the Ryukyu Islands. Ko So Kung smiled at his inability to make a lucrative career out of this trade.

The stories he had been told by his father included an episode in which Ma Tsu had single-handedly captured several powerful warlord robbers. He had heard a version of the story that claimed that the people captured were merely inexperienced young thieves, but he preferred to believe the former story. After all, wasn't Ma Tsu a great man of the martial arts?

There was more controversy about Ma Tsu. Handed down in the family transmissions was a peculiar tale pertaining to his supposed immortality. Ko So Kung personally doubted that one. He never believed what he couldn't see. He knew very well the exaggerated claims made by medicine sellers and mystics alike. You couldn't even trust the monks these days. Shaving your head and taking the robe and bowl had been an expedient method of going into political or criminal exile since before his great-grandfather's days.

He knew another tale as well—one about a young novice monk that Ma Tsu had rescued from the castle of the robber barons. The young lad had apparently been manacled and tied up with over one hundred feet of hemp rope, and was guarded day and night. Ma Tsu, after winning a fortune on a cockfight, had apparently breached the stronghold single-handedly and rescued the young man, who was on his way to become a Shaolin monk. Later the youth became head of the order.

Shifting position to try and get comfortable, Ko So Kung became aware of an object sticking into his back. Reaching behind him, he took a small leather pouch out from underneath him and, remembering its contents, he opened it. A large and flawless diamond fell out, followed by a ruby. He reached into the bag for the remaining stone. It was a perfect emerald. Believing that the stones had hidden powers, he'd never sold them. "What am I going to do with these now?" he thought.

◆　◆　◆　◆

Epilogue

"Bushi" Sokon Matsumura (1796–1893) became a celebrated Karate figure on the island of Okinawa, the largest in the chain that make up the Ryukyu islands. He (or others) named his art Shorin-ryu after the Shaolin Temple. His most celebrated student was Yasutsune Ankho Itosu (1813–1915). Itosu was the teacher of Gichin Funakoshi, the man credited with spreading the art of Ryukyu Kenpo on the Japanese mainland, where it became better known as Karate, now popular the world over.

◆   ◆   ◆   ◆

After the fall of the Shaolin Temple, various other adaptations or modifications of Shaolin methods appeared and became widespread.

The acrobatic Kung Fu of Fu Hsin was admired by a troupe of operatic performers who studied it to enhance their performance of the legendary exploits of the Monkey King. After that, it became common to see such performances in the repetoire of many such groups all over China.

The White Crane Chuan Fa of the Shaolin Temple came down through the lineage of *sifus* (teachers) Chou Tze-Ho, Wai Xin-Xian, Lin Liang Hsing, Ryu-Ru-Ko (Japanese rendition), Xie Zhonxiang (1852–1930), and others, whose methods found their way into what was to become *Naha Te* (Goju-ryu and Uechi-ryu Karate), popularized by the Okinawans Kanryo Higashionna, Chojun Miyagi, Kanbun Uechi, and the much-celebrated mainland Japanese teacher Gogen Yamaguchi, a student of Miyagi.

Near the start of the Ching dynasty, the unshaven monk Wang Lang (possibly a layman) regrouped Shaolin-based Chuan Fa into the a system later known as *Tang Lang* (praying mantis). The mantis is an excellent totem image for grappling. Once it grips, it will not let go, even if it is cut in half!

Using the Shaolin techniques as a base, it was possibly Chan Heung who founded Choy Lay Fut Kung Fu (*Fut* means Buddha). It is claimed that Chan Heung learned his Kung Fu from a monk called Choy Fook.

Other existing systems include, Hung Gar (also Hung Kuen), The Hung Fist, or Hung Family, Kung Fu system, various Hakka (dialect and people) types of Kung Fu, Shantung Black Tiger, Northern Long Fist, Tam Tui (Deep Legs), and many others.

About the empty-hand art, from its codification in the Shaolin Temple to the present time, it can be said:

A thousand mile journey begins with a single step

and,

From a seed, a tree.

Of the three gems, heirlooms of Master Chu's family, there was never a trace, but there is a rumor that somewhere in Korea exists a temple that has a statue of Bodhi-Dharma, dedicated by a person or persons unknown. The statue has gem-studded eyes, one green and one red. One of the gems of Master Chu is missing. Do you know where it is?

Irregularities in Orthodox Shorin-ryu Karate Kata

Naihanchi (Naifuanchin/Tekki): Original bedrock kata for Shorin-ryu, contains no kicks at all, only leg movements referred to in Japanese as *namni-ashi* (returning wave/sweep) and utilizes only sideways movement performed in a horse stance.

Anaku: No kicks at all.

Wanhkan (Matsukase): No kicks, but five knee raises, three for the right leg and only two for the left.

Rohai (Meikyo): One crescent-shaped kick called *Mikazuki geri* in Japanese, which is executed with the sole of the foot, right leg only. Three knee raises, all performed with the right leg only.

Wanshu (Empi): One abducted knee raise (similar to the returning-wave movement of Naihanchi) for the left leg only. One (standard) knee raise, with knee simply being lifted straight up, for the right leg only.

Passai (Bassai): Two knee raises, for the right leg only. One crescent-shaped kick, again using the sole of the foot, for the right leg only.

Gojushiho: One front kick for the right leg, and two for the left.

Chinto (Gankaku): One leaping kick for the right leg only. One knee raise for the right leg and two for the left, but finishing in different positions. One front kick for each leg.

Kushanku (Kwanku/Kanku Dai): One front kick off the front leg, for the right leg only, and three off the rear leg, again for the right leg only. Two (standard) knee raises for the left leg and one for the right. One crescent-style kick, again using the sole of the foot, right leg only. One leaping kick, right leg only.

A similar exercise, yielding the same results, can be conducted with the kata of the world's leading Karate styles—Goju-ryu, Shotokan, and Wado-ryu. Wing Chun forms have five movements in all that can be construed as kicks—two for the right leg and three for the left. I suggest that, aside from indicating that the forms be practiced commencing on both sides, the construction of forms may be based on symbolism and numerology. In any case, I never found a teacher who could provide a logical, technical reason for the anomalies described.

Glossary

(Please note that some names of Karate kata defy translation even for the best of translators.)

Abhaya: Ritual yogic and Buddhist hand gesture denoting fearlessness.

Aikido: "The way of harmony," a modern Japanese art focusing on harmonious interaction, locking, and throwing.

Akira Kurosawa: Japanese film director.

Anaku: Okinawan Karate kata.

Anglo-Saxon rune poem: Twenty-nine stanzas recorded in eighth-century England.

Anguttara Nikya: Vedic Indian scripture.

An'ichi Miyagi: Okinawan Karate teacher and one of the teachers of the contemporary international Goju-ryu teacher, Morio Higaonna.

Ankho Itosu (1832–1916): Okinawan Karate teacher and teacher of Gichin Funakoshi.

Bao (Pao): Chinese, leopard.

Bhakti yoga: Yoga of spiritual devotion.

Bodhi-Dharma: First patriarch of Zen.

Bon Shamanism: Indigenous Tibetan shamanism.

Brahma: Hindu creator god.

Buddha: Enlightened being; the Shakyamuni or other Buddhas.

Budo-Ka: Practitioner of the warrior ways of Japan.

Chan/Zen: See Dhyana.

Chang Sang Feng: Mythological 13th-century Taoist sage and alleged founder of T'ai Chi Ch'uan.

Chen Dzwo-Dzen: Contemporary White Crane and T'ai Chi Ch'uan teacher.

Chen Man Ching (1901–1975): Famous T'ai Chi Ch'uan teacher.

Chinto (Gankaku): Shorin-ryu Karate kata.

Chojun Miyagi (1888–1953): Founder of Goju-ryu Karate.

Choshin Chibana (1887–1969): Okinawan Karate teacher and student of Ankho Itosu.

Chou Tze-Ho (Zhou-Zi-He; 1878–1926): Chinese Tiger/Crane teacher; teacher of Kanbun Uechi.

Chuan Fa: Chinese, fist art (Gong Fu or Kung Fu).

Chuang Tze (369–268 B.C.E.): Alleged Taoist sage.

Daruma: Bodhidharma.

Dhammapada: Buddhist scripture.

Dharana, Sanskrit, concentration.

Dharma: Sanskrit, the teachings and their applications.

Dhyana: Sanskrit, meditation proper. Dhyana became Chan-na to the Chinese, which in turn became Zen-na—Zen in Japanese, now used universally.

Dravidian Indians: Early settlers of the Hindu Kush.

Eizo Shimabukuro (1925-   ): Okinawan Karate teacher.

F.A.I.: *Fighting Arts International*, British martial arts magazine.

Fong Sai Yuk: Mythological Han Ming/Ching dynasty national figure; the prototype hero for the Kung Fu films from the late 1960s.

Fuchow White Crane: Encompasses both Kung Fu and Karate. Fuchow is a city in Fujian province.

Fujian Shaolin boxing: Fujian is a southern Chinese province said to have inherited the Shaolin tradition.

Fukien: Alternate spelling for Fujian, a province in China.

Garuda: Hindu depiction of Vishnu.

General Choi: Founder of the modern Korean art of Tae Kwon Do.

Gichin Funakoshi (1868–1957): Okinawan Karate teacher and founder of modern Japanese Karate.

Goju-ryu Karate: Hard/Soft style founded by Chojun Miyagi.

Gojushiho: Japanese, fifty-four steps, Okinawan Karate kata.

Han: One of several races that comprise the Chinese peoples.

Hara-kiri: Japanese, belly cut.

He: Chinese, crane (bird).

Hinayana (Buddhism): Sanskrit/Pali, small or little vehicle.

Hironori Otsuka (1892–1982): Founder of Wado-ryu, the way of peace, a Japanese Karate style.

Honan: Province in China (also Henan, Hunan).

Horoku Ishikawa: Contemporary Okinawan Karate teacher.

Hsing Yi: Chinese, mind boxing.

Hu: Chinese, tiger.

Hui-neng: Sixth Patriarch of Zen.

Hwrang warriors: Korean warriors analogous to, but not identical with, the Japanese Samurai.

I Ching: Chinese philosophy of change, encompassing a mathematically based oracle.

Ikken hisatsu: Japanese, one-blow finish, or one hit one kill; a Japanese swordfighting principle.

Ikkyu Sojun (1394–1481): A Zen teacher.

Janna: see Dhyana.

Japa: Mantra, prayer, recitation.

Jiin: Japanese, temple ground; Okinawan Karate kata.

Jion: Japanese, temple sound; Okinawan Karate kata.

Jitte: Japanese, temple hand; Okinawan Karate kata.

Jiyu Kumite: Japanese, meeting hands (free fighting).

Jnana Yoga: Yoga of (abstract) knowledge.

Jou Tsung Hwa (1917–   ): T'ai Chi Ch'uan teacher and author.

Ju-jutsu: Soft technique; Japanese art of locking, throwing, and striking techniques, originally derived from Chinese sources.

Kahkie: Okinawan Hogen dialect for pushing or "sticky" hands.

Kali: Sanskrit, a manifestation of Shiva.

Kamakura Zen: Version of Zen Buddhism common during Japan's feudal period.

Kanbun Uechi (1877–1941): Okinawan founder of Uechi-ryu Karate.

Kanryo Higashionna (1853–1916): Okinawan Karate teacher and teacher of Chojun Miyagi.

Kapilavastu: Present-day southern Nepal, birthplace of the Shakyamuni Buddha.

Karate: Okinawan/Japanese word composed of two parts—"kara" and "te." Kara means empty (but formerly meant foreign, i.e. Tang/Chinese) and "te" means hand.

Karma: Sanskrit word that roughly translates as fate, consequence, or destiny.

Kata: Japanese word used to describe choreographed sequences of movements (usually performed solo).

Kendo: Japanese, the way of the sword; also a modern sport.

Kenwa Mabuni (1889–1957): Okinawan Karate teacher, student of Itosu and founder of Shito-ryu Karate.

Koan: Japanese, a precedent or statuette (Chinese, Kung-an).

Kofuku: Buddhist Temple in Nara, Japan.

Kongo Rikishi: Statue in the Kofuku Temple.

Kosaku Matsumora (1825–1898): Okinawan Karate teacher, alleged founder of *Tomarite*, one of the three fundamental Okinawan groupings of Karate (named after the three principal cities of Okinawa), the other two being *Naha-te* and *Shuri-te*.

Kosokun (Kushanku): possibly the name of a 17ᵗʰ-century Chinese envoy; also the name of an Okinawan Karate kata.

Kuen: Cantonese Chinese, fist.

Kundalini yoga: Tantric yoga.

Kung-an: See Koan.

Kung Fu: Cantonese Chinese, hard work.

Kushanku (Kwanku/Kanku): See Kosokun.

Kyokushinkai: Modern Karate style featuring knock-down tournaments, founded by the late Korean-born Masutatsu Oyama.

Lao Tze: Sixth-century B.C.E. Taoist sage.

Lin Liang Hsing: Mainland Chinese 19ᵗʰ-century Kung Fu teacher, possible teacher of Kanyro Higashionna.

Lin-Chi I-Hsuan (Rinzai): Ninth-century Buddhist master.

Lohan Chuan (Quan): Monk Fist (Kung Fu).

Lung: Chinese, dragon.

Mahayana Buddhism: Greater-Vehicle Buddhism.

Maitreya: The Buddha apparently yet to come.

Mandala: Sanskrit, arch, circle, section, diagram.

Mao Tse Tung: Father of Chinese communism.

Mara: Sanskrit/Pali word for (spiritual) murder or destruction and the embodiment of death.

Masatatsu Oyama: Founder of the popular Kyokushinkai Karate. Oyama was a one-time student of Funakoshi and Yamaguchi.

Masatomo Takagi: Senior student of Gichin Funakoshi.

Masatoshi Nakayama (1913–1987): Late chief instructor to the Japan Karate Association (JKA).

Master Hui-neng: Sixth patriarch of Zen.

Master Seng-ts'an: Third Patriarch of Zen.

Maya: Sanskrit, deception.

Meiji restoration: End of Japan's feudal era (1868).

Ming dynasty: Chinese dynasty from 1368 to 1644–1645.

Morihiro Matayoshi: Japanese reading of the name of a Chinese Kung Fu practitioner who allegedly worked as a servant to Kenwa Mabuni.

Morio Higaonna: Contempory teacher of Okinawan Goju-ryu Karate.

Mui Fa Chuan: Plum Blossom Fist, a Kung Fu style.

Mui Fa Jong: Plum Blossom Piles, a series of wooden posts driven into the ground and used to practice balance.

Naha: Okinawan city and a type of Karate (*Naha-te*).

Naifuanchin: Chinese Kung Fu form and, later, a Karate kata.

Naihanchi: Okinawan (Hogen) reading of Naifuanchin.

Neiseishi: See Gojushiho.

Pa Kua: Chinese, eight diagrams or directions; also refers to a martial art.

Pak Mei: Chinese, White Eyebrows, allegedly the name of one of the five survivors of the burning of the Shaolin Temple; also a Kung Fu style.

Passai (Basai): Okinawan Karate kata.

Pazuzu: Sumerian demon spirit.

Pechurin/Superinpai: Japanese, final one hundred and eight hands; Okinawan Karate kata.

Pinan Godan (Hein Godan in Shotokan): Last in a series of five Karate kata.

Pu: Chinese, (to) float.

Qi: Chinese word equating with internal energy.

Quan: Chinese expression for method; fist form (kata).

Quan Fa: Chinese expression for fist art.

Rentan Goshin Tote-jitsu: Title of a 1925 book by Gichin Funakoshi.

Rinzai: Mainstream Japanese Zen school.

Ritsuke Otake: Contemporary Japanese sensei (Japanese, teacher), principal instructor of the Katori Shinto-ryu, a traditional school of Japanese Budo.

Rohai (Meikyo): Okinawan Karate kata.

Rokushu: Japanese, six variations or varieties (hands). Originaly, a Kung Fu form from which Chojun Miyagi derived the Tensho kata.

Ryu-Ru-Ko: Japanese rendition of the name of one of Chojun Miyagi's Chinese Kung Fu teachers.

Ryukyu Islands: Chain of islands between China and Japan.

Sacred Science: Title coined by the French symbolist R. A. Schwaller de Lubicz to denote the teaching of a science of the divine.

Samadhi: Sanskrit, to establish, make firm.

Samyutta Nikaya: Yogic scripture.

Sanchin (Saam Chin or Chien): Chinese/Japanese, three conflicts.

Sangha: Community who support each other in the practice of Buddhist teachings.

Sanseryu: Japanese, thirty-six hands, Okinawan Karate kata.

Sanskrit: Ancient Asian Indian language.

Satsuma: Feudal Japanese mainland clan.

Seipai: Japanese, eighteen hands; Okinawan Karate kata.

Seng-ts'an: Third patriarch of Zen.

Sesan (Seisan): Okinawan Karate kata.

Shakya: Family clan of the Shakyamuni Buddha.

Shaman: Possibly Tungusic for "ecstatic one," medicine man/woman, healer magician.

Shaolin Temple (Cantonese, *Siu Lam* or *Siu Lum*): Buddhist temple, Honan Province, China.

Shi: Chinese, snake.

Shigoki: Japanese, savage training.

Shinpan Shiroma: Okinawan Karate teacher and a student of Itosu.

Shisochin: Four-monk conflict, Okinawan Karate kata.

Shiva: Hindu deity of destruction, part of a Hindu trinity.

Shiva-Shakti: Hindu male/female polar opposites.

Shorin-Ji: Japanese, Shaolin Temple.

Shorin-ryu: Shaolin-family Karate style.

Shoshin Nagamine: Late Okinawan Karate teacher.

Shotokan: Japanese, Shoto's Hall. "Shoto" was Funakoshi's pen name; "kan" means hall.

Shuri: Okinawan city and a type of Karate (Shuri-te).

Siddhartha Gautama: Given name of the Shakyamuni Buddha.

Sokon (Bushi) Matsumura (1796–1893): Okinawan Karate teacher.

Soto Zen: Mainstream Japanese Zen school.

Street-vendor Kung Fu: Kung Fu designed to attract crowds or customers.

Suddhodana: Shakyu State, Nepal.

Sung Shang: Mountain in Hunan Province, China.

Tae Kwon Do: Modern Korean martial art.

T'ai Chi Ch'uan: Chinese, grand ultimate fist.

Tang: Chinese dynasty.

Tang Lang: Chinese, praying mantis (Kung Fu).

Taoism: Chinese school of spiritual teaching (pronounced dow-ism).

Te: Okinawan/Japanese, hand.

Tekki: Gichin Funakoshi's renaming of Naihanchi (Naifuanchin) kata.

Tensho: Okinawan Karate kata derived from the form Rokushu.

T'm: Chinese, (to) sink.

To-de (te): Okinawan, hand way.

Toh: Chinese, (to) spit.

Tokugawa Ieyasu (1541–1616): Unified Japan in 1615.

Tomari: Okinawan city and a type of (largely redundant) Karate (Tomari-te).

Toshihisa Sofue: Contemporary Japanese Karate teacher.

Toshiro Mifune: Acclaimed contemporary Japanese film actor.

To-te' Sakugawa (1733–1815): Early Karate notable.

Tsutomu Ohshima: Contemporary Karate teacher and translator of Gichin Funakoshi's *Karate Do Kyohan*.

Tun: Chinese, (to) swallow.

Varada: Ritual yogic and Buddhist hand gesture denoting wish-granting.

Wado-ryu: Japanese, Harmony-Way Family or Way of Peace; a Karate style.

Wai Xin-Xian: 19th-century Kung Fu teacher, allegedly connected with Kanyro Higashionna.

Wanhkan (Matsukase): Okinawan Karate kata.

Wanshu (Empi): Okinawan Karate kata.

Wei: Chinese third-century dynasty.

Wing Chun: Popular southern Chinese Kung Fu style.

Wu-Shu: Chinese, to quell a spear.

Wu-Wei: Chinese, unmotivated action.

Xia Bai Hua: Director of the Theoretical Wu-Shu Research Institute, Beijing, China.

Xie Zhongxiang (1852–1930): Alleged by some to have been a teacher of Kanryo Higashionna.

Yama: Buddhist god of hell.

Yang Jwing Ming: Contemporary Chinese-American martial arts teacher and author.

Yin and yang: Chinese polar opposites.

Yoga: Sanskrit, to yoke, tie-back, unite.

Zen: See Chan and Dhyana.

Zen Koan: See Koan and Kung-an.

Zen Shorin Do: Modern, yet deeply traditional, Shaolin method.

Selected Bibliography

Blackstone, Judith and Zoran Josipovic. *Zen for Beginners*. London: Unwin, 1986.

Braverman, Arthur. *Warrior of Zen*. Tokyo: Kodansha, 1994.

Bukkyo Dendo Kyokai. *The Teaching of Buddha*. Tokyo: The Buddhist Promoting Foundation, 1979.

Chaplin, Greg. "A Meeting with Master Xia Bai Hua." *Fighting Arts International* 67, vol. 12, no. 1 (1990).

Comley, Andrew. Sports Science. Private letter, 1995.

Conze, Edward. *Buddhist Scriptures*. London: Penguin, 1959.

Dhammapada: Wisdom of the Buddha. Harischandra Kaviratna, ed. Pasadena, CA: Theosophical University Press, 1980.

Draeger, Donn F. *Classical Bujutsu: The Martial Arts and Ways of Japan*, vol. 1. New York and Tokyo: Weatherhill, 1973.

———. *Classical Budo: The Martial Arts and Ways of Japan*, vol. 2. New York and Tokyo: Weatherhill, 1973.

Franks, David. Several private communications, 1993-1997.

Funakoshi, Gichin. *Karate Do Kyohan*. London: Ward Lock, 1982.

Graves, Robert. *The White Goddess*. London: Faber and Faber, 1961.

Higaonna, Morio. *The History of Karate: Okinawan Goju Ryu*. USA: Dragon Books, 1995.

Horwitz, Tem and Susan Kimmelman. *Tai Chi Ch'uan: Technique of Power*. London: Rider, 1976.

Johnson, Nathan. *Zen Shaolin Karate*. Boston: Charles E. Tuttle, 1994.

Jou, Tsung Hwa. *The Tao of Tai-Chi Chuan*. Shoshan Shapiro, ed. Boston: Charles E. Tuttle, 1981.

Lao Tze. *Tao Te Ching*. London: Penguin, 1985.

McCarthy, Patrick. Private letter, 1995.

Nagamine, Shoshin. *The Essence of Okinawan Karate-Do*. Boston: Charles E. Tuttle, 1976.

Nakayama, Masatoshi. *Dynamic Karate*. London: Ward Lock, 1966.

———. "Karate Kata Shotokan." *Fighting Arts International* vol. 5, no. 6 (1985).

Noble, Graham. "The First Karate Books." *Fighting Arts International* 90 (1995).

———. "The Master Funakoshi and the Development of Japanese Karate." *Fighting Arts International* 34, vol. 6, no. 4 (1995).

Noble, Graham, with Ian Mclaren and Professor N. Karasawa. "The History of Japanese Karate: Masters of the Shorin-Ryu." *Fighting Arts International* 50, vol. 9, no. 2 (1988).

RA Un Nefer Amen. *The Metu Neter: Vol. 1: The Great Oracle of Tehuti & the Egyptian System of Spiritual Cultivation*. New York: Kamit, 1990.

Schwaller de Lubicz, R. A. *Sacred Science: The King of Pharaonic Theocracy*. André and Goldian Van den Broek, trs. Rochester, VT: Inner Traditions, 1982.

Smith, Robert. *Pa-Kua: Chinese Boxing for Fitness and Self-Defense*. Tokyo: Kodansha, 1967.

Turnbull, Stephen. "Samurai Genesis: The Origins of the Japanese Martial Arts." *Fighting Arts International* 46, vol. 8, no. 4 (1987).

Watson, Kirby. "Shito Ryu Karate: Discussions with a Master." *Fighting Arts International* 78 (1992).

Zwalf, W., ed. *Buddhism: Art and Faith.* London: British Museum Publications, 1985.

Index

NATHAN J. JOHNSON spent seven years learning about Buddhism from the monks and nuns in a contemporary monastery. He holds a fifth-degree black belt in Karate, a fourth-degree black sash in Chinese Kung Fu, and teaches the Chinese empty-hand arts and simple meditation techniques. He holds seminars and gives lectures throughout both Great Britain and the United States. His previous book, *Zen Shaolin Karate* (Tuttle, 1994), has had several printings. He lives in Hampshire, England, where he was born. Readers may contact him through his web site, http://www.zenshorindo.com.